Venus of Empire

THE LIFE OF PAULINE BONAPARTE

Flora Fraser

JOHN MURRAY

First published in Great Britain in 2009 by John Murray (Publishers)
An Hachette UK Company

First published in the United States by Alfred A. Knopf, a division of Random House, Inc.

2

© Flora Fraser 2009

Family tree © London Calligraphy Lettering www.calligraphystudio.co.uk

A CIP catalogue record for this title is available from the British Library

ISBN 978-0-7195-6110-8

Printed and bound by Clays Ltd, St Ives plc

John Murray policy is to use papers that are natural, renewable and recyclable products and made from wood grown in sustainable forests. The logging and manufacturing processes are expected to conform to the environmental regulations of the country of origin.

John Murray (Publishers)
338 Euston Road
London NW1 3BH

www.johnmurray.co.uk

CONTENTS

FAMILY OF PAULINE BONAPARTE, PRINCESS BORGHESE

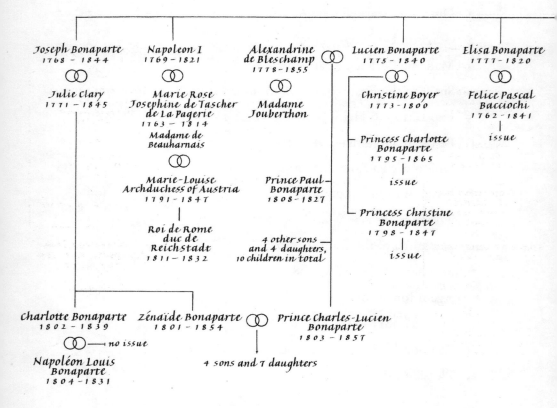

Joseph Bonaparte
1768 – 1844

Julie Clary
1771 – 1845

Napoléon 1
1769 – 1821

Marie Rose
Josephine de Tascher
de La Pagerie
1763 – 1814
Madame de
Beauharnais

Marie-Louise
Archduchess of Austria
1791 – 1847

Roi de Rome
duc de
Reichstadt
1811 – 1832

Alexandrine
de Bleschamp
1778 – 1855

Madame
Jouberthon

Prince Paul
Bonaparte
1808 – 1827

4 other sons
and 4 daughters,
10 children in total

Lucien Bonaparte
1775 – 1840

Christine Boyer
1773 – 1800

Princess Charlotte
Bonaparte
1795 – 1865

issue

Princess Christine
Bonaparte
1798 – 1847

issue

Elisa Bonaparte
1777 – 1820

Felice Pascal
Bacciochi
1762 – 1841

issue

charlotte Bonaparte
1802 – 1839

Napoléon Louis
Bonaparte
1804 – 1831

no issue

Zénaïde Bonaparte
1801 – 1854

Prince Charles-Lucien
Bonaparte
1803 – 1857

4 sons and 7 daughters

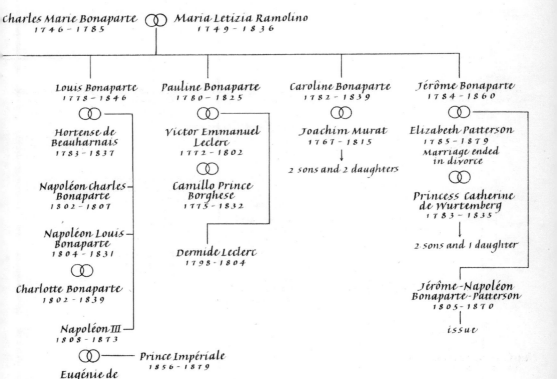

charles Marie Bonaparte 1746 – 1785

Maria Letizia Ramolino 1749 – 1836

Louis Bonaparte 1778 – 1846

Hortense de Beauharnais 1783 – 1837

Napoléon charles Bonaparte 1802 – 1807

Napoléon Louis Bonaparte 1804 – 1831

Charlotte Bonaparte 1802 – 1839

Napoléon III 1808 – 1873

Eugénie de Guzman 1826 – 1920

Prince Impériale 1856 – 1879

Pauline Bonaparte 1780 – 1825

Victor Emmanuel Leclerc 1772 – 1802

Camillo Prince Borghese 1775 – 1832

Dermide Leclerc 1798 – 1804

Caroline Bonaparte 1782 – 1839

Joachim Murat 1767 – 1815

2 sons and 2 daughters

Jérôme Bonaparte 1784 – 1860

Elizabeth Patterson 1785 – 1879 Marriage ended in divorce

Princess Catherine de Wurtemberg 1783 – 1835

2 sons and 1 daughter

Jérôme-Napoléon Bonaparte-Patterson 1805 – 1870

issue

•

ONE EVENING after dark in Rome some time ago I was walking with my husband between the via del Corso and the Tiber, and we stopped in a little piazza to let a car enter through the gateway of a massive palazzo. We saw, briefly illuminated within, a double courtyard with godlike statues surmounting the interior colonnade. Then the palace gates swung shut again, and we were left in darkness.

The building, I discovered from my map under the light of a street-lamp, was the Palazzo Borghese. So it was here, I thought, that Napoleon's outrageous sister Pauline Bonaparte had lived when she was married to Prince Camillo Borghese, here that she was immortalized by Antonio Canova in *La Paolina,* the near-naked, near-life-size marble statue that is now on public view in the Villa (or Museo e Galleria) Borghese, in the gardens of that name up above the Piazza del Popolo.

Two distinct memories came into my mind as I contemplated the palazzo's identity. First I remembered standing some years before in front of a portrait of Pauline Borghese at Apsley House in London. I was with a friend, Sabina Zanardi Landi, whose mother was a Borghese. And, as we gazed at Pauline's seraphic smile and at her diaphanous dress exposing rosy nipples, Sabina said, "You know, nobody speaks of her in my family. But you can see all her letters if you want. They're in the Vatican." The conjunction of scarlet woman, correspondence, and cardinals was immediately appealing, but I was busy writing another scarlet woman's life, that of Emma, Lady Hamilton, and we turned away from the picture.

And the second memory? While staying with Belgian friends on Corsica, in the course of writing about George IV's wife, Queen Caro-

line, I visited the Maison Bonaparte, a tenement house in Ajaccio
where Pauline and her brother Napoleon, as well as their six other siblings, were born and raised. No double courtyard there. Just a dowdy,
flat-fronted house in a side street running down to a small dark church
that bears the name "cathedral."

As we walked on that night in Rome, I reflected on Pauline's beauty
in her portrait and in her statue, on that tenement house, on the chain
of circumstances—insofar as I knew them—that had brought Pauline Bonaparte to the Palazzo Borghese, this acme of wealth and grandeur. And I thought about her unsavory reputation within the family
into which she had married—and outside it. I told my husband that
I would write about Pauline after completing the book I was then
working on, about the six daughters of George III. He nodded,
not especially impressed. Biographers have a habit of making such
pronouncements.

Time passed. I forgot my declaration and concentrated on writing
Princesses. When I finished I was resolved to write about a man, and a
man with a public career. I went to the British Library and looked
through the papers of various worthy candidates. And then one
evening on impulse I rang Bob Gottlieb in New York, my editor at
Knopf and good friend all my working life. "Can I pitch you an idea?"
I said, for some reason using the language of the Hollywood of yester-
year. Bob, it turned out, was about to head off to the ballet, but,
responding as a mogul might, he said he could give me three minutes.
"Oh well, I'll ring when you've more time," I said, reverting to shy and
retiring English type. "No, pitch it," he replied. And I said that I
wanted to write the life of Pauline Bonaparte, Napoleon's favorite sister, a legend both for her lovers and for her loyalty to her brother—not
least after his exile, first to Elba and then, following Waterloo, to Saint
Helena. "Done," came the answer. "And that leaves two minutes to
chat. How's your mother doing?"

So I began, in late 2004, and I was immediately engrossed by the
background to Pauline's story. For, as Stendhal has shown, the
Napoleonic Wars, from the point of view of French historical characters, are quite as colorful and varied in pace as they are when viewed by

the British—for instance, in *Vanity Fair*—or when surveyed from the
Russian perspective, as in *War and Peace*. In the case of Pauline, she was
sometimes at the side of, sometimes a thorn in the side of, but always
dearly beloved by the central character of this dramatic period, her
brother Napoleon.

She was with him in Milan following his victories with the Army of
Italy at Lodi and Rivoli. With her first husband, General Leclerc, she
lived modestly in Consular Paris, and visited Napoleon and Josephine
at Malmaison. Under the Empire, following her marriage to Prince
Borghese, she inhabited the sumptuous Hôtel Charost, which Wellington later bought when he was British ambassador to France, and which
is still today the British Embassy in Paris. She lived with Napoleon on
Elba and begged to be allowed to go and join him on Saint Helena.
Researching Pauline's life, I was examining the reverse of the coin in
which I had till now dealt, tracing the lives of eighteenth-century
women based in England.

When I wrote about Emma Hamilton, I came across a letter from
her lover, Admiral Lord Nelson, in which he holds out to her "the pro-
tecting shield of a British admiral." And George IV's wife, Queen Caroline, whom I wrote about next, felt an intense pride in the war record
of her father, the soldier Duke of Brunswick. "I am the daughter of a
hero," she said, "and married to a zero." To be fair, the six sisters of
George IV, whose lives I next considered, were very far from thinking
their brother a zero. With some reason they hero-worshiped him and
saw him as their protector. But in all cases these women had been men-
aced ultimately by the same aggressor—the Corsican-born emperor of
the French, Napoleon Bonaparte.

Although, in these previous books, I write little directly of the
Napoleonic Wars, that prolonged European conflict is always there in
the background, as are the suspense and danger and inconveniences
that were part and parcel of it. The vagaries of war, furthermore,
account quite as much as those of character or of any succession for the
course of Emma's, or of Queen Caroline's, or of the princesses' lives.
Two of their protectors—Nelson and the Duke of Brunswick—died
fighting Napoleon's forces. The other, George IV, triumphed when the

Duke of Wellington's army defeated the French emperor at Waterloo. Napoleon Bonaparte lurks like a dragon to be slain in the shadows of each narrative. But in *Venus of Empire: The Life of Pauline Bonaparte* he shares center stage with his sister and is both protector and, arguably, destroyer of his sister's welfare, as well as that of France.

I hope that readers will enjoy this account of the twists and turns in Pauline's career, which reflect her brother's rise and fall from grace. As his power grew, black and white lovers, lesbian affairs, nymphomania, gonorrhea, and even accusations of an incestuous relationship with Napoleon himself featured in the stories that gathered around her. Some were true, some not, but they lost nothing in the telling—by the enemy British press and, later, by the French government itself, after the restoration of Louis XVIII.

Pauline was indifferent when made the subject of scandal. She took lovers without regard for her brother, who wished his court to appear moral, at least, or for the feelings of her second husband, Prince Camillo Borghese. And while she cherished her reputation as the most beautiful woman in Europe, setting and resetting jewels, lavishing hours on her wardrobe, she was also matter-of-fact, speaking of her face and figure, which were commonly likened to those of the Venus de Medici, as "advantages of nature." In fact, whether Pauline was in Rome, where she was regarded as *nonconformista* when she behaved as she liked, or in Paris, where she was more often called *séduisante,* or seductive, she was always practical and as direct, in her way, as her brother. As a result her observations on imperial life are often pithy and frequently witty, none more so than her response to the lady who asked if she had not feared to pose, so lightly veiled, for Canova. Once heard, Pauline's answer, which I give later in the book, is never to be forgotten and only adds to the pleasure I take in making a pilgrimage to the statue whenever I am in Rome.

THERE HAVE BEEN many other pilgrimages to undertake in the course of researching *Venus of Empire,* all of them enjoyable and many of them accomplished owing to the kind offices of family and friends old and new. I wish to thank my uncle Michael Pakenham for introducing me to some of his many Parisian friends, including Ben Newick at the British Embassy. Marie-Eugènie de Portalès shared Bonaparte family lore with me during a most enjoyable stay in Corsica and subsequently in Paris. Penny Holmes, while British ambassadress to France, was a wonderful hostess, and knowledgeable guide to the embassy residence, formerly Pauline's home, in the rue du Faubourg Saint-Honoré. In addition, the Marquis d'Albufera kindly gave me a tour of the Château de Montgobert, which Pauline and her first husband, General Leclerc, owned. To my sister Natasha Fraser-Cavassoni, to Rana Kabbani and Patrick Seale, to Janine di Giovanni, and to Laure de Gramont I am, besides, infinitely grateful for their encouragement and good company.

In Rome, Scipione Borghese and Barbara Massimo made me most welcome at the Palazzo Borghese. Prince Borghese also arranged a very moving visit to the Borghese vault in the Basilica of Santa Maria Maggiore, where Pauline is buried with many of his ancestors. The late Giulia Cornaggia, in addition, was fascinating on the subjects of her Borghese forebears, while Giovanni Aldobrandini has also kindly shared with me information about the family. l wish to thank Pierre Morel, who, as French ambassador to the Holy See, showed me the delightful Villa Bonaparte by the Porta Pia—once, as the Villa Paolina, a residence of Pauline's. I am also grateful to Filippo di Robilant, Eduardo Ibáñez López, and Marino Serlupo Crescenzi, who arranged on different occasions for me to see the Circolo della Caccia and the Spanish Chancellery, apartments in the Palazzo Borghese once inhabited by Pauline and Camillo Borghese. Domenico Savini, who introduced me to many of those above, and also Laetitia del Gallo and Zenaïde Giunta, who shared with me their Bonaparte family memories, deserve special thanks. I thank besides Milton and Monica Gendel and all members of the di Robilant family for making every one of my trips to Rome so enjoyable and convivial.

In France again, Peter Hicks, at the Fondation Napoléon in Paris, has been continuously helpful in answering my many inquiries, and I have made much use of the Fondation reading room, the Bibliothèque Lapeyre. I am also grateful to Madame Danuta Monachon and her staff at the Bibliothèque Thiers in Paris, which houses Frédéric Masson's invaluable papers on Napoleon and his family. All at the Archives Nationales in Paris were unfailingly helpful, and I especially wish to thank Madame Martine Boisdeffre of the Archives de France. I also thank Madame Stéphanie Guyot-Nourry of the Archives Départementales de l'Yonne for her help when I was consulting General Leclerc's papers, and I am grateful to Jacques Grimbert of the Société Historique of Pontoise, the general's birthplace.

In Italy, Dottoressa Giulia Gorgone, director of the Museo Napoleonico in Rome, has been unfailingly kind in responding to my many queries. The staff of the Archivio Segreto Vaticano were most helpful, and in addition I thank Monsignor Charles Burns for helpful conversations about the Borghese papers there. To the splendid research of Anna Coliva and her curators at the Museo e Galleria Borghese into Canova's statue of Pauline I am greatly indebted. At the American Academy in Rome I wish to thank Adele Chatfield-Taylor and Christina Huemer for their enthusiasm for this project. In Florence, meanwhile, Niccolò Capponi has been very supportive; and I treasure the memory of a visit to the Marchese di Torrigiani's home in that city, where he showed me a lock of Pauline's hair. Farther south Carlo Knight in Naples was his usual erudite and helpful self, and in Venice I thank Giovanni Volpi. Marco Fasano and Carla Ceresa of the Fondazione Cavour of Santena besides gave me access to valuable correspondence between Pauline and the Comtesse de Cavour.

IN BRITAIN I thank the staffs of the Public Record Office at Kew, the National Archives of Scotland, the British Library, and the London Library for their patience with my inquiries. I thank Her Majesty the Queen for permission to read the diary Queen Victoria kept during her visit to Napoleon III's Paris, and am grateful to Pam Clark, registrar of the Royal Archives, for an interesting discussion about that royal journey. I am grateful also to the dukes of Devonshire and of Hamilton for permission to read their family correspondence. In addition I thank Charles Noble, the archivist at Chatsworth, for showing me the statue the sixth duke of Devonshire commissioned of my subject.

With Bernard Chevallier, director of the Château de Malmaison, I had a most helpful and wide-ranging discussion of the sources for Pauline's life. With Professor Jean Tulard, thanks to the kindness of Dr. John Rogister, I had an opportunity to touch on the myth and the reality of Pauline's existence. Meanwhile Béatrice de Plinval, curator of the Chaumet archives, kindly gave me a private tour of the Nitot jewelry commissioned by Napoleon and other members of the Bonaparte family, which was on exhibition in 2004.

Others to whom I am indebted for specific help or indeed inspiration of different kinds are: Laura Chanter, Guy de Selliers, Emilio di Campo, Edmondo and Maya di Robilant, Countess I. G. du Monceau de Bergendal, Jacques and Romy Gelardin, Jill, Duchess of Hamilton, Christopher Huhne, Mark Le Fanu, Jaclyn Lucas, Candia McWilliam, Eliza Pakenham, Clare Pardini, Roberta Martinelli, the Hon. Lady Roberts, Mark Roberts, Sam Stych, and the late Wendy Wasserstein.

I thank my cousin William Stirling for skillfully locating and photocopying references to Pauline in a mass of Napoleonic literature in the British Library. (It has been a feature of writing this book that very few former biographers of Pauline—and in that group I include Frédéric Masson—have seen fit to give references for their anecdotes and stories.) I have been fortunate once more in having Lesley Robertson Allen's assistance with this project, while to Leonora Clarke, as usual, go grateful thanks for typing the manuscript. At Capel and Land I thank Abi Fellows; at Knopf I thank Sarah Rothbard; and at John Murray I thank Rowan Yapp and Helen Hawksfield, all of whom contributed in great measure to its successful production. In addition I thank Helen Smith for the index, an invaluable guide to the Parisian, Roman and even Haitian salons Pauline adorned.

I thank Georgina Capel, my literary agent, for her enthusiastic and professional support of this project, and for reading and commenting on the chapters as fast as I could write them. I also thank Jonathan Lloyd, Alice Lutyens, and all at Curtis Brown for their encouragement and advice.

Meanwhile, Bob Gottlieb at Knopf has continued to be the editor a girl, or even a woman of nearly fifty, can only dream of. I thank Roland Philipps of John Murray, my friend and editor of many years, for his constant support for the project, and for his perceptive comments on the text. And I am happy to report that, following the book's cross-examination by Peter James, line editor supremo, Peter and I are still as good mates as ever. I hope that French speakers and historians will bear with my decision to abandon French Revolutionary dates well before January 1806, when that system of dating was in fact abolished.

I thank Philip Mansel for early and helpful advice about this book. My mother, Antonia Fraser, Professor Munro Price, and Peter Hicks have kindly read and commented on the manuscript at different times. I am grateful to my three children, Stella, Simon, and Tommy, for distracting me intermittently from my task of writing, but also for recognizing its place in the great scheme of things. To them and to my husband, Peter, who I hope is not too busy with schemes of his own to read it, I dedicate *Venus of Empire: The Life of Pauline Bonaparte*.

Venus of Empire

CHAPTER ONE

Dinner at Marseille, 1796

THE STORY OF PAULINE BONAPARTE, legendary beauty and seductress, begins, appropriately, with a meeting of three men. At dinner in the port of Marseille in the south of France were her elder brother General Napoleon Bonaparte, her fiancé, Citizen Stanislas Fréron, and her future husband, Adjutant General Victor Emmanuel Leclerc. According to the Gregorian calendar it was March 22, 1796. But that annual register had been suppressed, and, according to the Revolutionary calendar, which the national government had instituted with effect from September 1792, the day was 2 Germinal, Year Four.

We have no record of what Pauline Bonaparte herself was doing on that day in Marseille. Fifteen years old, with her widowed mother, Letizia, and others of her siblings she had been an inhabitant of the south of France since dramatic events had caused them to flee their native Corsica. The island was in the throes of a struggle for independence backed in its early stages by members of the Bonaparte family. Latterly Napoleon and his brothers had supported the French Revolution, an adherence that had brought them into conflict with Corsican patriots. The family had settled first at Toulon and then in Marseille in 1793.

Nor indeed until shortly before this dinner do we have much reliable information about Pauline's individual life. Her birth on October 20, 1780—she was the sixth of eight children—was recorded by her father, Charles, in his *livre de raison,* or commonplace book, which survives him. (He died when she was four.) The date of her baptism the next day in the small cathedral of Ajaccio in Corsica—Archdeacon Luciano Bonaparte, her great-uncle, stood godfather—is recorded in that town's archives. She was christened Maria Paola, and as she grew up was known as Paoletta. With the later fame of her brother Napoleon eclipsing all interest in the stories of his siblings, Pauline's childhood in the Maison Bonaparte in the harbor town of Ajaccio is distinguished by only a few mentions in the correspondence and anecdotes his admirers have so avidly collected.

When she was eleven, in 1792, Napoleon, aged twenty-two, sent her a fashion plate. Writing in the same month about her elder sister, Elisa, who had been educated far from Corsica at Madame de Maintenon's convent school of Saint-Cyr, and doubting the overeducated girl's chances in marriage, Napoleon mused that she was much less knowing than Paoletta. Both references, at once telling of Napoleon's affection for Pauline, of her love of finery, and of her mischievous character, might seem invented did they not come from reputable sources. Years later, while in exile on Elba, the emperor remembered that he and his sister had been caught mimicking their crippled grandmother, who was "bent . . . like an old fairy," and that Letizia punished Pauline rather than him—"it being easier to pull up skirts than undo breeches." If true, the story testifies to the harsh justice that the Bonapartes' mother meted out as well as to the taste this brother and sister displayed all their lives for unkind fun.

In the absence of other details about Pauline, these slivers of family life must represent her childhood years, her squabbles and games with elder brother Louis and younger siblings Maria Annunziata (always known as Caroline) and Jérôme. More generally her mother later spoke of a room in the Maison Bonaparte given over to the children, where they were allowed to play as they pleased, even scribble on the walls. That not much education—at most a dame school or the teaching of nuns—entered the lives of these younger Bonaparte children we know from later references to Pauline's deficiencies in this area. A good deal of healthy living was part of the picture, and through the difficult years when, following the early death of Pauline's father, Charles, the family might have been classed as *pauvre,* or unable to sustain themselves, they still summered at I Milleli, a substantial house in the *maquis,* or mountain scrub, above Ajaccio. It was here that Paoletta, her mother, and other siblings sheltered in the summer of 1793 when fleeing Corsican patriots, who had set fire to their home in Ajaccio following provocative remarks by her elder brother Lucien Bonaparte in a Jacobin club. From the nearby seashore they were sensationally rescued by Napoleon, and a French frigate bore them to the relative safety of the south of France. There Paoletta soon became known as Paulette, a gallicization that gradually gave way to Pauline.

But enough of vague accounts of a childhood we cannot reconstitute. Let us return to the dinner table in Marseille on March 22, 1796, and to the three men at it—Bonaparte, Fréron, and Leclerc. All three had been dedicated to the Revolution since it had first broken out in Paris on July 14, 1789, and all of them had played a distinguished part during its subsequent transformations. The Bourbon king Louis XVI had been executed in January 1793, and France, already steeped in blood at home, was now at war. Its enemies—Great Britain, Austria, Prussia, Spain, and Naples—had banded together to stop the French national government from spreading revolution throughout Europe and to support French royalists in their bid to restore the Bourbon monarchy. Although this struggle, which has since become known as the War of the First Coalition, provided the inescapable backdrop as the men dined that spring evening, we know that two of them at least had Paulette Bonaparte much in mind.

Despite the difference in their ages—he was forty-one to her fifteen—Stanislas Fréron had every intention of marrying Pauline within days, and her elder brother Napoleon favored the match, as well he might: Fréron was a person of consequence. He had been the national government's choice to take up the appointment of proconsul in Marseille the previous year and reestablish order in a city torn by faction and still bruised from the excesses of Robespierre's Revolutionary Terror of two years earlier. He had succeeded wonderfully well in his task, aided by one of the two younger men at the dinner, Adjutant General Leclerc, who had restored discipline to the disorderly troops in the town garrison. The third man at the table, General Bonaparte, had interrupted important preparations at Toulon for the launch of an Italian campaign to come and inspect the Marseille garrison, and this dinner marked the end of his visit and the successful conclusion of Fréron's and Leclerc's mission.

Some criticized the pomp and extravagance in which Fréron had lived at Marseille since his arrival the previous November, likening his behavior to that of a "Persian viceroy." The house he had commandeered was illuminated day and night by lanterns, and he never ventured out without a large suite of attendants. But he ordered theater and bullfights, which pleased the Marseillais. The salons of the city, slowly opening again following the overthrow of Robespierre and the installation of the new government called the Directory, marveled at his wit and address. He had been brought up, before the Revolution, in the household of Louis XVI's aunts, and among his attractions for the young Pauline Bonaparte was the lordly air he had preserved. When, exactly, over the past few months Pauline had come to the attention of this magnificent, decadent Parisian being, and where they had first met, we do not know. But it was almost certainly Lucien, acting as Fréron's aide-de-camp in Marseille, who introduced them. From political life in Paris Fréron knew the three eldest Bonaparte brothers, Napoleon, Joseph, and Lucien—and indeed had singled out for praise in the Convention, the national assembly that preceded the Directory, Napoleon's conduct in a royalist insurrection. Napoleon, meanwhile, noted with approval his brother Lucien's appointment to Fréron's staff.

What is certain is that Pauline and the other Bonaparte females would have known of Fréron long before they encountered him during this pacificatory mission to Marseille. For, after they left their native Corsica in the summer of 1793, they lived between Toulon and Marseille in the south of France. And in the summer of 1794 in the Midi, Fréron's name was synonymous with the Terror, after he had, with Paul Barras, been dispatched by Robespierre and the Committee of Public Safety to oversee in that region the national bloodshed in the Revolution's name that so horrified the rest of Europe. In Marseille he and his fellow commissioner, Barras, punished those who had backed the Girondins, moderate opponents of Robespierre's Jacobins. In Toulon they exacted vengeance on the royalist town for turning to the English. (It was at the siege of Toulon in late 1793 that the twenty-four-year-old Napoleon had first made his name, dispersing the British fleet in his capacity as captain of artillery.)

During this return visit two years later to the scene of his earlier crimes, however, Fréron had now succeeded by wise government in conciliating many. The day after the dinner, on March 23, 1796, General Napoleon Bonaparte reported from Toulon to Barras, now a member of the Directory, "Fréron has behaved well at Marseille. They seem to fear his departure and the renewal of assassinations." And on the thirtieth of that month from Nice he repeated his encomium to the same correspondent: "I found Fréron at Marseille. His departure has been a matter for regret—it seems he has behaved well there."

Fréron had certainly succeeded in attracting the heartfelt passion of Pauline Bonaparte, and already six weeks before Napoleon's visit to Marseille their imminent marriage was the subject of discussion between them. The fifteen-year-old girl was preparing herself to leave her family and follow Fréron, wherever the government might next send him. ". . . I swear, dear Stanislas, ever to love but you alone," Pauline wrote on 19 Ventôse (February 9). "My heart is not for sharing. It's given to you whole. Who could oppose the union of two souls who seek only happiness and who find it in loving each other? No, my love, not Maman, not anyone can refuse you my hand." She went on, "Laura and Petrarch, whom you quote often, were not so happy as us. Petrarch was constant, but Laura . . . No, my dear love, Paulette will love you as much as Petrarch loved Laura."

This rather surprising excursus into the world of Renaissance literature requires some explanation. We know that Fréron admired and translated into French the Italian poet's sonnets. That he shared his knowledge of Petrarch, and of the sonnets dedicated to "Laura"—the woman the poet claims to have first seen in a church in Avignon and who, being married, could never return his passion—with Pauline, an ignorant and more or less unlettered refugee from Corsica, says much for the power of love to transcend all boundaries. It is probable that Pauline had help from someone more literate than herself in framing this and subsequent letters, to her "idol" Fréron. Her brother Lucien and her sister Elisa have been suggested as possible secretaries. But Fréron's teaching left an indelible impression on Pauline. Later in life she was to take pleasure in reciting the lines from Petrarch he had taught her—to other lovers.

Pauline's reference to her mother shows that Fréron had not succeeded in conciliating all at Marseille: "No, my love, not Maman, not anyone can refuse you my hand." Following the early death of her husband, Charles, in 1785, Letizia Bonaparte had shared the duties that would have naturally fallen to him, as father of a family of five boys and three girls, with her two eldest sons, Joseph and Napoleon. Hence resistance from her to the match that Pauline and Fréron contemplated was to be taken seriously, even if Napoleon was in favor. (Within the family Napoleon was a figure of greater authority than his elder brother. In part this was because, unlike Joseph, he had spent months at a time at home in Corsica, helping his mother in her quest to make ends meet. In part he had the more dominant character.) That Madame Bonaparte objected, or at least wished the couple to delay their marriage, is made clear in a letter from Fréron to Napoleon days after his dinner with the young general. His mission concluded, Fréron was on the point of journeying north to Paris, where he had been called by the Directory, and intended taking Pauline with him as Madame Fréron:

Your mother is putting an obstacle in our way. I hold to the idea of marrying in Marseille in four or five days' time. Everything is arranged for that. Independently of possessing this hand that I burn to unite to mine, it is possible that the Directory will name me straightaway to some distant post, which will mean an immediate departure. If I am obliged to come back here, I will lose precious time. Moreover, the government, which, rightly, occupies itself little with matters of the heart, might blame an absence that could retard [the object of] the mission entrusted to me.

On what ground Madame Bonaparte objected to her daughter's marriage to Fréron we do not know. The bridegroom's age may have been a factor—or, indeed, the bride's youth. Or, being endowed with a remarkable ability to see which way the wind was blowing, Madame Bonaparte may have had some inkling, either from her links with the Corsican community in Paris or from information from the merchant community of Marseille with whom the Bonapartes were friendly, and indeed into which her son Joseph had recently married, that Fréron's earlier crimes in the south were about to come back to haunt him. She may even have known of and objected to the five-year liaison that Fréron had enjoyed with an actress from the Italian theater. Two children had been born, and the actress was pregnant with a third. But her objections were certainly not shared at this point by her son Napoleon. Indeed Pauline later reminded him, "You consented to my marriage to Fréron," and referred to "the promises you made me to smooth all obstacles."

It was perhaps surprising that Madame Bonaparte made objections to her daughter's marriage. When she and her children had fled Ajaccio for the mainland after the Maison Bonaparte had been burned down, the modest income they derived from the produce of vineyards and other smallholdings on their native island had come to an end. Indeed Corsica was now in British hands. In addition the support of a close-knit if quarrelsome structure of relations—paternal and maternal—had been lost to them. In Toulon, where they landed in June 1793, and afterward in Marseille, they had had to depend on small sums that the new republican government meted out to refugees from Corsica. Legend even has it that the Bonaparte women resorted to taking in laundry and washed it in the public fountain.

Now, however, in the spring of 1796, Napoleon had been appointed to head the Army of Italy, which had as its mission the expulsion of the Austrians from northern Italy and the introduction of republican government into that region. As a result he was able to supplement his family's income from his salary. Equally Madame Bonaparte's stepbrother, François Fesch, who had escaped with them from Corsica, had recovered some of his Swiss father's patrimony and could also help. Fesch, whose vocation was the priesthood and who had earlier been archdeacon of Ajaccio after Luciano Bonaparte's death, had been living a secular life since religious orders were suppressed under the Revolution.

But the times were still unsure. It was as easy to fall into disgrace as to win a command, as Napoleon had found to his cost two years earlier when he had come under suspicion and been briefly put under house arrest at Nice. Surely any bridegroom, especially one with a position and prospects like Fréron, was preferable to refugee life? But the Bonapartes had what some would call a remarkably inflated idea of what was due their status. A house above Antibes in which the family summered shortly after Napoleon was freed, for instance, was a property of some dignity, with pepperpot turrets. The family disapproved strongly when Lucien, appointed to a commissary post in Saint-Maximin, promptly married the daughter of the innkeeper with whom he lodged and had a daughter by her. Again, Napoleon directed that a "Citizen Billon" at Marseille who wished to marry Pauline in October 1795 should be rejected, as he seemed to have no occupation. And he refused Pauline's hand in marriage to a subaltern, Andoche Junot: "She has no money. He has no money. No money, no match."

Shortly before the dinner in Marseille took place, both of the eldest Bonaparte brothers had committed themselves to marriage. Joseph made what all agreed to be an excellent match—to Julie Clary, the plain and slightly backward but very rich daughter of a merchant family based in Marseille who had interests as far afield as Smyrna.

Napoleon was for a time engaged to her sister, Désirée, but broke it off. (Désirée later married another officer, Jean-Baptiste Bernadotte.) There were to be no further worries about Joseph's career, as he entered the Clary house of business. But Napoleon's subsequent marriage in March 1796 to Josephine, the beautiful widow of an aristocrat called de Beauharnais who had been guillotined in Paris during the Reign of Terror, did not please his mother. As part of his mission to Marseille later that month, Napoleon hoped to persuade Madame Bonaparte to acknowledge his bride.

General Bonaparte did not doubt, on parting from Fréron, that the proconsul's marriage to Pauline would take place within days, or that she would then accompany Fréron to Paris as his wife. During his brief visit to Marseille he therefore promised the proconsul a letter of introduction for Pauline to his new bride, Josephine, whom he had left with her two de Beauharnais children in Paris. When the letter did not materialize, Fréron sent a courier after Napoleon to Toulon, to try to extract it from the busy general. Fréron wanted it, he wrote, "so that she [Josephine] will not be astonished by the sudden apparition of Paulette when I present her." Fréron needed no introduction to Josephine as he knew her well already, not least because she had between the end of one marriage and the beginning of the next had an affair in Paris with his southern fellow commissioner Barras. Josephine de Beauharnais was, with Madame Tallien and Madame Récamier, an extremely fashionable member of Paris society. Pauline's life, despite her mother's objections, seemed set to take a dazzling, metropolitan path that would remove her all at once from the uncertainties of refugee existence in Marseille.

AND THEN EVERYTHING CHANGED. But before we follow the very different course that Pauline's life took over the next few months, let us look at the man who made a third at the dinner in Marseille on March 22—Adjutant General Victor Emmanuel Leclerc. This young man was awaiting a fellow adjutant general, Alexis Grillon, whom

Napoleon had ordered to take over as garrison commander at Marseille. Once his transfer into a suitable regiment had been effected, Leclerc was to join the Italian campaign that Pauline's brother had been chosen to head.

Blond, slight, and with a bony face, Victor Emmanuel Leclerc was certainly known to Pauline, as he had worked in concert with her fiancé, Fréron, to subdue the town over the preceding months. Moreover Leclerc, a merchant's son from Pontoise near Paris, had another claim to Fréron's attention. He was a protégé of Fréron's brother-in-law, the Marquis de la Poype, who was a landowner in the Pontoise region. Patriotism had led nineteen-year-old Victor Emmanuel to join up within days of the French Revolutionary Army's formation in September 1792. In so doing he abandoned his life as the promising scion of a prominent burgher family in Pontoise, an important town on the Seine, and in the Val-d'Oise near Paris, where his father had held the grain concession up to his death.

Victor Emmanuel's widowed mother, Madame Musquinet Leclerc, like his father from a prominent Pontoise family, no doubt had a hand in arranging his entry into the regiment commanded by the Marquis de la Poype. However, it was Victor Emmanuel's own military talents and flair for organization that led to his rise through the ranks. As early as 1793 he distinguished himself (like Napoleon) at the siege of Toulon, the following year he served in the Ardennes, and finally he came to Fréron's attention, perhaps after a commendation from de la Poype. His powers of organization and the confidence with which he had subdued the unruly garrison in Marseille now won him greater rewards—the attention of General Bonaparte.

Neither Leclerc nor Pauline dreamed in the spring of 1796 that within a year they would be publishing their banns in Milan with a view to marriage. Pauline, of course, was preparing for marriage to Fréron and a life as the wife of an administrator in some part of the expanding French republic. And in the coming months Leclerc was to be entirely occupied with the campaign in Italy, which began in April with successes in Piedmont and which he joined a month later in Lombardy. In June, commending a young cavalry general, Joachim Murat, under whose command the cavalry had performed "prodigies of valor," Napoleon also singled out the brigade chief of the tenth Regiment of Hussars, Leclerc, who had "equally distinguished himself." Later that month Napoleon sent Leclerc as a special envoy on a reconnaissance mission, masquerading as a diplomatic visit, to the Swiss canton of Grisons on the Tyrolean frontier, to see if that republic chose to acknowledge the government of France. His envoy Leclerc, announced Napoleon, "joins to excellent conduct a pure patriotism."

Meanwhile, in Marseille, Pauline's life had taken a very different turn, and one could say that thanks to Napoleon she had been saved from a marriage that would have brought her not grandeur but penury and disgrace. Fréron, delay as he might in Marseille, could not succeed in overcoming Letizia Bonaparte's objections to his marriage to her daughter, and willy-nilly set off for Paris—still affianced but without his bride-to-be. On arrival in the capital he learned that he had been denounced on March 30, the very day Napoleon had written his second encomium of the man he confidently expected to be his brother-in-law. The charges were of peculation and embezzlement during the proconsul's first mission to Marseille. And despite immediately penning a memorial in which he skillfully answered the charges, opinion in these volatile times swung against him. Fréron was disgraced. To add to his troubles, his Parisian mistress, Mademoiselle Masson, heard that he was about to marry and, on the point of giving birth to their third child, informed the Bonaparte family of her situation.

Not surprisingly, then, Napoleon changed his tune when he wrote to his wife, Josephine, in May following success at the Battle of Lodi. "Let Fréron know the intention of my family is for him NOT to marry Pauline, and that I am prepared to take whatever part is necessary to achieve this. Tell my brother." The next day he wrote to Barras, of the Directory, "Do me a favor, persuade Fréron not to marry my sister. This marriage suits no one in my family. He is too reasonable to persist in marrying a child of sixteen [in fact she was still fifteen]. He could be her father. And one doesn't look for another woman when one has two children by another woman already." And in a letter to Joseph on the fourteenth of that same month, Napoleon came down firmly against the match: "All goes well. I beg you, arrange Pauline's affair. I have no intention of letting Fréron marry her. Tell her that, and tell him to tell her. We are masters of all Lombardy."

But Pauline was not concerned with her brother's victories, or with anyone's disapproval of her love for Fréron. On 30 Floréal (May 19), ill in bed, she replied to a letter her lover had written to her after "a silence" and in which he addressed the subject of "that woman." Pauline told him that she was very anxious to hear of "the outcome for that woman," and added, "I put myself in her place and feel for her"— she referred to the impending birth of Mademoiselle Masson's third child. She added that a portrait of Fréron that he had given her was the greatest consolation to her. "I pass days with it, and talk to it as though you were here." She promised him her own, as soon as she was better able to support the fatigue of sittings.

Lucien, who remained attached to Fréron despite the commissioner's disgrace, tried to plead the lovers' cause when he joined his brother at headquarters in Milan in June. But Napoleon, the conquering hero of Rivoli and Lodi, Mantua and Bologna, was too busy to discuss anything but his plans for an assault on Rome. Lucien reported: "No family news could be discussed between us. His object occupies him so exclusively that it is impossible to make him take an interest in anything else." Meanwhile Pauline continued to write to Fréron, apparently reconciling herself to his relationship with Mademoiselle Masson and making little mention of his political disgrace.

On 14 Messidor (July 2) she told him that she had been to the country, where she had fallen into a river while trying to jump into a boat. "You nearly lost your Paulette," she wrote. She was still hopeful that a way would be found to unite her with Fréron and relied on Lucien, who was leaving for Paris, to promote their interests. "I don't talk more about your mistress," she wrote. "All that you say reassures me. I know your honest heart, and approve the arrangements you are making in that respect. The water I drank in the river has not cooled the warmth of my heart for you. It was more likely nectar I swallowed."

Breaking into Italian, she added, "Addio, anima mia, ti amo sempre, mia vita" (Adieu, my soul, I will love you always, my life), and ended by copying the words to a popular aria, written to be sung with a guitar accompaniment:

> *Non so dir se sono amante;*
> *Ma so ben che al tuo sembiante*
> *Tutto ardor pressa il mio cuore,*
> *E gli è caro il tuo pressar.*

> [I don't know if I am in love
> But I know when I see you
> My heart burns with ardor
> And your embrace is sweet.]

Pauline's cheerful mood did not last long. Only four days later, on July 6, she wrote again to Fréron:

All the world conspires against us. I see by your letter that your friends are ingrates—including Napoleon's wife, who I thought was for you. She writes to her husband that I would be dishonored if I were to marry you, so she hopes it can be stopped. What have we done to her? I can't bear it, everything is against us! We are wretched indeed! But what am I saying . . . no, while we love, we are not unhappy. We may experience setbacks, we have troubles, it's true, but a letter, a word, "I love you," consoles us for the tears we shed.

The girl went on determinedly:

All these difficulties, far from diminishing my love, only increase it. Courage, my beloved, our constancy will see a time when all these obstacles are swept away, I hope. I advise you to write to Napoleon, I would like to write to him. What do you think? It seems to me my letter wasn't strong enough to persuade him fully of my feelings for you. Maybe he will be moved by the tears of a sister and the prayers of a friend. You know that he is capable of much. I will do my best to send you my portrait. You can send your letters to Maman's address. Adieu, my love, for life your faithful lover.

Her letter ended again with sentences in Italian, the language she had spoken growing up in Corsica: "Il mio coraggio cominciava ad abbandonarmi, non ch'io dubitassi dei tuoi sentimenti, ma tante contradizioni m'impazientavano. . . . Sta di buon cuore, malgrado le tue disgrazie, mi sei sempre più caro; forse le cose camberanno; amami sempre, anima mia . . . mio tenero amico, non respiro se non per te; ti amo." (My courage began to abandon me, not because I doubted your faith, but so many obstacles made me impatient. . . . Be of good heart, despite your misfortunes, you are ever more dear. Maybe things will change. Love me ever, my soul . . . my dear love. I live only for you.)

Only one letter from Pauline to Napoleon survives from this period, during which, as she writes, he was "in the middle of brilliant victories." Without a date, it cannot be assigned a secure place in the developing drama of love blighted and marriage denied that forms this first chapter of her life. Nevertheless it is worth reading carefully, not least for the acknowledgment that Pauline first makes here of her obligation to her brother, as the head of the Bonaparte clan:

I have received your letter. It caused me the greatest pain. I didn't expect this change on your part. You had consented for me to marry Fréron. After the promises you had made me to smooth all obstacles, my heart was given to this sweet hope, and I regarded him as the one who would fulfill my destiny. I send you his last letter; you will see that all the calumnies that have been heaped on him are not true.

As for me, I prefer by far to be unhappy all my life than to marry without your consent and to draw down on me your malediction. You, my dear Napoleon, for whom I have always

had a most tender love, if you were witness to the tears your letter made me shed, you would be touched, I am sure. You, from
whom I expected my happiness, you want me to renounce the
only person I can ever love. Although young, I have a firm character; I feel it is impossible to renounce Fréron, after all the
promises I have made to love only him. Yes, I will honor them.
No one in the world can stop me keeping my heart for him,
receiving his letters, replying, repeating that I love him. I know
too well my duty to deny it. . . . Goodbye, this is what I have to
say to you. Be happy, and in the middle of these brilliant victories, of all this good fortune, remember sometimes the life full of
bitterness and tears that is P.B.'s every day.

Whether Napoleon accepted Pauline's rather unusual promise that
she would not marry Fréron but would continue to love him and cor-
respond with him, we cannot know. The last letter extant from her to
Fréron she wrote on July 6, following more days spent in bed, and
when she was on the point of changing residence at Marseille. "You
must have been worried not to receive my letters, but I suffered also
not to be able to chat with you. . . . You know that I idolize you. And
to see that we are so sinned against and so unhappy. No, it is not possible for Paulette to live at a distance from her dear friend Stanislas," she
declared.

She had had the comfort of opening her heart to her elder sister,
Elisa, on the matter of her lover. However, the seriousness of Fréron's
disgrace appears to have penetrated Pauline's consciousness at last,
three months after he had been denounced. "Lucien showed me your
letter," she told him. "I see that your situation is still the same. . . . I
would like to be with you, I would console you for all the injustices
that have happened to you."

In Italian she concluded:

Che soffranza d'essere separati così molto tempo! Ma conservo
la speranza che saremo presto riuniti; addio dunque, cara mia

speme, idol mio, credo che alla fine la sorte si stancherà persegui-
tarci. . . . Ti amo, sempre, e passionatissimamente, per sempre ti
amo, ti amo . . . sei cuore mio, tenero amico. [What suffering to
be separated for so long a time! But I keep up my hopes that we
will soon be reunited. So adieu, my dear, my idol, I believe that
in the end fate will tire of persecuting us. . . . I love you, always,
and so passionately, for ever I love you. I love you . . . my heart,
my dear love.] Ti amo, amo, amo, amo, si amatissimo amante.

But Napoleon, whose star continued to rise, had other plans for his
beautiful younger sister, and Pauline turned sixteen at Marseille in
October 1796, still a spinster, still without having set eyes on Fréron
since he had been called north that March. Two months later
Napoleon gave orders for Pauline, escorted by their uncle Fesch, to
meet him and Josephine at his Italian headquarters at Milan. Pauline
Bonaparte's adolescence at Marseille, marked by financial uncertainty
and emotional turbulence, was at an end—as was her vow of constancy
to Stanislas Fréron. Napoleon had plans for her in Italy, and they
involved Adjutant General, now Brigade General, Victor Emmanuel
Leclerc.

Meanwhile Fréron's career and prospects slipped away from him,
and even an attempt to gain a salary as a deputy for New Guinea failed.
Of his former life he was left only with Mademoiselle Masson, whom
he seems to have married and with whom he lived in slowly increasing
poverty. Strange to think that this woman's fate would have been
Pauline Bonaparte's had not the will of her mother intervened.

CHAPTER TWO

Garrison Bride, 1797–1798

T OWARD THE END OF APRIL 1797 there was cannon fire in Paris in the middle of the day. "It's probably a new victory for the Army of Italy," someone said. Since Jean Victor Moreau, Napoleon's contemporary and commander of the French Army of the Rhine, had retreated back across that river, General Bonaparte's campaigns were being followed all the more eagerly in the French capital. It was indeed news from the Italian front. On April 16 Napoleon had signed at Leoben in Austria the preliminaries of peace with the Austrians, the overlords of northern Italy, and the general officer who now brought the resulting treaty to the Directory was Brigade General Victor Emmanuel Leclerc.

As the Directors had not authorized peace negotiations, they were privately not pleased with Bonaparte or his emissary. But, as all Paris was delighted at the prospect of an end to the war with Austria, they had to affect enthusiasm. In addition Leclerc had inspected the different movements of the enemy troops as he passed through Germany en route to France, while he bonhomously shared with them the news that the peace treaty had been signed. The enemy consequently relaxed its guard, and, on Leclerc's arrival at the Rhine and at his suggestion, the French general Moreau recrossed the river with four thousand men and twenty cannons, and gave the Austrians a bloody nose. This was all in accordance with General Bonaparte's instructions to Leclerc, and he had once again proved himself an able second-in-command—in recognition of which he was promoted to brigade general. Six months later, under the Treaty of Campo Formio, France would acquire former Austrian territories in northern Italy and in the Netherlands. The War of the First Coalition had thus ended in triumph for the Revolutionary forces, and only Britain now remained in the field against them.

"I beg you to send [Leclerc] back to me straightaway," Napoleon wrote on April 19 from Leoben to the Directory. "All the officers I send to Paris stay there too long. They spend their money and lose themselves in pleasure." That evening Leclerc appeared, as if in echo of Napoleon's words, at a ball in Paris to celebrate the marriage of two persons of fashion. There two of his friends, the poet Antoine Arnault and another intimate, the actor Lenoir, congratulated him on following their advice the previous year when he had chosen to enlist in the Army of Italy rather than serve with the Army of the Interior, where he would have been confined to the antechambers of the Directory in Paris. Now Leclerc was the toast of the town. He was a brigade general at twenty-five, he represented that evening the most illustrious army in Europe, and he could indeed have lingered and enjoyed being feted, as his superior had feared.

However, Leclerc was not one to disobey Bonaparte, and he made haste to return to headquarters in Italy. But he had some private business to attend to before he left France, as his superior was well aware. The day after he left Napoleon at Leoben, Leclerc had appeared before General Louis Alexandre Berthier, chief of staff at the French army headquarters in Milan, armed with a copy of his baptismal entry from the Church of Notre-Dame in his native Pontoise. At his side was Pauline Bonaparte, and on that day, April 20, 1797, they gave notice of their intention to marry. The banns were duly read and posted, with their names, dates, and places of birth for all to read, before Leclerc resumed his journey to Paris as the envoy of Pauline's brother.

At the Parisian ball Leclerc declared to his friends that this honor, to have won the hand of his general's sister, outdid all the others lavished on him. And his friends agreed with him. Not only had word of the beauty of sixteen-year-old Pauline Bonaparte by now spread to Paris, but her brother's renown gave Leclerc's bride additional cachet. Leclerc's mother, Madame Musquinet Leclerc, no doubt agreed and had an opportunity to tell him so when he visited her and his younger sister, Aimée, at their house in the town of Pontoise before returning to Italy. Leclerc's mother was not especially literate, unlike her sophisticated son, but she was an experienced businesswoman, having now managed the family business for five years since her husband's death. The details of the dowry that Pauline Bonaparte would bring to the family—an unimpressive forty thousand francs—were no doubt discussed. But what was most remarkable was that General Bonaparte's plans for his sister and Leclerc's feelings for her should dovetail. For according to Leclerc's friend Arnault, who now traveled with him to Milan to be present at the couple's marriage, Leclerc had loved Pauline for three years, even before her brother's rise to power had added to her attractions.

WHAT OF PAULINE in all this? We last saw her in Marseille, mourning the end of her relationship with Fréron. Was she content with her new life at her brother's Italian headquarters? Was the match with Leclerc an arrangement made by her brother in which she had no part to play but to acquiesce? And did the love affair with Fréron of the previous year cast no shadow over this marriage that she now contemplated? The answer seems to be that she embraced the coming marriage with delight.

There exists a terse letter from Napoleon to his uncle Fesch, who was at Marseille in early December 1796 and whom he had appointed a commissary, or victualler, to the Army of Italy. In it he writes: "I beg you to come as soon as possible to Milan with Paoletta, whom my wife wants to have with her. . . . You can go to Nice by land and then embark for Genoa." Two days later he called on his brother Joseph, who was in Ajaccio taking the first steps toward restoring the Maison

Bonaparte following the British evacuation of the island, to join the family party in Italy. Napoleon wrote: "I think my wife is pregnant. I expect Fesch and Paoletta at Milan in a fortnight."

Josephine, after much prevarication, had reluctantly left Paris and joined Napoleon in Italy the previous summer. Accordingly, after the sea voyage from France with Fesch, it was under this fashionable Parisienne's chaperonage that Pauline, in the last days of December, made acquaintance with her brother's headquarters at Milan—the Palazzo Serbelloni, all shimmering pink granite and classical proportions. Here General Bonaparte held court. His recent victories—at Rivoli, at the bridge of Arcola—had guaranteed him a reputation for invincibility, and all at headquarters shone in his reflected glory.

Officers of the Italian campaigns—giants like André Masséna and Auguste de Marmont, lumbering provincials like Pierre Augereau— dined in the marble and porphyry salons and the colonnaded galleries opening onto terraces and gardens at the Serbelloni. Their companions were Josephine and the ladies she had prevailed on to follow her from Paris, all of "immodest behaviour," with their arms, bosoms, and shoulders uncovered, as the Milanese noted. The Milanese disapproved of the very arrangement of the Parisiennes' hair, adorned with flowers and feathers and crowned with little military helmets from which untidy locks escaped. The ladies' fashionable tunics, revealing their legs and even their thighs, clad in flesh-colored tights, were another matter for scandal, and finally their manners matched their clothes. It was all arrogant talk, provocative looks, and meat eaten on Fridays. Needless to say Napoleon was delighted by the arrival of Josephine and the sophisticated troupe she brought with her.

In addition there were the staff officers, led by round, fat Berthier, who had been brought up at Versailles and was Napoleon's trusted chief of staff. There were Henri Clarke, the Directory's representative; Karl Ludwig von Haller, the financier; Jean-Pierre Collot, the munitioner. And envoys and ambassadors crowded in from all over Italy—Tuscany, Naples, the Papal States, and the Republic of Venice. Over them all presided Napoleon, a slight, even scrawny figure whose gray gaze was glacial and whose reserve in the midst of the assembly seemed bound-less. Berthier, Charles Kilmaine, Clarke, Jacques-Pierre de Villemanzy, Augereau, noted an observer, all waited in silence till he addressed them. Never, in short, had a headquarters so resembled a court; it was like the Tuileries in its heyday, the royal palace in Paris that Louis XVI and Marie Antoinette had inhabited before the abolition of the French monarchy and their own execution.

Now that Pauline Bonaparte had joined the party, she would sit before dinner with her sister-in-law Josephine and her intimates Madame Visconti and Madame Berthier in the gallery that resembled, a Parisian said, "the foyer of the Opéra" in the French capital. In Milan the via degli Orefici, or Street of Goldsmiths, afforded her opportuni-ties to bedeck herself, the Scala opera house opportunities to display herself. In Marseille, Pauline had had the attention of individuals. Now an entire headquarters admired her, and Victor Emmanuel Leclerc most of all. What did she look like? One has to turn to later portraits, to surviving dresses with court trains, even to slippers that belonged to her, but most of all to a famous later statue for evidence of the sixteen-year-old's appearance.

Simply put, Pauline Bonaparte was exquisitely lovely—dark haired, with pale skin, dark eyes, and a well-cut, mobile mouth. Her counte-nance, it was sometimes said, bore a strong resemblance to that of her brother Napoleon. At other times, it was said, she looked like her mother, who had been a beauty in her day. She was always inordinately proud of her feet and hands, milk white, like the rest of her. Whether or not her figure had by now gained the perfect proportions later cele-brated in Canova's statue, we cannot say. She was about five feet five, or at most five feet six—the same height as her brother Napoleon and as her sister-in-law Josephine. As with Napoleon, what Pauline lacked in stature she made up in personality.

Napoleon still had work to do before he could follow the Direc-tory's standing instructions to invade Austria from the south in order to meet up with the other French generals who commanded the French armies on the Rhine. Accordingly Pauline accompanied Josephine to campaign quarters in Bologna and Modena, until Mantua fell to the French in February 1797, and Napoleon departed for Austria. It would seem very likely that by this time the marriage between Pauline and Leclerc had been agreed, as a copy of that officer's baptismal certificate, a necessary document for marriage, was obtained from Pontoise on February 22. Thereafter there was little time to dwell on personal matters. Leclerc was sent by Napoleon to urge the French generals on the Rhine to halt their offensive, and by the end of March, Napoleon himself was just outside Vienna, with the Austrian court packing up to flee. In April he and Leclerc were both, as we have seen, in Leoben in Austria, and for the bridal couple events then moved swiftly.

At the beginning of May, with the brigade general's return to headquarters, Leclerc and Pauline were reunited. "Pretty Paulette," whom Leclerc's friend Arnault pronounced "eager to become Mme. Leclerc," did not, however, behave with the decorum that might have been expected either from her venerable brother's sister or from the fiancée of her distinguished young husband-to-be. Shortly after Leclerc's return to Milan, Napoleon set up a summer headquarters a few leagues outside the city at the Château of Mombello, and there Arnault was placed next to Pauline at dinner. General conversation being impossible, as a medley of military marches and Italian patriotic airs was played throughout the meal, the poet had ample opportunity to study the character of the young beauty, who treated him with disarming familiarity. Although she had seen him before only at Marseille, she knew him to be in her fiancé's confidence.

"Singular mix of all that was most complete in physical perfection, and most bizarre in moral qualities," wrote Arnault, long years later.

Although she was the most beautiful person one could imagine, she was also the most unreasonable. No more deportment than a schoolgirl, talking inconsequentially, laughing at nothing and at everything, she contradicted the most serious people and put out her tongue at her sister-in-law when Josephine wasn't looking. She nudged my knee when I didn't pay enough attention to her rattling on and attracted to herself from time to time those ferocious glances with which her brother recalled the most intractable men to order. But this didn't work with her. A minute later she would start again. To have the authority of the general of the Army of Italy checked thus by the giddiness of a little girl! A good child, besides, by nature rather than by effort, since she had no principles and was likely to do the right thing only by caprice.

One wonders who was more glad, the sorely tried Arnault or saucy, show-off Pauline, to rise from the table and take coffee and ice cream out on the terraces after dinner. Did the malice she displayed toward her sister-in-law arise from Josephine's earlier opposition to her match with Fréron? Or was it simply jealousy of her sister-in-law's primacy at headquarters?

Either way, the time of Pauline's marriage drew near, while Napoleon and his officers came and went, exacting terms from the Venetians and negotiating the final clauses of the peace with Austria to be signed at Campo Formio. Napoleon's stepson, Eugène de Beauharnais, and Jérôme, the youngest Bonaparte, who were at the Macdermott School in Paris together, joined the Mombello party. At the beginning of June, Pauline's mother arrived from Marseille with her elder sister, Elisa. Elisa was regarded as ill favored, with "those things we call arms and legs . . . haphazardly stuck on to her body," as a contemporary, the Duchesse d'Abrantès, put it. However, she had found a husband, a Corsican named Felice Bacciochi. (The match was blighted only by his unfortunate fondness, given his lack of talent, for playing the violin.) And so it was decided that, following Pauline's civil marriage to Leclerc, which took place on the morning of June 14 at Mombello, the two couples should go through a religious ceremony that same evening in the Chapel of San Francesco. Archbishop Visconti, from Milan, gave his dispensation—the banns had been posted for the civil marriage but not read in church—the priest of a neighboring parish was hauled in to officiate, and Uncle Fesch and Leclerc's brother Nicolas stood witness while the nuptial benediction was given. Leclerc, we know, was religious in an irreligious age, and though it was Napoleon who requested the dispensation for this ceremony, it may have been at the urging of his new brother-in-law. Pauline was no doubt more occupied with her appearance than with spiritual affairs.

The double marriage was a focal point of a summer whose "unique spell" was felt by all, as General Marmont observed. It had "a character of its own which no later circumstances could re-create. There was grandeur, hope and joy. We were all very young, from the supreme commander down to the most junior officers; all bright with strength and health and consumed by love of glory . . . we felt unlimited confidence in our destinies." There were those who found the tendency of Napoleon's officers, Marmont and Leclerc among them, to imitate his mannerisms, his way of walking, his gravity, his silences—they even copied his practice of wearing a simple gray riding coat—laughable or even irritating. But Leclerc took the appellation "the blond Bonaparte" as a compliment.

Napoleon, meanwhile, unbent in the presence of his trusted fellow officers. He told ghost stories, "stories that frightened the imagination," improvising and using actors' tricks with the inflections of his voice. He even showed a sense of humor. Walking in the garden at Mombello, he noticed one of the cooks jump out of his way and inquired as to the cause of the man's alarm. It transpired that the cook's dog had fatally bitten Fortuny, a lapdog precious to Josephine and her children, Eugène and Hortense. Josephine had since acquired a new dog, and Napoleon asked the cook: "Where is your dog now? Don't you have him anymore?" "I keep him in," came the reply. "Well, let him out," said the general. "Maybe he'll get rid of this one too."

There was another important matter in the affair of Pauline's marriage that required attention—the signing of the marriage contracts before a notary in Milan, whereby Pauline's brother settled forty thousand francs on her, to be conveyed to Leclerc. In return she gave up all claim on the Bonaparte family property. In monetary and household matters she was later to have what the French call a good head on her shoulders. However, at this point she was probably more interested in the honeymoon journey to Lake Como that took place a few days after the marriage ceremonies, and in which most of the staff joined. While Napoleon parleyed with the Neapolitan ambassador to Vienna, the Marchese di Gallo, Pauline and Leclerc voyaged on the lake, rode in carriages flanked by Polish officers, and attended meals prepared in the lakeside villas.

The golden holiday atmosphere slowly dissipated. Napoleon was recalled to Paris, and with his departure and that of Josephine most of the assembly dispersed, and Milan resumed its workaday northern aspect. From Pauline's point of view, if Milan was not Paris, at least Leclerc took over Napoleon's duties as commander in chief of the Army of Italy, which gave her a position of importance as the general's lady. Meanwhile General Berthier was in due course replaced as chief of staff by General Guillaume-Marie-Anne Brune.

Pauline's brother Joseph had already left for Rome, where he had been appointed French ambassador, and had taken her younger sister, Caroline, with him. Letizia Bonaparte returned to Ajaccio with Elisa and Bacciochi, where they intended, as a matter of family piety, to further the work of restoration on the Maison Bonaparte that Joseph had begun the previous autumn. Pauline and Leclerc settled down to a life at headquarters in the Palazzo Serbelloni, and she soon performed the first duty of the wife of a republican officer: She became pregnant.

In October, Leclerc's friend the waspish Arnault, who had been on a tour of Italy, returned to Milan and visited the Leclercs at home. *He* was bathed in domestic happiness, he reported. *She* struck him as very happy too—not only to be married to Leclerc but to be married at all. Her new state had certainly not imbued Madame Leclerc with as much gravity as her husband, whom Arnault found even more serious than usual. "As for her, it was still the same folly. 'Isn't that a diamond you have there?' she asked me, pointing at a brilliant of the most modest nature that I wore as a pin. 'I think mine still better.' And she started comparing with some vanity these two stones, of which the better was not much bigger than a lentil."

Pauline remained pleased with her husband, with her jewel box, and in due course with her child, a boy who was born on April 20, 1798, at the couple's home in the Palazzo Graziani. As a measure of the respect Leclerc felt for his brother-in-law, he left it to Napoleon, who was appointed one of the godparents (Leclerc's mother would be the other), to name the child. The baby was not only an heir to the Pontoise family fortune; at this point this Leclerc child was the only heir Napoleon acknowledged, as he regarded his brother Lucien's marriage to the innkeeper's daughter Christine Boyer as a misalliance and the birth of their child, Charlotte, in 1795 as a further outrage. The birth of another niece, Christine, later that year, he would simply ignore. Unaccountably, although a mother of two by her first marriage and despite numerous false hopes during two years of marriage, Napoleon's own wife, Josephine, had not become pregnant. On the point of setting out for Toulon and the expedition to Egypt which was to blaze his name still more boldly in the journals of Europe, Napoleon therefore gave the matter of his small nephew's name some thought and replied: "Thank you, my dear brother-in-law, for the agreeable news you have given me. I am sending my proxy to General Brune [who was to stand in his place at the baptism]. I name my little nephew Dermide."

This unusual name was that of a hero in the poems of Ossian, supposedly translations from a Gaelic epic, which had been published thirty years earlier and which Napoleon, among others, greatly admired. "I beg you to give this little fan to my sister while a small jewel that I am having made for her is being finished," the godfather went on. Then, looking ahead, he wrote, "When my sister is better, General Brune could allow you to spend a month at Paris. Then, depending on circumstances, you could either join me or return to Italy. You cannot doubt the pleasure I would have to have you with me."

While Napoleon and his Army of Egypt, accompanied by archaeologists and botanists, embarked at Toulon, Leclerc arranged for his child to be baptized, and on the evening of May 29, 1798, at the Capuchin Church in Milan the six-week-old infant duly received the names of Dermide Louis Napoléon Leclerc. The garrison marked the event with every attention, cannons were fired and Milan rejoiced—for all the world as though an Austrian archduke had been born. The proud father celebrated further by buying an estate at Novellara, between Parma and Guastalla, for 160,000 francs.

If Leclerc intended Novellara as a residence rather than as a speculative purchase, he was to be disappointed. Ill health led to his resignation as commander in chief of the Army of Italy, which General Brune accepted on 5 Fructidor (October 14), and he was transferred to Paris. While Pauline Leclerc certainly did not wish ill health on her husband, there can be little doubt that she looked forward with immense excitement to the move to the French capital. A visit that she had made "in search of diversion" to Florence that August found her, according to Madame Reinhardt, the French minister's wife there, "keen . . . to talk fashion. The new vogues are of the utmost importance to her." Madame Reinhardt noted further of her "young and pretty" guest that she was "very natural, gay, a good child." When they went out sightseeing, Pauline's "elegant appearance, the animation with which she speaks," attracted attention. "A small circle gathered around us wherever we went."

Pauline was no doubt delighted with the attention. Victor Emmanuel Leclerc, on the other hand, was later to express some disappointment that, despite his efforts in Italy, both administrative and in the field, and despite public approval for those efforts, he had no great gains to show for them. He could, with some justice, deplore the ill luck that had left him languishing in Milan when so many less able had joined Bonaparte on the Egyptian adventure and were to return to Paris having gained greater rewards and renown. It remained to be seen if his fortunes would alter with the move to Paris. For Pauline, young and confident, the only fly in the ointment appears to have been worries about her health, as well as that of her husband. The birth of Dermide, though a welcome event, had apparently not been without its problems, and she would be plagued for years to come by troubles arising from it.

CHAPTER THREE

Madame Leclerc in Paris, 1798–1799

GARRISON LIFE IN MILAN had had its advantages for Pauline Leclerc—there she had easily carried off the palm for beauty. The foray to Florence and the attention she had attracted had also been delightful. It had been enough in Italy, in short, to be the wife of an ambitious officer, a young mother, and the admired sister of General Bonaparte. But in Paris she faced challenges of a different kind.

First of all, within a month of their reaching the capital, Leclerc was dispatched on October 14, 1798, to Rennes in Brittany, to serve under General Kilmaine, who commanded the Army of England. This was a force of ships and troops that had been drawn up on the French littoral facing the Channel some months before Bonaparte left for Egypt in May that year. It had been hoped by the Directory that the French fleet accompanying the general south would inflict such a defeat on the British navy in Mediterranean waters that its home fleet would be unable to patrol the Channel. In consequence an invasion of England could be attempted.

In the event, Nelson had destroyed the French fleet at the Battle of the Nile that August, and it was now plain to all that the invasion of England would never take place. The Army of England, however, had still not been disbanded, and Leclerc, as ever not in good health but in demand as a noted administrator, was sent to northern France to keep order. He went without much hope of improving his financial position—or, indeed, the morale of the troops.

Pauline meanwhile had to make what she could of the unknown capital without her husband, who knew the city well from his university days. She stayed at the house in Paris that Leclerc had taken in the rue Ville-l'Évêque. It belonged to an army contractor friend of Leclerc's, Monsieur Michelot, who lived next door, and Pauline soon became intimate with her landlord and his wife, calling them "Poulot" and "Poulotte." She relied on them, as seasoned Parisians, to help her navigate her new life in the capital and her obligations to her husband's family. Besides her mother-in-law, or "Mama," as she called her, and two Leclerc daughters still unmarried, there was another brother-in-law to encounter—Jean Louis, bachelor partner with his mother in the milling business in Pontoise and, in Paris, member of the Corps Législatif (legislative body). Nicolas, who had stood witness to Victor Emmanuel's marriage to Pauline in Milan, was meanwhile absent with the Army of Egypt.

"My dear friend, Leclerc has just told me," writes Pauline to Madame Michelot during one of her husband's leaves of absence from the army, "that we are engaged at Mama's . . . for tomorrow. This really puts me out as I had counted on the pleasure of dining with you and Madame Alcan. But all can be saved if you can put off the party till six." Pauline could take satisfaction from the fact that Leclerc was usually not particularly anxious to see much of his mother, much less spend time in his native Pontoise. Indeed, when he bought a country house, as he did shortly before leaving for Rennes, it was to the north of Paris, near Senlis, while Pontoise lies to the capital's west. Montgobert, as the imposing property set in parkland high above church and fields was named, bordered the land of a friend of his, Montbreton, rather than that of any Leclerc family member. (It was, however, close to a house at Plessis-Chamant that Leclerc had bought and then sold to Pauline's brother Lucien.) Montgobert was to occupy Leclerc's imagination as he did his unpalatable duty in Rennes and elsewhere in the bleak northwestern winter. Plantations, woods, allées, gardens—all were planned to bear fruit when he would retire from his soldiering and live there with Pauline, Dermide, and children to come. Pauline too took an active interest, but it was limited to the house's interior. Meanwhile there were more practical matters to consider.

Dermide's wet nurse, having completed her term, had to be dispatched to Milan in the *diligence,* the public coach service. A visit from Pauline to Leclerc at Rennes in February 1799 occasioned a demand for a wool shawl to be sent to her from Paris as a shield against the cold. A month later she wrote again from Rennes to Madame Michelot: "I cannot tell you if I will be away long. It depends entirely on where Leclerc is sent. I see here several officers' wives, and go sometimes to the theater, which is passable for a provincial theater." Pauline reveals herself as an equestrienne. She wanted her amazons, or riding habits, from her wardrobe sent, as well as her linen chemises, for going on horseback.

Whether Madame Michelot performed these errands out of friendship, or whether she was already employed by Pauline at this point, these notes are the first examples of a long correspondence between the two women. Perfectionist Pauline Bonaparte relied on Madame Michelot as a woman of taste and with a good eye, who could be trusted to act as an agent in the important matter of clothes and linens. In addition, Madame Ducluzel, who was to be a stalwart member of Pauline's household, joined the establishment at the rue Ville-l'Évêque as Dermide's nursery nurse. From the beginning of her employment she appears also to have acted as a secretary who took dictation. All her life Pauline liked to dispatch letters in number and at speed but did not always care to write herself. She was to tell one correspondent that the act of writing fatigued her, while promising that every word had been dictated by herself. The truth may have been that she did not wish to expose her poor spelling and grammar.

Pauline had, besides the Michelots and Madame Ducluzel, the occasional company of her sister-in-law Aimée, who was two years younger than she and living at Madame Campan's celebrated school in

Saint-Germain-en-Laye outside Paris. Jeanne Campan had in her time educated the sisters of Louis XV and served Queen Marie Antoinette. Now she had among her pupils, apart from Aimée Leclerc, Josephine Bonaparte's daughter, Hortense, and the daughter of the American Republic's ambassador to France (future U.S. president James Monroe). Although education was the focus of the establishment, cavaliers and followers were not wholly discouraged, and in years to come the distinguished preceptress would boast that among her former pupils were the wives of eight marshals of France—including Aimée Leclerc.

Leclerc had removed Aimée from his mother's care in Pontoise on their arrival in Paris, and Madame Campan wrote to Joseph Bonaparte on January 20, 1799: "Citizen Leclerc entered my establishment six months ago. Her progress in all has been astonishing, and she did not know how to read or write." Impressed by this, Joseph in due course placed his younger sister Caroline among the scholars of the school. For in December 1798 Joseph's embassy to Rome came to an abrupt end when feeling against French occupation resulted in the assassination of one of his colleagues. Joseph, in whose care sixteen-year-old Caroline had been living, headed for Paris, where he established himself in the rue Rocher and Caroline at Madame Campan's school.

The name "Citizen Leclerc" has been taken to refer to Pauline, and it has been proposed that she spent six months, when a wife and mother, at Madame Campan's. But Leclerc's correspondence with Aimée over the next three years shows that she was the pupil in question, and one whose progress Leclerc encouraged. "I am glad to see from your letters . . . that your style in composition is improving," he wrote in 1801. Pauline Bonaparte, wartime bride, was to make her way in the world without a formal education, unlike her sisters, Elisa and Caroline, and her sister-in-law Aimée. Leclerc might have wished it otherwise, but, as with so many other aspects of Pauline's personality, he accepted it.

Pauline Leclerc was nevertheless at a disadvantage in Paris, where the salon was the meeting place of society and that meeting place traditionally a forum of ideas. In the drawing rooms of Madame Necker and of Madame de Geoffrin the *philosophes* of the Enlightenment had exchanged ideas, and the nature of the Revolution itself had been forged. The salons of the Directory—those of Madame Récamier, Madame Tallien, Madame de Staël, and Josephine, Pauline's own sister-in-law—were less numinous affairs, the conversation centering on the republic's army movements and the diaphanous fashions of the day. But the *incroyables,* as these sophisticated women were known, were admired for the elegance of their conversation as much as for that of their dress, for their interest in the arts as much as for their looks. Indeed, in the case of Madame de Staël, her conversation was said to be so intoxicating that men forgot that she was plain and happily fell into bed with her. For a feature of Directory society in general, most vividly seen in the lives of the *incroyables,* was that women began to seize the lead and initiate sexual relationships, taking the Revolutionary watchwords "Liberty, Equality, Fraternity" rather literally. And, of course, while these women knew how to be alluring and seductive to the men they desired, they knew also how to be cruel to other women. Pauline Leclerc, ignorant, young, and vibrantly beautiful, was meat for these cats.

Fortunately she had a protector in the shape of Madame Permon, a wealthy widow of Corsican origin who kept a salon in her house in the rue Sainte-Croix in Paris. Here Madame Permon seamlessly entertained both the members of *ancien régime* society who inhabited the Faubourg Saint-Germain and the men and women who had made their names since the Revolution.

Madame Permon, who had been brought up on Corsica as part of the Greek community at Cargèse, had known the Bonaparte parents well. When living in Montpellier she had nursed Pauline's father, Charles, when he fell ill while visiting doctors before his death there of liver cancer in 1785. She felt warmly toward all the Bonaparte children and made a pet of Pauline upon the latter's arrival in Paris. "My mother, who put herself out for no one," remarks Madame Permon's daughter, Laure, in the highly colored memoirs she later wrote as the Duchesse d'Abrantès, "loved Paulette with as much tenderness as if she had been my sister." Perhaps significantly, Madame Permon's other daughter had recently died at the age of eighteen, Pauline's current age. Madame Permon was indulgent to Pauline in all her butterfly moods, and encouraged the young wife and mother to come to the house as often as she wished, not just on salon days.

As we have seen on her trip to Florence, Pauline was enthusiastic about fashion, indeed preoccupied by it. Nothing had occurred to change her disposition following her journey to Paris and establishment there with Leclerc and Dermide. In the French capital, as a newcomer, she "still felt the need to make great efforts to please," as Laure d'Abrantès put it in her memoirs. But Pauline quickly grew ambitious, too, and a ball planned by Madame Permon gave her the opportunity to show her mettle.

Culture, letters, and musical knowledge Madame Leclerc could not supply. But Pauline had another claim on people's attention. In Egypt her brother Napoleon, in command of a massive force en route to do battle with the British for the riches of India, was winning glory for France and making illustrious the name of Bonaparte. At the Battle of the Pyramids in July 1798 he had routed the fearsome Mamelukes. Though balked—by Nelson's victory at the Battle of the Nile—in one objective, to pry the wealth of India from the British, Napoleon went on to march on Palestine, sacking Jaffa and besieging Acre. Meanwhile the archaeologists and naturalists on the expedition claimed the sites of Thebes and Karnak in Egypt. Pauline, enjoying her brother's renown, was resolved to have her day in the sun too, and told the Permons she would prepare a toilette for their ball that would "immortalize her." Not only did Pauline turn this toilette into "the serious affair of an entire week, according to her custom," but she insisted that her couturier Madame Germon and her coiffeur, Charbonnier, keep it the darkest secret. In addition she asked permission to dress at Madame Permon's, as she had several times before, so that her ensemble would appear as dazzling as possible.

Pauline chose the best possible moment to appear. There was plenty of company in the salon, but the room was not too crowded to allow her to be seen and appreciated. She was dressed as a bacchante, with golden grapes and bands of panther skin in her hair. A Greek tunic, clasped at the shoulders with cameos and under the bosom with an ancient intaglio, fell over a dress of fine Indian muslin, hemmed with vine leaves of gold thread. "As Madame Leclerc had dressed in the house, she had not put on gloves," Laure d'Abrantès recorded, "but had left her lovely round, white arms on display, decorated with gold bracelets and more cameos. . . . Nothing can give an idea of this ravishing figure. She truly lit up the salon when she entered." And a crowd of the young men who frequented the Permons' house and who had been bent over other ladies' chairs, murmuring praises, drew away and followed Pauline as she took her place by Madame Permon.

Now that Pauline's week of work had had its effect, she was content. But her hostess now had her own work to do, as the other women, deserted at their stations, recovered themselves and began to mutter jealously. Such brazen display—and from a Corsican who had had to beg for her dinner three years before—stuck in the gullet, they said. Madame Permon moved about to quell this envious friction. But one woman, the aristocratic Madame de Contades, escaped her. Seizing the arm of an unfortunate gentleman, Madame de Contades propelled him toward Pauline, who had established herself in a graceful attitude on a sofa in Madame Permon's boudoir.

This room was small and brightly lit. Madame de Contades, a statuesque beauty with the gaze of a goddess, bent her stare on her diminutive and recumbent rival. She admired it all—toilette, figure, face, hairstyle. And then she exclaimed to her companion: "Oh God, God. What misfortune! And such a pretty woman. But how has this defect never been noticed? God, how unfortunate!"

Pauline went bright red, so that she looked almost ugly, while someone asked, as Madame de Contades had intended, "What do you mean?"

"What?" she replied with relish. "Why, those two enormous ears planted on either side of her head. If they were mine, I would have them cut off. In fact, I will advise her that's what she should do." All eyes were now trained on Pauline, this time not on her many charms but on two parts of her anatomy that, Laure d'Abrantès happily tells us, were indeed slightly less than perfect. Pauline's ears, although not enormous, in Laure's opinion lacked the elegant curl of real beauty, being flat and shapeless. Madame de Contades had triumphed, and the evening ended with a crumpled Pauline in tears and home before midnight.

The next day, however, Pauline was prepared to do battle, although it was a battle she conducted lying in bed and with her ears hidden under a cap thick with lace. Receiving a concerned Madame Permon, she spoke indignantly of Madame de Contades as a great long stick of a woman and declared she had no idea what any man could see in her. Madame Permon was patient with her, but then Pauline went on to laud the appearance of a woman at the ball who was famously ill favored, tempering her praise only with the reflection that she was not fair enough to wear silver. The older woman ended her visit, saying genially, "You are quite deluded."

Madame Permon was an invaluable and frank guide for Pauline in these early days. There were traps galore for the incautious in Directory society, and it is impossible to know how many others Pauline fell into. There were temptations too, but one titillating note written by a certain Guillaume in February 1799, shortly before Pauline left to visit Leclerc in Rennes, suggests that at this date she was still a virtuous wife and mother: "To the beautiful dancer, to the amiable Madame Leclerc, to the woman uncaring of all one writes. . . . If you want me to amuse you, to sing to you while waiting as another beautifies you, employ your moments of leisure to reply to me . . . I will not be amorous toward you. That cannot be. If I love you, it will be only with an affection tender but chaste."

While Pauline's admirers, whether chaste or not so chaste, swelled in number, Leclerc was promoted to general of division and transferred at the end of August 1799 to a command in Lyon. There he had the charge of troops who had been the Austrians' prisoners of war at Mantua and elsewhere and who now required clothing, arming, and redeploying. Pauline meanwhile was occupied with the arrival in Paris of her mother, whose ill health had prompted her to leave Ajaccio and settle with her son Joseph and his wife, Julie, in the rue Rocher.

In the unfamiliar city Letizia Bonaparte made the acquaintance of her one-year-old grandson Dermide, and was glad to become reacquainted with her old friend Madame Permon, with whom she could speak in Italian. Madame Bonaparte's French, explained Laure d'Abrantès, was incomprehensible, despite her years in the south of France. Besides, Laure adds, Madame Bonaparte had an absolute ignorance of literature in her own language, as well as that of France, and she assumed a stately manner and forbidding air in Parisian society so as to ward off exposure of her ignorance. Madame Permon was someone to whom Madame Bonaparte could speak freely of her home in Ajaccio and of her network of relations in Corsica. "And everyone who knows Madame Bonaparte knows that, once on that subject, she did not get off it very easily," Laure remarks.

While the two older women conversed, Pauline Leclerc did her own kind of filial duty at the Permons' house, seating herself on her favorite sofa and admiring herself in a mirror. Playing with the folds of her dress and shawl, she reminisced with her mother about their escape from Ajaccio after the patriots had set fire to their house. They spoke of the treacherous path along the coast in the darkness, the appearance of her brother Napoleon wading ashore from the boat that had come in search of them, the vagaries of the weather as they voyaged north to Toulon. Now, six years later, Pauline and Madame Bonaparte could recite the details with tranquil pleasure.

While Napoleon and the Army of Egypt penetrated Palestine and the kingdoms of the Upper Nile, the Bonaparte family was gathering in Paris in force, but not necessarily in amity, as Laure d'Abrantès records. Pauline's sister Elisa and her husband, Felice Bacciochi, and her brothers Louis and Jérôme joined their siblings over the course of the year. They found that Pauline was learning to be cruel, as befitted a beauty of the time. Entering and seating herself on the sofa next to her hostess at the Permons' one day, she said, "So where's Joseph? I saw his carriage at the door. And is Julie here? Poor Julie, she is so ugly. Don't you agree, Laure?" She appeared stupefied to receive a negative. "No? What! Julie isn't ugly? Do you hear your sister, Albert?" she said to the son of the house, apparently at the top of her voice. At that moment Joseph and Julie entered. To someone desperately making signs, Pauline merely said, "Oh pooh, Joseph knows perfectly well his poor wife is plug-ugly."

On another occasion, Laure reports, Pauline appeared in great elegance, with Aimée her foil, at a soirée at the Permons'. In attendance hovered a Monsieur Auguste de Montaigu, alive to every wish that Madame Leclerc could express, her willing slave. And then Pauline's mother entered, bringing with her Caroline, the youngest Bonaparte sister, who was at school with Aimée. Caroline, all golden curls, white shoulders, and rosy skin, displayed a general air of pleasure at being out in the world and particular excitement at seeing her sister. She fell on Madame Leclerc to embrace her. But Pauline had noticed Auguste de Montaigu admiring the pretty picture Caroline made. "My God, Maman," said Madame Leclerc, ruthlessly repulsing her sister's advance, "she is as clumsy as a peasant from Fiumorbo," naming a savage part of Corsica. Now Caroline was the one to weep and retire from Madame Permon's salon, as Pauline herself had done not so long before.

Laure d'Abrantès relates a curious conversation between her brother, Albert, and her mother, in which Madame Permon asked her son if a certain notorious thief was targeting passersby in the rue Ville-l'Évêque. Albert answered innocently that he did not believe so. In which case, asked his mother, why had he escorted Madame Leclerc to her home in that street every evening for the last eight days? When Albert had the grace to blush, his mother warned him, "Paulette is a madcap, a pretty madcap." And she exhorted him to leave the business of escorting her to a certain "Ajax." Monsieur de Montaigu, she suggested, could meanwhile serve as her page. A private exchange in Greek followed, after which mother and son burst out laughing.

So runs Laure d'Abrantès's narrative. The implication is that "Ajax" was Pauline's lover and de Montaigu an aspiring admirer. As Laure offers an identity for "Ajax"—General Pierre de Ruel, later Marquis de

Beurnonville—we can add from army records and other sources that this soldier was in his late forties and had, after a distinguished appearance at the Battle of Valmy and a spell as an Austrian hostage, recently been inspector of infantry with Leclerc in the Army of England. But Laure does not stop there. She declares that Pauline was dividing her favors between Beurnonville and General Moreau—who had been in Paris for some time without occupation, following the Peace of Leoben and the end of his leadership of the French army in Germany. To the reader's gratification, there is more. The Duchesse d'Abrantès declares General Étienne-Jacques Macdonald, who had fought against the Russians under Suvarov and was now governor of Versailles, to be a third lover. And all three generals were great friends with one another. It was a comic opera indeed.

According to Laure d'Abrantès, Pauline successfully kept all three generals in the dark about her relations with the other two, until she made the mistake of repeating to each of them hostile comments the others were supposed to have made. She "put them at each other's throats." At that point, unfortunately for Pauline, one of the generals, wishing to preserve his friendships, made overtures to the others. They compared notes, discovered the source of their disagreements, and resolved one and all to break with their troublemaking mistress. To this end Beurnonville handed over to Pauline letters in which his friends repudiated her, and in person announced his own resignation as her lover. Pauline apparently admired Beurnonville for his candor and persuaded him to continue their relationship.

How far we can trust this story is unclear. Laure d'Abrantès tells us she had the story from General Lannes, who was told it by Pauline herself long after the trio of generals had ceased to be her satellites. We can say only that the twenty-five volumes of d'Abrantès's memoirs are an entertaining source for stories about Pauline Bonaparte in Paris at this period, when we have few of Pauline's letters preserved, and when Madame Leclerc of the rue Ville-l'Évêque was not of sufficient importance to attract more distinguished attention. Laure's mother's house in the rue Sainte-Croix did offer the Bonaparte family an asylum in the early days in Paris, when they were still nostalgic for their Corsican heritage. But those days were about to end, and Pauline Bonaparte Leclerc's position in Parisian society was about to alter.

TO RETURN TO THE HISTORICAL RECORD, Napoleon had left Egypt unexpectedly in August 1799 and landed on the French mainland in October. During his absence his wife, Josephine, had been conducting an affair with Hippolyte Charles, formerly one of Leclerc's aides-de-camp. Napoleon learned of this affair while in Egypt and swore that he would divorce his wife, but Josephine managed to placate him. He was anyway otherwise occupied immediately upon his return to Paris, planning a coup d'état to overthrow the unpopular Directory government and browbeat the Conseil des Anciens (Council of Elders) and the Conseil des Cinq-Cents (Council of Five Hundred), the upper and lower chambers of the Corps Législatif established in 1795, into framing a new constitution, giving him draconian powers.

The 18 Brumaire (November 9) saw the first upheaval. Of the five members of the Directory, three resigned voluntarily and two resisted to no effect. Meanwhile the two councils, falsely warned that they were in danger from a Jacobin rebellion, had removed to the Château of Saint-Cloud, west of Paris, where General Bonaparte assured them they would be safe with the troops he commanded. With him went not only Joachim Murat, the cavalry officer who had distinguished himself at the Battle of Abukir and then accompanied Napoleon from Egypt to France, but Victor Emmanuel Leclerc, who had been recalled from Lyon to Paris a few days earlier.

The following day both councils were in an uproar. Napoleon Bonaparte dealt with the Council of Elders himself, marching into the chamber with an escort of grenadiers and accusing the deputies of destroying the republic's constitution. He then proceeded with his grenadiers to the château's Orangery, where the Council of Five Hundred was meeting, and met with a stormy reception. He was assaulted by Jacobin deputies, and a motion was raised, after he had fled the chamber, to declare him an outlaw. At this point Lucien Bonaparte, who was president of the council, left the chamber and called on Leclerc and Murat to enter and restore order. He declared that a group of deputies brandishing daggers were holding the assembly hostage inside and motioned to Napoleon's bloody face as proof. If his brother was a traitor, said Lucien, seizing a sword, he would himself plunge it through the traitor's heart.

Leclerc and Murat duly entered the chamber and, between them, successfully expelled the disputatious deputies. Characteristic of the two men were their orders. Murat, the flamboyant Gascon, cried: "Foutez-moi tout ce monde dehors" (Get this mob out of here). Victor Emmanuel Leclerc was more restrained: "Représentants, retirez-vous, c'est l'ordre du général." They were obeyed, the council dispersed, and the Directory years, in which General Bonaparte, Murat, and Leclerc had served as comrades, were at an end. Under the new constitution that was soon approved, Napoleon Bonaparte became first consul of the French republic, the other two being the Abbé Sieyès and Pierre Roger-Ducos.

For an account of these stirring events, as viewed from the perspective of Pauline and the other denizens of the Permons' salon, we turn once more to the gossipy *jeune fille* of the maison Permon.

The 18 Brumaire was a highly charged day in Paris, during which rumor was rife, without substantiation being possible, to the irritation of all. The Permon ladies, paying a visit on Madame Letizia Bonaparte, found her superbly calm. Madame Leclerc, on the other hand, they found dictating a letter every quarter of an hour to General Moreau to solicit news of developments. Whether her lover or not, he was closely involved in the coup and had charge of the Directory members at the Luxembourg Palace. (She was not to be deterred, Laure informs us, even when told that Moreau was not at home and was not necessarily expected back that night.)

The next day, Saint-Cloud being remote from Paris and Fouché, chief of police, exercising a remarkable control of information issuing from that quarter, the Bonaparte women knew nothing of what had passed there until halfway through the evening. Pauline and her mother were at the Théâtre Feydeau with Madame Permon and Laure when the performance was interrupted by a dramatic announcement: "Citizens, General Bonaparte has narrowly missed being assassinated at Saint-Cloud by enemies of the republic."

A general hubbub erupted, Pauline reeled backward, then burst into tears. Her mother, tight-mouthed, urged her to compose herself. Setting about organizing an exit from the theater, the Permons had their carriage brought around. For once in her life Madame Bonaparte chose to make her first port of call her daughter-in-law Josephine's house in the rue Chantereine, where the most news was to be had. They found the road outside packed with horses, carriages, and curious onlookers. But a comedy developed, as Madame Permon, who did not know Josephine, swore that, whatever the circumstances, etiquette was etiquette and she could not accompany the Bonapartes into the house.

While they were arguing the point, an opponent of the coup leaders pulled down the carriage window and said to Laure, "Your friend Lucien has made his brother the general a king." The Bonaparte women hurried inside to find that Fouché had brought to Josephine a more sober account of the proceedings at Saint-Cloud. All were safe, Leclerc included, and Napoleon, they learned, was to be sworn in within hours as first consul.

In reward for Murat's part in the Brumaire coup, Napoleon consented to his marriage to the eighteen-year-old Caroline Bonaparte, which took place in January 1800. Murat had hurried to her with an account of events late in the evening of 19 Brumaire, alarming all at Madame Campan's with his ferocious knocking on the door. But there were rewards for others who had played their part. To Moreau was assigned the command of the Army of the Rhine, and, in the campaign against the Austrians that now opened in Germany, Leclerc was appointed head of a division. Pauline and Leclerc could hope for advantages from his service there, and Napoleon gave every indication that he intended to honor not only his mother but his seven siblings too at his Consular court. These were heady days.

CHAPTER FOUR

Sister to the First Consul, 1800–1802

FIRST CONSUL BONAPARTE DECLARED that, with the coup d'état of 18 Brumaire, the Revolution was "perfected," although those visiting the splendid Tuileries Palace, formerly the residence of Louis XVI and Marie Antoinette, where he made his home in February 1800, might have begged to differ. Caustic as ever, Napoleon said to his valet Benjamin Constant, with reference to the Tuileries' previous occupants, that the art lay not in obtaining entry but in staying there. But some were in no doubt that Napoleon possessed the black arts necessary for dominion. Madame Permon had said on 19 Brumaire, "He is a monster fish who will swallow whole the other consuls." Pauline continued to exhibit the lively pride in her brother that she had always displayed. She also maintained her animosity toward her sister-in-law Josephine.

Josephine Bonaparte had a strange existence now that her husband was first consul. She had no official status as consort, and indeed to a degree preferred it that way. Napoleon had the architect Fontaine draw up plans to adapt for him the royal château of Saint-Cloud, where the events of 18 Brumaire had taken place. But Josephine refused to abandon Malmaison, her small country retreat west of Paris at Rueil, and, busy with her garden and greenhouses there, and with her daughter

Hortense's upbringing, did not always appear in what now became known as Consular society. Nevertheless both she and Hortense attended the ball that followed Laure Permon's wedding in October 1800 to General Andoche Junot—a bridegroom, now commander of Paris, whom Napoleon had once spurned for his sister Pauline.

In the memoirs she wrote as Duchesse d'Abrantès, Laure Junot gives no details of Pauline's toilette for an event at which most of the Bonaparte family was present. But she indicates that Madame Leclerc was "as ever charming, as ever elegant"—until naughty Pauline chose to comment on her sister-in-law's appearance. Josephine's dress was embellished with poppies and golden wheat sheaves, and she wore a garland in her hair to match. "Really," said the twenty-year-old Pauline. "I can't believe someone of forty putting flowers in her hair." (Josephine was thirty-seven.) Embarrassed, Laure Junot pointed out the bunches of jonquils that adorned the turban and dress of her own mother, Madame Permon. Pauline looked astonished at this intervention. "That's quite different," she said firmly. "Quite different."

First Consul Bonaparte did not himself always appear at the balls and parties that marked Consular society. There was a new constitution to establish, a central administration, the Bank of France, and a legal system, the Code Napoléon, to initiate. Meanwhile a lasting peace between the state and the Catholic Church was being engineered, which was to be formalized in the Concordat of 1801. But some things did not change. Officials and military officers continued to be appointed to posts and commands, and Napoleon's family benefited from his exaltation. Lucien became minister of the interior, Caroline's husband, Murat, became chief of the Consular Guard, and Louis Bonaparte, aged twenty-two, took charge of a cavalry brigade. Even sixteen-year-old Jérôme left school and became a naval lieutenant. And Pauline in Paris awaited news of her husband's fortunes in the Rhine campaign, where he had been serving since December 5, 1799, as commander of the Second Division of the center. (Moreau was commander of the entire force.)

The Allies had taken advantage of the absence of Napoleon in

Egypt to open a further offensive—the War of the Second Coalition. In June 1800 Leclerc's division received the order to take the Bavarian town of Landshut, which was in the hands of the archduke Ferdinand. The Austrians had about 120,000 men in all, deployed in the Black Forest north of the Alps, under the command of General Paul Kray, to obstruct any French advance along the Rhine and Danube rivers to Vienna. Although the town, on the river Isar, appeared impregnable, such was the verve of Leclerc's attack that in short order much of the enemy had been put to flight and of those remaining, four hundred were dead and six hundred taken prisoner.

Despite this success Leclerc had received a wound in the leg and had to retire to the rear, so he saw no more action on the Rhine. Furthermore Moreau's Army of the Rhine, although ultimately successful in December 1800 at the Battle of Hohenlinden, was quite outshone by the Army of Reserve that Napoleon led that summer over the Alps and into northern Italy. In a journey that piqued the imagination of Consular artists, who depicted Napoleon on horseback amid frozen masses, this force crossed the Alps by the Great Saint Bernard pass, which was still snowbound in May. By a mixture of luck and vigor Bonaparte and his troops then defeated the Austrian force mustered south of the Alps, at the Battle of Marengo in June 1800, and threw the enemy out of Italy. Once again Leclerc had, by bad luck, been attached to the less glorious fighting force.

However, in consolation for his troubles, if it was no sop to his ambition, Leclerc was to spend much of the summer of 1800 with his wife, to whom he remained devoted. The faults Laure Junot and others were quick to note in Pauline, Leclerc seems to have easily overlooked. He was, a friend wrote, hard on himself and indulgent toward others. Laure Junot had her own view of this "singular" marriage: "Madame Leclerc treated her husband despotically, and yet she went in fear, not that her husband would rebuke her but that the first consul would."

The Leclercs were to have as their rendezvous the watering resort of Plombières-les-Bains in the Vosges, where Pauline arrived in June, some weeks before her husband. She struck a General Jean Hardy, who was there taking the cure, as "a fine little woman, very sweet and very kind." She begged the general to visit her, and he told his wife that Madame Leclerc was there to reestablish her health, and tend to her pelvis, "which had been weakened by childbirth. . . . She knows no one at Plombières and seems very happy to have as a neighbor a comrade of her husband's." (Hardy had served under Leclerc in Italy.) "I owe her the care that I would wish for you, were you in her place. Besides, without reading the future, one cannot foresee what will result by chance of a meeting; good intentions are not always fruitless." And indeed when Leclerc arrived, weeks later, Hardy's solicitude for Pauline may have been a factor in stirring the senior officer to promote the other's career. "I will write to Bonaparte myself," Leclerc was to declare. But privately he was beginning to despair, and to doubt that he had any influence with his brother-in-law. Although Bonaparte had anxiously asked after Leclerc's health each time he had corresponded with Moreau after the Landshut action, he seemed to wish to do nothing for him now.

This was the first of many visits that Pauline was to make for her health to fashionable watering resorts or bathing stations. As on future visits, she now made a habit of living retired, and, as now, on future occasions there would always be those who sought to develop an acquaintance with her. But late as she might dance into the night in Paris, as a valetudinarian in Plombières she was dedicated to a regime of waters, exercise, and rest. Besides, the society available in the town was not designed to please her. At a dismal ball that General Hardy attended, there were sixty women—but no more than a dozen men, and only four among them young and fit enough to dance.

Pauline's sister-in-law Josephine had earlier sought at Plombières a cure for the continuing infertility that beset her relationship with Napoleon. Hardy's claim that Pauline's visit to the resort was occasioned by her need to recover following childbirth is somewhat surprising, given that Dermide was now two years old. But Dermide's birth appears to have presented his mother with long-lasting complications. Certainly in the autumn of 1801 and again some years later Pauline was to order a girdle to support her pelvis. (Today women faced with sacroiliac pain and pelvic instability following childbirth wear a special belt.) She added to that order two bidets, and there is evidence to suggest that later in life she suffered from salpingitis, or inflammation of the fallopian tubes. This can occur after childbirth, although multiple sexual partners and gonorrhea are other causes, and possibly she was already affected when she was at Plombières. Symptoms of salpingitis include lower abdominal pain, which can cause difficulty in walking. In other words Pauline's apparently capricious desire to be carried everywhere may have had its root in either sacroiliac or abdominal pain, or perhaps both.

Content with her cure for the moment, Pauline wrote to Madame Michelot on July 11, "I am well. I have benefited enormously from the waters and still more from the exercise that I take here. I have seen Brulière, whom my husband sent to tell me to stay here longer. I hope you are happy about my health." Leclerc duly arrived himself later in the month, much worn by his fatigues on the Rhine, and pursued, like his wife, a regime of baths, exercise, and rest. But in this letter to Madame Michelot, Pauline added, "How are you coping with your big stomach?" Madame Michelot was to have a baby later that summer. Although Pauline was full of concern for her friend as the day neared, she appears, with this question, to feel the distaste of one who had regretted seeing her own stomach grow big with child, her fashionable silhouette distended.

Although Dermide was now more than two years old, there is no suggestion that Pauline was at Plombières to improve her fertility. As we shall shortly see, she was not above claiming that she was pregnant to try to avoid unwelcome duties. But there is no speculation in Leclerc's correspondence with his family, or in that of the Bonapartes—both of which refer freely to pregnancies and childbirths—about another pregnancy for Pauline. If she was indeed suffering from salpingitis, then she would have been most unlikely to fall pregnant again. And her doctors would have known that, and have made her and Leclerc aware of it. But for want of firm evidence on the matter we cannot say whether her first pregnancy had left her unable or unwilling to reproduce again.

A few weeks later the Leclercs settled at their estate, Montgobert— an invalid couple with a small son, enjoying themselves in the Picardy landscape with visits from Leclerc and Bonaparte relations and friends. The couple amicably planned decoration inside the château and reno- vation of the garden and lands without. Leclerc changed the parterre garden *à la française* that summer into a landscaped English garden and to that end planted thousands of trees and bushes. Pauline appears to have remained in charge of the interior decor for the rooms they occu- pied, but her husband had ambitious plans to add another floor to the house and had already consulted Fontaine, the architect from Pontoise who, with his associate Percier, was making a name for himself in Paris. (Fontaine, meanwhile, was relying on Leclerc to protect him at the Ministry of the Interior, where Napoleon's plans for him to alter Saint- Cloud were calling down on the alien architect from Pontoise the wrath of the ministry's architects.)

At Montgobert, Leclerc made "improvements" as though he were a returning general who had amassed a considerable war chest during campaigns. In fact, it would seem from his papers, he had amassed con- siderable debt, and that year, when sending him three thousand francs for decoration that Pauline had instigated, he told his brother Jean Louis, who was overseeing the works, that he could do no more. One wonders what his mother, living modestly at Pontoise, made of his extravagance. But Leclerc was in the grip of an obsession, and the expenditures continued.

There were visits to be made to neighboring properties. Leclerc's friend Montbreton owned the property that bordered Montgobert. Joseph and Julie Bonaparte had meanwhile bought and embellished the Château of Mortefontaine, which lay close to the forest of d'Ermenonville between Montgobert and Paris, where they made all the family welcome. And Pauline's brother Lucien was nearby at Plessis. Although Lucien's wife, Christine, died in May, he put off mourning that summer to play host to amateur theatricals, in which the Bonapartes' eldest sister, Elisa, played an active role. Pauline informed Madame Michelot in late August that she was to take part in a comedy that was being staged at Plessis. "I am very happy with my role as a servant girl," she wrote.

The legend runs that, upon his return from Marengo, Napoleon was outraged by the lascivious gestures and diaphanous costumes that were a feature of his siblings' theatricals and banned Lucien and Elisa from performing Voltaire's *Alzire*. If so, he seems to have taken his time, as he had returned from Italy to Paris by early July, and this performance of which Pauline writes was scheduled for late summer. Moreover, if Napoleon felt distaste for his family's amateur theatricals, he relished the professional stage. A young actor from the Midi, Rapenouille, took the name of Lafon and dazzled audiences on his debut that May in Racine's *Iphigénie* at the Comédie Française. Napoleon told the star of the troupe, the great Talma, that he should welcome the advent of the younger actor. "It's a stimulant you needed. You were acting in your sleep, now you must wake up."

Lafon is said separately to have been taken under the protection of Lucien Bonaparte and may have been involved at Plessis in tutoring the Bonaparte family in their theatrical roles. Pauline, moreover, is credited with having embarked on an affair with the handsome young southerner, all flashing black eyes and deep seductive voice. But Leclerc's correspondence with his family contains no hint that summer of marital discord. "Paulette has left this morning for Paris and won't return here this year," he records placidly from Montgobert, on September 23. "I follow her once they have finished planting." And he goes on to write of harvests and donkeys, of mares to be sold and carpenters to be paid. If a cuckold, he was a remarkably complacent—if not an unwitting—one.

In Paris the Leclercs, with Dermide and his nurse, had been occupying apartments in the house of Victor Emmanuel's brother Nicolas, as they had left the Michelots'. But now they signed a contract to buy for 20,500 francs an elegant house in the rue de Courcelles, close to the Faubourg Saint-Honoré and next to the Church of Saint-Philippe-du-Roule. The house, although not large, was commodious, with a salon, a boudoir, a dining room, a billiard room, and a library, as well as an upper floor of bedrooms, with a "grotto" and a swing in the garden.

Pauline had indicated that they would wait for the general to receive command of an army before they purchased a house. But perhaps it had proved too galling to see the other Bonapartes in the smart Parisian houses they now occupied. Pauline's mother enjoyed the hospitality of her half brother Fesch in a luxurious *hôtel,* as these large town mansions were known, in the rue Mont Blanc. Joseph and Julie were now in the Hôtel Marboeuf in the rue du Faubourg Saint-Honoré, which had belonged to the governor of Corsica. (On that island at least, the Marquis de Marboeuf was popularly believed to have been Letizia Bonaparte's lover.) Caroline and Murat were installed in the Hôtel de Brienne, to the north of the Tuileries. And Lucien, with Elisa and Felice Bacciochi as lodgers, occupied the Hôtel de Brissac in the rue de Grenelle.

While Pauline decorated her boudoir to her satisfaction, Leclerc was at last given a command, but it was not one to please him. He was dispatched in December 1800 to Dijon, to command the Army of Reserve, which had now returned from northern Italy and was in winter quarters. If there is any doubt that Leclerc was unhappy with this stagnant posting, a letter exists from his former commander, General Berthier, written shortly after his departure for Dijon: "I have seen your wife, and I have tried, with her, to persuade the First Consul to let you come to Paris." Pauline's efforts to obtain her husband's return to Paris, where he might himself press the War Ministry for a more advantageous posting, do not preclude her simultaneously conducting one or even more than one affair. It does show, however, that she was still ambitious for him and eager to see him singled out. Leclerc himself later recorded, "I was vexed that I was forgotten during the war. . . . Although I was full of admiration for Bonaparte, who sacrifices himself all day long to assure France's well-being, I was indignant to see these wretches who, by the worthlessness of their resources, ought never to have had a role to play, not content with the fine place he had assigned them, try to put themselves at his side and even in his place." Leclerc had in mind General Bernadotte, Désirée Clary's husband, and other officers who had earlier curried favor with Bonaparte before attempting to stage a coup during his absence in the east.

Between them Berthier and Pauline were successful, and Leclerc was agreeably surprised with the new post assigned him in March 1801, after the War of the Second Coalition had been brought to an end by the Peace of Lunéville. He was made lieutenant general of the Army of Observation of the Gironde that was assembling in Bordeaux, preparatory to going to Spain. Once there the French corps would support Spain in the so-called War of the Oranges that it was conducting against Portugal, Britain's oldest ally. On arrival at Bordeaux, Leclerc wrote to his sister, Aimée, at Madame Campan's school: "The roads getting here were terrible, but the beauty of the town and the affability of the inhabitants are compensation enough." When Pauline joined him there, attending balls and concerts with him, he was more than content.

But once Pauline had returned to Paris, and the Army of Observation set off for Spain, Leclerc was grumpy. He wrote to Aimée in mid-June from Ciudad Rodrigo, in western Spain, "I have been constantly on the road for a month, and always in the most frightful rush. This is a horrible country, five centuries behind France." Furthermore, for all his exertions, once more the campaign to which Leclerc was assigned failed to provide him with a proper theater of war. Once more a great destiny was denied him, for Spain and Portugal rapidly signed a peace. And, no doubt mindful of his expenditure on the new house in Paris, of the building works at Montgobert, he appealed on August 7 from Salamanca to Lucien Bonaparte, who had recently become ambassador to Spain: "If you find an opportunity at Madrid to help me increase my fortune, I will be obliged to you."

While Leclerc labored in Spain, Pauline spent most of the summer at Mortefontaine, at her brother Joseph's house, with some excursions to Montgobert, where her brother-in-law Jean Louis Leclerc was still overseeing the improvements. "You see, my dear brother," wrote Leclerc from Spain, "that I have more and more ambitious plans for the property." And again he wrote, "This year we should begin to have a little fruit from the vines we planted."

What made her husband's stymied campaign all the more galling for Pauline was the successful career of her younger sister Caroline's husband, Murat. A description of the two pretty sisters tormenting an elderly Italian poet by repeatedly seizing his wig when he was sitting out in the sunshine shows that Pauline and Caroline could be the best of friends. But they were also all their lives jealous of each other, and now Caroline had a small baby, Achille Louis Napoléon Murat, and was pregnant with another. Murat, moreover, had been named commander in chief of the French forces in Italy, while Leclerc battled against fatigue and loss of morale in Spain and fell prey to anxiety about his loved ones in France. "I see with pain that you do not speak to me of Paulette," he wrote from Ciudad Rodrigo on July 28 to his sister, Aimée. "Has there been some coldness between you? I would see with pain a rift between two people who are so dear to me."

And then in early October, just as Leclerc had taken his men into winter quarters in Bro, near Valladolid, Napoleon addressed the following momentous dispatch to General Berthier, the minister of war: "Send an order by special courier to General Leclerc to come to Paris with all speed. He should bring his aides-de-camp, two adjutants-commandant, and five artillery and reconnaissance officers of quality to serve under him in an overseas expedition. . . . He can leave the command of the observation corps to the most senior general." Leclerc left Spain the moment he received the dispatch. At last his chance had come.

Napoleon went on to outline, in this and further dispatches to Berthier, the details of the vast overseas expedition that Leclerc was to head. It was to comprise a fighting force of more than twenty thousand men, with an equal number of sailors supplied by the Admiralty—and commanded by Admiral Louis Thomas Villaret de Joyeuse—to man the seventy-one vessels, including twenty-five ships of the line, that would transport the army. One squadron was to set sail from Brest, another from Rochefort, and others from Lorient, Toulon, Cádiz, and even Vlissinden in Holland. The force also included Spanish and Dutch contingents. And the object of this powerful expedition? To recover for France the formerly profitable sugar colony of Saint-Domingue, known as the Pearl of the Antilles and now in the hands of rebel slaves led by Toussaint Louverture. Saint-Domingue, present-day Haiti, forms the western part of the Caribbean island, which, with its much larger eastern part, Santo Domingo—the present-day Dominican Republic—was originally claimed for Spain by Columbus in the fifteenth century as Hispaniola. Spain ceded Saint-Domingue to France in 1697.

A recent endeavor of Toussaint's, to frame a new constitution according to which he would be governor-general for life, had incensed his former masters. The National Convention of 1794 had granted the slaves of Saint-Domingue, as well as those of other French colonies, their freedom, and by degrees Toussaint had won control of the country, as well as of Spanish Santo Domingo. Now that the preliminaries of the Peace of Amiens, which would tie up the loose ends left dangling by the War of the Second Coalition, had been settled, and now, indeed, that the protracted expedition to Egypt had ended in defeat—the French surrendered Alexandria to Sir Ralph Abercromby in March—Napoleon had troops and ships at his disposal, and was eager to bring the unruly former colony to heel. In particular he meant to recover the enormous revenues of Saint-Domingue for France—and, to that end, he planned to reestablish slavery.

In Toussaint, however, Napoleon had an opponent of extraordinary charisma and intellect, who was in addition a proven warrior. Over the years the former slave had won the loyalty of local chiefs and trained a large army in guerrilla warfare against the Spanish and the British. Now he was expecting an attempt by the French to regain control, and he was ready.

As Leclerc learned when he arrived in Paris, it was the express wish of the first consul that he should take his wife and small son with him to Saint-Domingue. For this was no short military campaign that awaited the commander, as Napoleon's instructions made clear. Once Leclerc had subdued Toussaint and the other island commanders, he was, as captain general of the colony, to introduce and oversee the implementation of a series of legal, administrative, and fiscal reforms. He might be away for some years in this latter capacity, and in the circumstances it was deemed by the first consul only proper that Leclerc's family go with him. Nevertheless there were those who were startled by the proposition that Pauline and Dermide Leclerc were to accompany the expeditionary force.

In the first place Toussaint, the chiefs who served him, and their guerrilla forces would almost certainly resist the French expeditionary force. But in addition the history of Saint-Domingue was a violent one, checkered with rebellions by the slave population of five hundred thousand and with massacres they perpetrated among the thirty thousand plantation owners who farmed coffee, sugarcane, and indigo. Toussaint had subdued most of the country, but news of battles between his forces and the mulattoes under General Rigaud, who occupied the south of the colony—of voodoo crimes, of atrocities—continued to percolate back to France. And then there was the ever-present threat in the Americas of yellow (or, as it was then called, Siamese) fever, with hemorrhage, high temperature, and black vomit preceding death. It would, in short, have been hardly surprising if Pauline had not felt some dread at the idea of leaving her settled life in Paris for unknown, fearsome Saint-Domingue. But diminishing all other concerns, there was always the prospect of glory and fortune to be won, debts to be eliminated, in the distant Caribbean.

According to one account, Pauline was positively ebullient the evening after Leclerc arrived in Paris from Spain. Their neighbor from Montgobert, Montbreton, called at the rue de Courcelles with his brother, Jacques de Norvins, to congratulate the couple. (There had been rumors since the peace with England had been signed that an expedition to Saint-Domingue would take place, but it had been thought that the command would be given to General Bernadotte.) "Leclerc and his wife received us with the greatest friendship," Norvins tells us. "I was astonished to learn that she, so young, so delicate, so happy in Paris, would follow her husband to Saint-Domingue with her son, aged about three. The first consul had decided it, and she spoke with frank pleasure of this great adventure." Norvins explains that everyone in Paris had been somewhat thrown by the news of the expedition. "I said, 'My God, madame, I would go with you too, if Leclerc wants me to come.' 'Yes, yes, you must come with us!' And she called her husband who was talking to General Davout: 'Listen, Norvins says he wants to come with us.' 'You're joking,' replied Leclerc. 'Norvins is not a man to leave Paris, where he is so well off. Aren't I right, Norvins?' 'No, you're quite wrong, and if you want, I'll be of your number.' Leclerc looked at my brother, Montbreton. 'What do you say?' 'I say, in my brother's place, I'd do the same.' 'Then shake on it,' said Leclerc, extending his hand."

The general was not usually so cavalier in choosing his regular staff. "I only take notice of good conduct and talent," he had written from Spain to his sister, Aimée, when she asked him to advance a protégé's military career out there. Now General Charles-François-Joseph Dugua, who had served in Egypt, was co-opted for the Saint-Domingue expedition, as was General Hardy, with whom Pauline had dined in Plombières. "I hope to acquire legally and honestly funds to assure your well-being and educate our children," Hardy wrote optimistically to his wife. Despite Leclerc's love of order, everything now took place in the most tremendous hurry. "It is just as you would expect," he grumbled to Davout, "when the commander is appointed at the last minute." He was kept constantly busy, answering requests from those who wished a son or a godson or a protégé to form part of the army and share in its glory. Nor were his own and Pauline's families unrepresented. Leclerc's elderly uncle General Jean-Charles Musquinet de Beaupré joined the force, and Pauline's younger brother Jérôme was to accompany the expedition as a naval lieutenant.

Madame Campan's nephew Pannellier won a place as secretary to the general, even as the schoolmistress lost Aimée Leclerc, with Hortense de Beauharnais one of her prize pupils, to matrimony. Leclerc wanted to see Aimée married to his friend and colleague General Davout before he left France, and the ceremony was duly performed on November 9, 1801. But it could have been set for a month later. The date of the expeditionary force's departure was constantly postponed, as preparations were not complete, and arms, clothing, hospital supplies lacking. In the meantime, according to legend, Pauline began to fret and told her brother she could not accompany her husband as she was pregnant. The first consul promptly sent around his physician to examine and declare her mistaken. Laure Junot gives this account of visiting the general's lady in the rue de Courcelles:

"Oh, little Laure," said Pauline, throwing herself in the other's arms. "Lucky you! To stay in Paris. Good God, I am going to be so bored. How can my brother have so hard a heart, so mean a soul as to exile me in the middle of savages and snakes. . . . And I am ill too. Oh, I'll die before I even get there."

Laure Junot talked to the disconsolate beauty "as one would to a child, of toys and pom-poms." Pauline would be queen in Saint-Domingue, said Laure, she would be carried in a litter. A slave would be attentive to her every wish, and she would walk through arbors of orange trees and flowers. There were, besides, no snakes in the Antilles, and the people weren't savages. Getting nowhere with these arguments, Madame Junot had the canniness to suggest that Pauline would look very pretty in Creole dress.

Pauline's tears dried instantly, and she set to imagining the costume. "Oh, it would be pretty. A madras handkerchief, tied Creole fashion, a little corset, a skirt of pleated muslin?" Immediately she rang for her maid and had her entire stock of Indian cotton, a present from Madame Permon, brought out. As that lady had habitually worn a madras handkerchief at home in bed, her daughter, Laure, proved adept at knotting the four corners of the cloth selected and fitting it to Pauline's head. And Madame Leclerc was thrilled with her coiffure *à la créole*. "'Laurette,' she said, arranging herself on her sofa, 'do you know how I love you? You prefer Caroline to me, but let's see if we can't change that. Here's a proof of my love for you. . . . Come to Saint-Domingue. You will be the first lady of the island after me. I'll be queen, as you say. Well, you'll be vicereine. I'll talk to my brother about it.' 'Me, go to Saint-Domingue,' I cried. 'What are you thinking of?' 'Don't worry, I'll talk to Bonaparte, and as he likes Junot, he'll let him come.'"

Pauline then enumerated the balls she would give, the parties in the mountains—"something every day." And she ticked off on her fingers the couturiers, milliners, and jewelers that Laure must patronize before she would be fit to travel—"Mademoiselle Despaux, Madame Germon, Le Roi, Copp, Mesdames Roux . . . no, Nattier is better." In the end, as she would not take no for an answer, according to Laure, Junot himself intervened to ask how his wife could possibly travel, given that she was vastly pregnant "Oh," said Pauline. "So you are."

Frivolities aside, Pauline and Leclerc had sober legal action to take before they left Paris. Such were the risks of the journey to come that they each signed a bond leaving to the other their property on death. It is said that Leclerc even picked out at Montgobert the site of a grave, should the need for burial arise. In any event he gave his brother Jean Louis a proxy so that works at Montgobert could continue, and received a proxy from Josephine Bonaparte, who, by coincidence, and although a Martinique Creole by birth, had property in Saint-Domingue.

"Don't bother me about money anymore," Napoleon is said to have told Leclerc, on bestowing on his brother-in-law this prime command. And when Leclerc and Pauline embarked with Dermide on the flagship L'Océan, at Brest, and set sail for the Caribbean on December 14, 1801, the general had every hope that he would return a rich man. At the last minute, and it seems to have been a matter of regret for Pauline, their house in the rue Courcelles, which she had so recently decorated, was sold. But, although she sighed for Paris and for her boudoir there, she had what Norvins describes as sumptuous quarters on L'Océan, and at Le Cap, the former capital of Saint-Domingue, she would inhabit the governor's palace. On board the ship, as the bad weather off the French coast gave way to balmy breezes in the Canary Islands and farther west, Pauline played with Dermide on deck.

It was a picture that Norvins, for one, appreciated, but another member of the expedition had preferred to wait and find a separate passage at Brest. Stanislas Fréron, down on his luck now for years, had obtained a post as subprefect at Les Cayes in Saint-Domingue, but on finding that his berth was booked on *L'Océan,* chose not to travel on the same vessel as his former fiancée and her husband. He had to wait four months for another berth.

There were others who found the sight of *L'Océan* and the rest of the fleet from Brest more than off-putting. As the ships sailed into the Bay of Samana in eastern Hispaniola at the end of January 1802, Toussaint Louverture was on the lookout. "Friends," he addressed his lieutenants, "we are doomed. All France is come to Saint-Domingue." And he sent a message to the vassal chief General Henri Christophe, who occupied Le Cap, ordering him to set fire to the town when the French troops threatened it.

CHAPTER FIVE

Expedition to Haiti, 1802

U NAWARE OF TOUSSAINT LOUVERTURE'S grim words, the combined fleets that had set out from Brest, Rochefort, and Lorient the previous year made their way slowly south from the Bay of Samana and sailed in a westerly direction along the southern shore of Hispaniola, a tropical landmass of thirty thousand square miles. Soon they left behind the eastern two-thirds of the island known as Santo Domingo. Although it was still nominally in Spanish hands, it was in fact now under Toussaint's control. At last they entered the waters of Saint-Domingue, the mountainous and fertile western third of the island, humid and forested, rich in minerals, flora, and fauna—and their destination.

Not for nothing was this colony, French since the late seventeenth century, known as the Pearl of the Antilles. Adam Smith had called it in his 1767 *Wealth of Nations* "the most important of the sugar colonies of the West Indies," but Saint-Domingue's indigo, coffee, and cotton plantations were nearly as lucrative. It was hardly surprising that the French regretted losing control of its income, and indeed Toussaint had long expected a challenge to his hegemony. When warned by the British in neighboring Jamaica that an expedition was forming against him in France, he had placed his generals and troops in a state of readiness to do battle, as Leclerc and his forces would all too soon discover.

Now, sailing westward, the French expeditionary force passed Les Cayes, the small town where Pauline's former lover Fréron was to be subprefect. Proceeding up the western coast, they sailed past the wooded island of La Gonâve and entered the harbor at Port-au-Prince, capital of the colony since 1770. There the black Jacobin, General Jean-Jacques Dessalines, occupied the governor's palace and commanded twelve thousand troops. Now Admiral Louis-René Levassor de Latouche-Tréville's squadron, carrying General Jean Boudet's division, anchored here, while General Jean-Baptiste Rochambeau with two thousand men was dispatched to Fort Dauphin. Pauline and Leclerc continued northward on *L'Océan* with the rest of the fleet that had set out from Brest under Admiral Villaret de Joyeuse's command, all the time watched by Toussaint's lookouts. Finally, proceeding along the northern shore of the colony toward the east and passing the small island of Tortue, once a base for French pirates, they anchored on February 3, 1802, in the Bay of Le Cap.

This opulent French colonial town, founded in 1711 and capital of Saint-Domingue for much of the eighteenth century, had been dubbed "the Paris of the West," in allusion to the fashionable shops, theater, and concerts that the Creole merchant and plantation families enjoyed there. Besides eight or nine hundred substantial houses of stone and brick, fine churches, and two hospitals, there were two handsome squares with public fountains and a governor's palace. This elegant residence, which successive governors had occupied, however, was not as yet to house the Leclerc ménage. For, at Le Cap, the former slave General Christophe commanded a total of five thousand troops and flatly refused Leclerc's request to surrender the town. Deputations came and went in canoes between Leclerc and the black general, but in vain.

In consultation with General Dugua, his chief of staff, Leclerc therefore resolved to disembark in the night some nine leagues to the west and, with his brother Nicolas, General Hardy, and six thousand troops, cross mountains and plains in order to lead an attack on the rebel town, under cover of cannon from the fleet. Meanwhile, according to Jacques de Norvins, her husband's amanuensis, Pauline reclined gracefully on an ottoman in the great cabin of the flagship *L'Océan*. He found her "beautiful as any angel, suffering"—the seas had risen high—"and caressing her son, a stalwart child of nearly three." (Dermide was actually nearly four.) Norvins remarked that the boy exhibited "a singular strength which made one fear as much as hope for his well-being."

But that very night, while Leclerc and Hardy were making their way painfully through the darkness, Christophe set fire to Le Cap, as he had threatened to do. From *L'Océan* Pauline and her fellow voyagers had a clear view of what Norvins described as "immense clouds of red and black smoke billowing above the town, shedding horrible shadows and shafts of light. At the will of the winds they illumined by turn rocks, woods, and sea. The sinister clouds ventured even as far as the fleet, and so every ship became palpably aware of the destruction." What Toussaint had ordered, Christophe had enacted, and the inferno was to rage for three days.

Meanwhile Leclerc and Hardy, ignorant of what lay ahead, traversed unknown plain and mountain. As Hardy wrote to his wife, their minds were not eased by the intermittent appearance of the inhabitants of the interior, who loomed threateningly out of the night. Two leagues from Le Cap a disparate force actually attacked Hardy's men but was dispatched without too much difficulty. And then they too saw the ominous red clouds. When they arrived in the town of Le Cap, the gracious buildings that they had seen from the ships and that had ringed the bay like an amphitheater were charred and burned, the inhabitants homeless in the high hills that lay behind.

Leclerc's courage did not desert him, although with Le Cap in ruins it would be more difficult to implement Napoleon's instructions to restore order to the colony. He and his troops did battle with Christophe and his men and, at a cost of five hundred casualties, gained the advantage. Leclerc then announced to the inhabitants of Le Cap that reconstruction would begin as soon as he had suppressed insurgency elsewhere. He published proclamations—of his own, of Napoleon's, in French and in Creole, the bastard French that was spoken in the colony—all of which declared that he and his forces represented legitimate government but emphasized that the inhabitants of Saint-Domingue were free Frenchmen and would remain so.

"Blancs, nègues, tout cé zenfant de la Répiblique" (Black, white, all are children of the Republic), declared Bonaparte in Creole. "Zabitans de Saint-Domingue," ran Leclerc's text:

> Lire proclamation Primié Consul Bonaparte. Voyez pour zote, Zote à voir que li vélé nègues resté libre. Li pas vélé ôté liberté à yo que yo gagné en combattant, et que li va mainteni li de tout pouvoir à li. [Inhabitants of Saint-Domingue, please read First Consul Bonaparte's proclamation; see for yourselves that he wishes all blacks to stay free. He does not wish to take away that liberty for which you have fought so hard, and he will do all in his power to maintain it.]

And Leclerc proclaimed that the first consul's promises would be faithfully fulfilled. To think otherwise would be a crime.

Finally Leclerc dispatched to Toussaint Louverture, who had retreated to his home at Ennery on the west coast, the black leader's two sons, who had been educated in France. They took with them their tutor and a letter begging their father to submit to Leclerc's governance, but Toussaint gave the French general no reply.

While her husband moved rapidly about the former colony, Pauline was left on board *L'Océan* at Le Cap with Dermide. The heat at this season of the year, according to Hardy, was no worse than on a June day in France. But Pauline had no previous experience of a climate in which heavy skies, thunderstorms, and showers followed brilliant sunshine twice or three times a day. She did not like the motion of the sea at the best of times. And there was the anxiety she felt about the outcome of each of Leclerc's successive forays against Toussaint's generals.

"Madame Leclerc is at the moment at Le Cap," wrote Leclerc to Napoleon on March 5. "She is fairly well. The disastrous events in the midst of which she found herself wore her down to the point of making

her ill. Today, now that all that is over, she has recovered her spirits."
(Pauline had indeed made herself popular with the officers who formed
her guard, distributing wine among them. On hearing that one of them
was the son of a notary and from Paris, she said, gesturing with her fan
to his shoulder, "When we leave this island, I will have you enter my
brother's private guard.") As for Dermide, Leclerc assured Napoleon,
he was well and had survived the crossing from France better than anyone. Even of young Jérôme, Pauline's naval lieutenant brother, Leclerc
had good reports: "He has the makings of an excellent officer."

Leclerc was writing to Napoleon from Port-au-Prince, where he had
given thanks to God for their successes. "Confidence returns," he said.
"Yesterday I had a Te Deum sung, which I attended with all my staff.
All the inhabitants of the town, who could not get into the church,
pressed about my path, and everywhere I received the strongest proofs
of their satisfaction."

A month later he wrote to the first consul that he was sending his
brother Nicolas to Paris with an account of his situation at Saint-
Domingue. "I have made one of the most exhausting campaigns possible and I owe my position to the rapidity with which I moved." He
spoke of his altered health (he had been pulled down by bouts of fever):
"Once I have reestablished order, I will ask to return to France."

He wrote to the minister of marine and colonies on March 26 from
Saint-Marc giving details of that campaign. They had besieged a
stronghold at Crête-à-Pierrot, "an extremely important position" in the
interior occupied by Dessalines, one of Toussaint's most feared
generals, who had formerly held Port-au-Prince. "I didn't know of its
existence or its importance," Leclerc rebuked the minister. He had
three generals attack it from different points, but Dessalines and his
men within the fort fought fiercely. One day saw six hundred of the
attackers killed or wounded, among them fifty officers. Leclerc wrote,
"It was the hottest affair I have seen in my life." There was no alternative but to besiege the position and hope to starve out the inhabitants.
But at night the French officers in their tents were discomfited by the
sound of the "Marseillaise" and other French Revolutionary songs

floating out from within the stronghold's walls. Dessalines had convinced his men that they were the true heirs of the Revolution and that the first consul and the expeditionary force he had sent to Saint-Domingue had perverted its cause.

When at last Leclerc took the stronghold, he found within, besides bodies of those killed during the prolonged siege, and cannon and gunpowder, "all of Dessalines' music"—the orchestral instruments that had so disturbed his soldiers' peace of mind—"and many crates of tambours." "You can have no idea of the atrocities committed here," he told the minister of marine and colonies. "More than 10,000 white and black or mulatto inhabitants have had their throats cut on the orders of Toussaint or Dessalines and Christophe. In our expeditions we found more than 6,000 men, women, and children whom they had led into the woods and whom they intended to kill."

The tide turned when Leclerc took Crête-à-Pierrot. Soon all the black generals, with the exception of Toussaint, had surrendered. As Napoleon's instructions allowed, Leclerc enrolled them and their troops in his army with due honor and with a rank equivalent to the one they had held in Toussaint's. Meanwhile Pauline and Dermide joined Leclerc at Port-au-Prince, and husband and wife could exchange news of their experiences in this demanding colonial habitat while the heat of the day grew more onerous as March gave way to April.

DURING THE DAY small boys chased away flies and fanned the Leclercs with long feathers, while butterflies fluttered around the governor's palace and plumes of smoke rose from the hills behind the town, denoting the manufacture of sugar. To drink there was fresh lemonade, made from cane sugar, lemons, and red apples; to eat, apricots, sapodillas, and fig-bananas. The smell of jasmine and of orange flowers pervaded the town. But sleep was difficult, the night air pernicious. Even with mosquito nets it was difficult not to feel dread of the spiders, scorpions, and bloodsucking creatures native to the colony.

Leclerc's work took him, after this short respite with his family, to

Le Cap in mid-April to oversee the work of reconstruction in the town. Norvins, who accompanied him, gives an idea of how quickly the town had been reerected. "Nine weeks earlier we had left a town in ashes; imagine our astonishment when we saw a totally new town rising above the bay. The white wooden roofs of a thousand houses glistened there, forming an elegant amphitheater, and the crowded quays spoke to the town's renaissance."

Leclerc wrote to Napoleon, "My situation is fine and brilliant." In only forty days he had subdued the whole island, and, once he had completed his preparations, Pauline could look forward to reigning at Le Cap as her consort's queen just as long ago in Paris with Laure Junot she had imagined she would. Moreover, Leclerc had conceived the idea of asking for the forested island of La Gonâve, which lay off Port-au-Prince, as a gift from the first consul in recompense for his efforts. The Leclercs would thus have a colonial property and an annual income of as much as two hundred thousand francs from the timber.

At Le Cap, Leclerc waited for a response from Paris, while framing judiciary reforms and penal law. In addition he called for skilled botanists and mineralogists to be sent to the colony—"the richness in medicinal plants here is incalculable"—as well as mechanics to conduct mining experiments. He dispatched to France for the Museum of Natural History in Paris an example of an exotic animal—"which Buffon calls the 'little *lamantin* [manatee] of the Antilles.'" It was ten feet long, and its flesh, which he had tasted, he informed the minister of the interior in Paris, was like beef.

There is no doubt that the "blond Bonaparte," Leclerc, hoped that the fruits of his expedition to the Pearl of the Antilles would fascinate the French, just as Napoleon's expedition to Egypt had awakened interest in the ancient and modern civilizations of that country. With the naturalist Descourtilz, who had visited the colony three years earlier, he might have asked, "Oh, why is Saint-Domingue, made for its climate, by the fertility of its soil, by the beauty of its sites, to be an enchanted isle, inhabited only by lovers of money and not those of nature?"

But Leclerc's desire to showcase the flora and fauna of Saint-

Domingue ran parallel with, not contrary to, his colonial ambitions, and, despite his words to Napoleon, he had reservations about his position that he felt he had to express to the government in Paris. It was essential that they dispatch, he wrote, besides money, food, and hospital supplies, a further twelve thousand men from France. With five thousand men in hospital and another thousand dead, he had only six thousand fit for action of those who had voyaged out with him. He could not count, he said, on the loyalty of the black troops who had come over to him. Without these reinforcements, he believed, he must lose control of the colony within two months. "Once I have lost it, imagine what it would take to regain it," he warned.

General Hardy reported to his wife in France that, at Port-au-Prince, Madame Leclerc was bored to death, and he was content to have left Madame Hardy at home. However, in the years following the expedition to Saint-Domingue, exotic rumors circulated about the six weeks that Pauline had spent in the capital without her husband, and, as her fame spread, so did the tales of her infamous doings during this period. She succumbed to the "island vice," runs one account, and indulged in lesbian affairs with two women at a time, then passed from their arms to those of General Jean-François Debelle, known as the "Apollo of the French army." Another lascivious report asserts: "The tropical sun was, they say, astonished by the ardor of her passions." A third source claims that she experimented with white and black lovers to see which she preferred. Finally there is the accusation that she conducted an affair with General Jean Robert Humbert, a notoriously cruel French administrator. Her later employment in France of a large black page to carry her to her bath and act as outrider on her carriage did nothing to dispel the rumors.

Few of those who attacked her reputation were with Pauline or Leclerc in Saint-Domingue. Many of the allegations formed part of a later mudslinging campaign by the British in which Napoleon's family was condemned for a multitude of vices. Alternatively they were written after Napoleon's fall from power and the restoration of the Bourbons to the throne of France. However, Pauline received two letters from her brother Napoleon, one written in mid-March, the other in July 1802. The first was mild and encouraging:

> I have received your letter, my good little Paulette. Remember that fatigue and suffering are nothing when one shares them with one's husband and when one is useful to one's country . . . make yourself beloved by . . . your affability, and behave prudently, never thoughtlessly. They are making you the outfits, which the captain of the *Sirène* will bring out to you. I love you very much. Make sure all the world is pleased with you, and be worthy of your position.

The second letter began well: "I have learned with pleasure that you have bravely withstood the ardors of the campaign." However, a stern note follows: "Take care of your husband, who, from what they tell me, is a little ill, and don't give him any ground for jealousy. For a serious man, all flirtatious ways are insupportable. A wife must be good and seek to pleasure, not demand. Your husband is now truly worthy of the title of my brother, given the glory he is amassing. . . . Unite with him in love and tender friendship."

Napoleon's information about the state of affairs in Saint-Domingue was necessarily not current, given that it took six weeks for a ship to reach France from the West Indies. But if he alludes in this second letter to specific misdeeds on Pauline's part, his admonitions hardly amount to a condemnation of much more than flirtation. Lesbian relationships, sex with the natives of the island, affairs with his officers, orgies—transgressions of this magnitude would have called forth a different response. In fact there is no real reason to think this July letter anything other than a general lecture of the kind that Napoleon thought it necessary periodically to deliver to his younger sister. And as Napoleon's harangues to Pauline on the subject of her behavior usually proved unavailing, if she was indeed not behaving with circumspection at Port-au-Prince, his letter was unlikely to have had much effect. Nevertheless, if the embers of sexual fire that gave rise to the clouds of smoky rumor that later wreathed Pauline are anywhere to be found, they are at Port-au-Prince, where she lived in the palace that Toussaint Louverture had so recently vacated.

At any rate Pauline's husband was looking forward to her arrival at Le Cap in early May. "I left her for six weeks in Port-au-Prince, not wanting her to live in the middle of ruins. She is coming here in a few days," he told his brother-in-law Davout on May 8. In addition Leclerc had the news to impart that Toussaint had come to parley with him. After the black general had protested his loyalty to France, he had refused to join the French army, pleading age—he was nearly sixty— and the wish to live retired with his wife and children at his home in Ennery. All the while his cavalry guard in fine uniforms had waited outside in the courtyard, leaning on their swords. Neither side trusted the other, and when they sat down to eat together Toussaint accepted only a piece of Gruyère, fearing poison. Leclerc agreed, however, to the other's plan of retirement, while he counseled Toussaint to use his influence with the inhabitants of the colony wisely.

On leaving, Toussaint said, "Providence will save us," a remark that infuriated and alarmed the French. Providence was the name of the hospital in Le Cap, and the season when yellow fever could sweep the West Indies was near. It was believed that Europeans were particularly at risk. At any rate Leclerc considered that this was a good time to establish a hospital free of "an air poisoned by fire, massacre and battle- fields," as Norvins put it. The general chose the island of Tortue, north- west of Le Cap, and, settling there with Pauline and Dermide on a former plantation owner's estate, the Habitation Labattut, set about staffing a hospital of four hundred beds.

Army headquarters were established in outlying houses and former slave quarters in the village, while the Leclercs and a guard detachment occupied the main house on the estate. A small population of farmers, who had lived on the plantation since their former masters left, "philo- sophically set about serving us and provided vegetables, fruits, and fish," Norvins tells us. He adds that the chief duty of the general's guard on what he called the "enchanted isle" was to protect his wife from the adoration of the inhabitants of Tortue. They appear to have mistaken Pauline for some deity when she first arrived. "Their admiration on setting eyes on her was so energetic that, despite us and also her who was the cause of it, they all tumultuously followed us into the house, from which we had some trouble in evicting them. During our stay," Norvins continues, "they stationed themselves constantly before the door, peering in at the windows in hopes of catching sight of the goddess; it needed a cordon sanitaire to stop them from entering. But nothing could prevent them from following us on the promenade too, although the guards kept them at a safe distance."

The problem was how to acknowledge the homage that the people wished to pay to Madame Leclerc. Norvins reports that "knowing the passion negroes feel for dance, we conceived the idea of hosting a chica for them all." A great clearing in a neighboring wood was chosen as the site of the spectacle—a *chica,* the French understood, was a traditional dance—and some of the old West Indies hands among the French sailors were told to arrange the event.

Old, young, children of both sexes—the whole population of the Habitation Labattut estate went on ahead, and, when the Leclerc party set out, they heard cries coming from the clearing, indicating that the dancers had not waited to begin. Upon arrival, writes Norvins, it became evident that "we had surprised the strange pantomime of the chica at its climax, a point of exaltation cheered on lustily by our soldiers and sailors." The dancers' costumes were scanty, their movements suggestive. "We were really very embarrassed, for our ravishing *madame la générale,* and then for ourselves."

Whether Madame Leclerc was so embarrassed is not clear. As the guest of honor, she took her place on a big seat of banana leaves, under an arbor of frangipani and scented roses, that the sailors had placed at a distance from the "pandemonium." She watched from that place of safety what Norvins termed the "infernal bacchanal" in her honor, all "wild chants and barbaric cries." Tom-toms and tambourines beat out an infectious rhythm, while couples fell exhausted to the floor and then rose to writhe together again in their unbridled dance. The Leclercs retreated back home, but the dancers continued their "abominable orgy" till daybreak. In Norvins' opinion, "A month earlier or several months later, these same blacks who knelt when Mme. Leclerc passed by, would have cut her throat with the same fervor, she and her child both, fine as he was. We knew it when we had them dance."

TORTUE AND ADULATION at the Habitation Labattut soon became a distant memory for Madame Leclerc, when, with the hospital there functional, she, her husband, and her son returned to Le Cap in early June. As the heat was still sweltering, they settled in a summer residence in the hills, the Habitation L'Estaing, while officers instructed by Leclerc performed an unpleasant duty. Only a month earlier Leclerc had guaranteed Toussaint his safety, but now he had grown suspicious of the black general. Around his estate at Ennery more and more of his supporters had gathered, and Leclerc feared an insurrection. He decided, with fateful consequences, that the security of the colony made it imperative that he break his word to Toussaint.

Following Leclerc's orders, General Jean-Baptiste Brunet asked Toussaint to meet near the town of Les Gonâves, under the pretext of military discussions. The French then disarmed his guard, and Leclerc's aide-de-camp Ferrari demanded Toussaint's sword. Under arrest, the black leader was then embarked with his wife and two sons for France, where he was to be imprisoned. On leaving his native land, with whose destiny his own had been so closely tied, Toussaint pronounced, "You have axed the trunk of the tree of liberty, but it will grow again, for its roots are numerous and deep." Meanwhile Leclerc warned the minister of marine and colonies, "You must make sure his prison is both secure and as far from the sea as possible. This man has fanaticized this country to a point that his presence would put it once more in combustion." His directions were followed, and, on his arrival in France, Toussaint was separated from his wife and children and imprisoned in a cold stronghold in the Jura. Alone and forgotten except in his native land, he died there of cold and malnutrition the following April.

Toussaint had gone, but his prediction that yellow fever rather than his troops would lay low the French command might yet come true. Leclerc wrote to his brother Jean Louis in early June, "We have here a terrible sickness. Men die in twenty-four hours. Few are exempt. I have lost four generals and five of my aides-de-camp." Among the officers who succumbed early on was General Hardy, who had dined two years before at Plombières with Pauline. The symptoms of the dread disease, borne by mosquitoes, were paralysis of the nervous system accompanied by vomiting, high fever, and delirium, and all too often it had a fatal outcome.

"Soon every day the yellow fever filled our hospitals, and every day death emptied them," wrote Norvins. Nevertheless Leclerc, expecting reinforcements, was content. The colony was tranquil. He was still optimistic, and proud of his campaign and of those who had served in it. "This brave army," he wrote to the first consul, ". . . has undergone a campaign that would astonish Europe in its energy, despite suffering deprivations of all kinds. Today it withstands the ravages of a hideous disease and still isn't discouraged." When his uncle Beaupré, who had accompanied the expedition as an adjutant commandant, returned to France to take the waters for a wound in his leg, Leclerc wrote begging his brothers-in-law Davout and the first consul to recognize the old soldier as "one of the warriors of the army of Saint-Domingue."

Leclerc received his own encomium, and promise of riches, in the form of a letter Napoleon wrote in early July, shortly before he was confirmed first consul for life:

Great national rewards are being marked out for you, and for the principal officers and soldiers who have distinguished themselves. Act in the best interest of the Republic, and it will be grateful and take care of your private interests. . . . Defeat for us these gilded Africans, and we have nothing left to ask of you. . . . You are en route to acquiring great glory. The Republic will enable you to enjoy a suitable fortune, and the friendship I have for you is unalterable.

Leclerc had, to all appearances, fulfilled the task that Napoleon had set him, and, as the first consul knew, he was driven by a desire for recognition as well as for pecuniary reward. Those days in Rennes, in Landshut, in Spain, where Leclerc had lamented the lack of opportunity to shine were now mercifully over. At Le Cap the victorious captain general of Saint-Domingue awaited the reinforcements promised him, as well as sugar and coffee traders, from France. "Commerce is activating and heading for Saint-Domingue," Napoleon told him.

Leclerc wrote to Davout of his hopes of handing over to a successor at Saint-Domingue, and of returning to France in the spring. "The arrival of Toussaint in France will give pleasure," he continued, and emphasized the tranquillity of the colony. "Those in Paris who laughed at my chances here will have to change their tune." Thinking ahead, Leclerc purchased hunting dogs from Norvins's brother Montbreton, his neighbor at Montgobert, to await his return with Pauline and Dermide to France. In addition he issued a series of letters to his brother Jean Louis with instructions for embellishing Montgobert at considerable expense. The fashionable architect Fontaine was to add two wings to the main house, but the floors were not to be laid. "I will bring with me exotic woods to panel and parquet Montgobert and my house in Paris," Leclerc announced. Moreover he wished a hothouse to be built near the château. "I want to bring back all the trees and flowers of this island. I think they will do very well," he declared ambitiously. In the park a lake was to be dug, and the English garden embellished, as well as a dairy and milking parlor constructed at a picturesque spot.

Leclerc, as a good servant of the republic, continued also to attempt to interest the authorities in France in the remarkable flora and fauna of the region. In July he sent a stuffed cayman and from Caracas a live "American tiger" (ocelot) just a few months old, with the remark that the latter hated cold. If it died, it would still make a fine exhibit at the Museum of Natural History, stuffed with straw. In addition, as he informed the minister of the interior, he had dispatched an officer— Norvins—to South America to search out llamas, vicuñas, and other exotic species. "Let me know if there are any items—mineral, vegetable, or animal—native to Saint-Domingue that the museum of natural history lacks," he urged, "and I will send them." He believed that mineralogists would find supplies of gold, silver, iron, copper, and even platinum in the interior. As for the botanical garden he envisaged, he advised that its staff—he thought of a director, two deputy directors, and four gardeners—should arrive no sooner than September. "Then they will have nothing to fear from this climate, which is no longer fatal in that season."

Leclerc's request to his brother in July to send out a waiting woman for Pauline and a "good nurse" for Dermide, as well as a cook, indicates that the previous incumbents of these posts had fallen victim to yellow fever. But Pauline and Dermide, as well as Leclerc, remained healthy in their summer residence, the Habitation L'Estaing, on a "wooded eminence" above Le Cap, while a miasma of heat hung over the island. Leclerc wrote in his wife's praise to Napoleon: "Considering how cruel it has been for her to stay in a country where she has had before her eyes only the spectacle of those dead or dying, I have often pressed her to go to France. She has never agreed to do so, saying that she will share my misfortunes and my successes. Her stay here is indeed agreeable for me."

Loyalty was always to be Pauline's strongest suit. She had stood by her husband through all the vicissitudes of his earlier career. Now that Leclerc had defeated the "gilded Africans" of whom her brother had written, she could look forward, beyond her time in Saint-Domingue, to a life in Paris and at Montgobert, enriched by the fruits of her husband's success. But not for long. For, as quickly as Leclerc had won control of the colony, he was to lose it.

CHAPTER SIX

Pestilential Climate, 1802–1803

LECLERC WROTE CONFIDENTLY to Napoleon in early July 1802 of his intention—at the celebrations he planned for the tenth anniversary of the republic in September—to declare Saint-Domingue formally restored to France. Three elements, however, now conspired to loosen the captain general's control of the colony. First, isolated insurgencies followed the arrest and dispatch of Toussaint to France, and in addition, as Leclerc wrote to Decrès, the minister of marine and colonies, "some of the colonial troops have had the air about them of insurrection . . . at the moment they hide their discontent, but licentiousness operates." The chilling end of the insurrections, he suspected, would be the massacre of all the Europeans.

In early August, however, Leclerc believed that he had dealt with this threat, informing the first consul that he had hanged thirty chiefs who had led risings in different parts of the island, and that he had given orders for any disaffected colonial troops to be shot. The colony was disarmed and once again tranquil. He was battling, however, more than ever to maintain a fighting force as well as an administrative staff that were being ravaged by yellow fever. Pauline was ill, although not dangerously so, but he had lost five thousand men in the last few weeks alone. The hospitals were in crisis, and most of the medical staff were dead, while the fever had also swept through the French ships, leaving devastation and yellow corpses in its wake.

No one was immune. Men who had survived the ardors of Moreau's campaigns in Germany, the desert heat in Egypt, and Alpine bivouacks now succumbed. All of Leclerc's generals of division were abed, as he wrote, and most of his generals of brigade. Many of these were to die, including fat General Dugua, Napoleon's chief of staff during the Egyptian campaign; and Debelle, the "Apollo of the army" with whose name Pauline's was to be linked, was already dead. Among those who died elsewhere in the colony was Pauline's former lover Stanislas Fréron, only weeks after he had at last arrived to take up a post as underprefect at Les Cayes. (In Paris, Lucien Bonaparte was to solicit a pension for his widow and children.) All they could do was wait till this murderous phase of the epidemic subsided, as it was expected to do in September, when the extreme heat of summer would be over and the heavy, pestilential atmosphere that hung over the colony dissipated.

The third cross Leclerc had to bear was the hardest of all. "All the blacks here," he wrote to Decrès, "are persuaded by letters coming from France, by the law reestablishing the slave trade, and by General Richepanse's orders reestablishing slavery in Guadeloupe, that we mean to make them slaves once more." A law had indeed been passed in France in May sanctioning the slave trade, and slavery had been reintroduced in Guadeloupe in July as part of the peace treaty signed with the British. Leclerc wrote bitterly, "On the eve of ending everything here, these political circumstances . . . have all but ruined my work. I cannot any longer count on my moral authority here, it is destroyed. . . . Now I can only manage the blacks by the force of arms. For that, I need an army and funds."

Of the twelve thousand men he had requested months before, three thousand only had come, and half of them were already in hospital. Moreover, none of the funds he had asked for had been forthcoming. To Napoleon, Leclerc wrote, "If you abandon us, as you have done till now, this colony is lost, and, once lost, you will never get it back." The black inhabitants of Saint-Domingue, who prized their liberty above pearls, began once more to arm against the French. The insurgencies, which had been sporadic, became more organized, and by mid-August the rebel forces had set a date a month thence to combine and attack Leclerc and his forces at Le Cap.

Norvins, who, with Leclerc's old comrade Lenoir, acted as the captain general's secretary, has left us a description of those dog days of August up at the Habitation L'Estaing, while Leclerc tried desperately to combat the rising tide of destruction. To fend off the "thousands of bloodsucking insects" that threatened them, they removed the general's bed from his room, replaced it with a table, and, seated there together beneath a mosquito net, dealt with business as best they could, while the sweat streamed from their every pore down onto the dispatches over which they bent.

Miraculously, while so many of his staff and household had died of yellow fever, Leclerc himself—and Pauline and Dermide—had suffered only passing episodes. It was possible to survive the fever, and indeed Norvins had a severe bout of it at this time, complete with vertigo, loss of consciousness, paralysis, and fearsome sweating. But sickness, the climate, and the scenes of death and destruction all around seem not to have shaken Pauline's resolve to remain at her husband's side—until a letter arrived from her younger sister, Caroline, in Paris.

Caroline, with her husband, Joachim Murat, had been *en poste* in Italy when Pauline set out for Saint-Domingue. Now that Murat was commandant of Paris, Caroline was enjoying both Consular society and, in her more beautiful sister's absence, the compliments she received there. Pauline shared the contents of Caroline's letter, outlining her successes, with Norvins, whom she invited during his convalescence to a tête-à-tête dinner. "Imagine, my sister Murat has a carriage. She has written it to me to enrage me, talking of parties and balls and all that Bonaparte does for her."

Norvins tells us that he had been sure she would ask something impossible of him that Leclerc had already refused her. He was right. "You know Leclerc wants me to leave for Paris," Pauline went on tempestuously. "I consent on one condition. He must give me a hundred thousand francs." This enormous sum, it transpired, was to fund a carriage to trump her sister's and a *parure* of jewelry to put any baubles

Madame Murat might be wearing at the Tuileries court quite in the shade. Pauline repeated, "Get the hundred thousand from my husband . . . and I'll go."

Norvins duly learned from Leclerc that there was no such sum available, and indeed that there was no question of Pauline's departure. With a heavy heart he went to give Madame Leclerc this unwelcome news but found her in a sunny mood. "The ravishing creature, utterly sanguine, said, 'My sister Murat has a carriage like all the bourgeoisie of Paris. She's just one of them, while I reign here like Josephine, I am the first lady. . . . Anyway, I'm perfectly happy. . . . I don't want to go anymore.'" And indeed, according to Norvins, Pauline had constructed her little court to be as gay as possible. She dressed her band of musicians in brilliant uniforms and, surrounding herself with officers' pretty wives, entertained her husband and his general staff as well as could be managed in the ominous circumstances, when the absence of habitual attendants from Pauline's soirees often presaged their death.

There were still moments for the shrinking French colony to enjoy. Before his death Dugua, coiffed in a madras turban and wearing a white chemise, had pursued the various butterflies of the island with a net. Now Leclerc proposed making a tour of the entire island to find items for the natural history museum. In addition, he told the interior minister, he proposed working on an edition of the flora of the colony. "This work could be finished within five years, with the plants drawn exactly from nature—not from the dried state in which they appear in herbals. I have noticed here how far the engravings in the *Encyclopédie* are from the reality." He also wrote to his brother Jean Louis, instructing him to add to the other buildings at Montgobert an aviary for the birds he was acquiring in Saint-Domingue: "It must be made so that it can be easily heated in winter."

The most bizarre moment came when the governor of Cartagena in Colombia, responding to Leclerc's efforts to recruit animals for the menagerie at the Jardin des Plantes in Paris, sent to Saint-Domingue a vast collection of beasts. Cages of lions, tigers, panthers, and bears were duly unloaded, to be admired at Le Cap before continuing their journey to France. Sailors bore monkeys and parrots on their arms, and tambourines and music preceded the noisy menagerie as it wound its way through the streets. Mongrel dogs came running, as well as the town's inhabitants, attracted by the hullabaloo. While the wild animals stayed in the palace stables in Le Cap, Leclerc arranged a courtyard planted with trees and roofed over with sailcloth, where they let loose the parrots and monkeys.

Against the cries of these new companions, Pauline wrote to her friend and former landlady, Madame Michelot, in early September:

> It has been impossible to write more often. This climate is so hot and humid that I suffer nearly all the time. . . . This is a truly sad country. . . . Disease has accounted for many deaths, but thankfully Leclerc and Dermide and I have survived several passing illnesses. I hope, my dear, good friend, that in seven months I will be back in Paris, never to leave it again. I have suffered too much, and I suffer still. Leclerc is fearfully busy, and works day and night. . . . In a few days I will go down to Le Cap.

As we have seen, Leclerc had proposed to make 1 Vendémiaire (September 22) the occasion of a grand fete at Le Cap. But all thoughts of that were driven out by the news that the mass insurrection that Leclerc had long feared was appointed for the sixteenth of the month. Mulatto and black troops deserted Leclerc's army in the days before and reverted to their former generals' command. Meanwhile some of the white inhabitants of Le Cap, providing themselves with a sword and a horse, declared themselves ready to help Leclerc and save the colony. Others, fearing massacre, pressed about the government palace, where Leclerc and Pauline had their quarters. The women, in particular, begged to be embarked with their children rather than face the rape and death they feared.

The odds appeared hopeless. There were thousands in the hospitals. At most Leclerc had two thousand troops to deploy, and the black generals headed a force estimated at nine or ten thousand men. But, mounting his horse and preparing to lead his army out to do battle, Leclerc was coolly in command. Pauline, bidding him adieu, was no less composed. "Her charming face," Norvins tells us, "was suffused by a supernatural beauty, where dignity and courage mingled." But uppermost in everyone's minds was the conviction that the black generals and their troops would rape Pauline and cut her throat and that of Dermide without compunction if they gained the town. Leclerc therefore put Norvins and his other secretary, Lenoir, in charge of his wife and son. "I leave you these four sergeants," he said, "and this piece of cannon. If I am defeated, you will receive the order to embark my wife and son, and their attendants."

Norvins followed Pauline inside the palace to her apartments, but they were pursued by a crowd of supplicant officers' wives and townswomen. Pauline in reply was magnificent. With an energy in her gestures and her voice of which Norvins had not believed her capable, she said, "You may be afraid to die, but I am the sister of Bonaparte. I am afraid of nothing." "Oh madame, if you knew what those monsters are capable of," the women responded. "They will find me dead—and my son, too," said Pauline with "an inflexible sangfroid." Then, turning to Norvins, she said, "You promise to kill us both?" Norvins replied grimly that he had confidence in God and in her husband. "But if the order comes to embark you, I will execute it," he warned her.

The order duly came, brought by an aide-de-camp, but Pauline refused to cooperate. A long hour passed, the echoes of cannon and gunfire from the battlefield of Haut Le Cap above the town audible below. Then another aide appeared at the palace and, without even getting off his horse, told Norvins, "The general orders you to embark Madame Leclerc—by force if necessary." And off he galloped back to Haut Le Cap.

Norvins called the four sergeants Leclerc had left him and ordered them to carry Pauline, just as she was, in her armchair, down to the port. Dermide was apportioned to a grenadier, and the child played with the plume of his porter's helmet. Meanwhile Norvins and Lenoir and a few others, sabers in hand, formed an escort, but during the journey from palace to sea Pauline repeated, "I don't care. I'm still not leaving." Then, mockingly, she said, "Do look, Norvins, we're like a masquerade at an Opéra ball in Mardi Gras. If your brother Montbreton could see us, how ridiculous he would think us." And she laughed and pointed at Lenoir, who had tucked his sword under his arm like an umbrella.

Just at the point when Lenoir was going to force Pauline aboard the waiting ship, a third aide arrived. "Victory!" he cried. "The general has routed the blacks. Madame, he begs you to return to the palace, where he will join you shortly." Pauline, so happy she would willingly have kissed the messenger, said only, "I said I wouldn't leave." Back up to the palace she was carried, and when Leclerc arrived, covered in dust and glory, Pauline told him after a thousand embraces, "I swore I wouldn't go back to France without you." That day, said Norvins, who when she was on board *L'Océan* had likened Madame Leclerc to the nymph Galatea, and during subsequent days in Saint-Domingue to the enchantress Armide, she showed the courage and determination of a Spartan woman.

But Leclerc's victory was short lived. Every day the rebels launched some new guerrilla initiative. "The men I am against are fanatically brave," wrote Leclerc to Davout. "Richepanse's orders reestablishing slavery at Guadeloupe have launched this general unrest. They would rather be killed than surrender, and they kill those of my men whom the yellow fever spares." He had given up attempting to control the interior, concentrating on maintaining in French hands Le Cap, Port-au-Prince, and Port-de-Paix, and awaited anxiously the reinforcements without which he had no hope of restoring order.

How altered was the general's opinion since he had boasted to Napoleon in July of his hold on the colony, when he had been proud of his good government! Now he wrote in September to the minister of marine and colonies, "I have not had one day's satisfaction since I have been in this country." A month later, on October 7, he wrote to the first consul, "Here is my opinion about this country. All the blacks in the mountains, men and women, need to be destroyed, and children older than twelve. Half of those in the plains must also be killed, and not a single black who has worn rebel uniform should be left alive. Otherwise every year, especially after the murderous fever season, you risk civil war." Already, in pursuit of this policy, he was employing Dessalines, the black general who had previously led attacks against the French, as "the butcher of the blacks. I get him to perform all the odious measures necessary."

In a bitter, private letter addressed to Napoleon the same day, Leclerc wrote: "Since I have been here, I have had only the spectacle of fires, of insurgencies, of assassinations, of deaths, of the dying. My soul is wounded, nothing can make me forget these hideous scenes. I struggle here against the blacks, the whites, the misery and lack of money, against my army which is discouraged, against yellow fever." For Pauline, however, he had nothing but praise: "Madame Leclerc is . . . a model of courage. She is well worthy to be your sister." Napoleon's opinion of Pauline was similarly high: "I am very content with my sister's behavior. She need not fear death, because she would go to her death with glory in dying with an army and in being useful to her husband. All passes swiftly on earth, except the opinion we leave imprinted on history."

Both Leclercs had now abandoned hope of glory from Saint-Domingue. They were looking ahead to a time when he would be succeeded on the island by some other unfortunate, and, turning his mind to life in Paris, Leclerc asked his brother to rent a house there—somewhere between the Tuileries and the Italian theater. It should be on a quiet street, with a courtyard and garden, and needed to be of a certain size, to accommodate five or six officers, as well as Pauline and Dermide and their immediate entourage. Pauline began to think of the styles that next spring would bring into fashion in the French capital, Leclerc of future postings.

Conditions, meanwhile, had not altered in the colony. The yellow fever season was abnormally prolonged that year, and fifty to sixty men a day were still dying at Le Cap. But Pauline continued to host her little receptions, summoning her band of musicians to play each evening.

A welcome energy was injected into these assemblies when the young General François Watrin, with a pretty wife, arrived with a small detachment from France and with promises of further reinforcements. But then disaster struck.

Leclerc was about to get into his carriage early on the morning of October 22, when he suddenly found himself unable to move, and he was carried to his bed. The director of the army hospital at Le Cap, Peyre, was summoned, and diagnosed the ailment as a slow, nervous fever, "caused by the bodily and mental hardships the general had suffered." But the symptoms were those of yellow fever.

Five days after he had taken to his bed—and despite the entreaties of his wife and doctor that he should stay there—Leclerc insisted on showing himself to the inhabitants of the town, fearing that there would be a general loss of morale if his condition was suspected to be serious. Then he collapsed. Two days later he revived. But he spoke strangely to Norvins, saying that he intended to leave Saint-Domingue in secret and return with Pauline and Dermide to his forest retreat of Montgobert.

In the evening the general attended his wife's assembly, entering the salon with Pauline at his side and with General Watrin supporting him on the other. But, as he walked over to the window to inspect his beloved menagerie, he fainted. The fever was back with a vengeance, and it seemed very unlikely that the general would survive this bout. Certainly Leclerc, between bouts of sweating and vomiting, now made arrangements for what should happen after his death—not least detailing General Boyer to oversee Pauline and Dermide's passage to France. In the event of Leclerc's death the administration of the island was to pass, following Napoleon's instructions, to General Rochambeau— a succession that no one relished, as that officer's cruelty and irascibility were notorious, and the threat of which added to the sense of gloom as Leclerc's condition grew worse. But no one dared to counter the first consul's orders.

Two nights after the assembly, Leclerc said he longed to die, such was his agony. The next day he was delirious, his spirits as high as his fever. And then the delirium passed, leaving him once more conscious of his suffering. At eleven o'clock in the evening of November 1, his purgatory ended. Peyre pronounced the "blond Bonaparte" dead at thirty years and seven months. It seems that Pauline and four-year-old Dermide were at Leclerc's bedside at that moment, for Norvins, waiting with other staff and officers outside the private apartments, heard a high-pitched cry: "My father is dead!"

Almost before she could absorb the shock of the death of the husband she had called "mon joli petit gamin," Pauline was embarking for France on November 8 with Dermide. On board the *Swiftsure* frigate with them was Leclerc's corpse, embalmed and in a lead coffin placed within another of rich cedar. Separately his heart and brain made the voyage in a lead box, later to be enclosed in a gilded urn bearing this inscription: "Paulette Bonaparte, married to General Leclerc on 20 Prairial, Year V, has enclosed in this urn her love with the heart of the husband with whom she shared dangers and glory. With this sad and dear inheritance of his father her son will inherit his virtues."

Nor did this inscription alone bear testament to Pauline's distress. In the hours succeeding her husband's death, when Peyre and other surgeons were embalming the body, she had cut her hair and had them place a cushion of it under the bandages on Leclerc's face impregnated with embalming ointment—"as a gauge of her conjugal love." In return she had asked for Leclerc's own blond hair. And so it was with her hair cropped close and dressed in black that the widow Leclerc returned to France. On New Year's Day 1803 she wrote to Napoleon from the Bay of Toulon, having anchored at the isle of Hyères two days earlier: "I am arrived . . . after a dreadful crossing and am in abysmal health, but this is still the least of my sorrows. I have brought with me the remains of my poor Leclerc. Pity poor Pauline, who is truly unhappy."

Whatever the truth of Pauline's relationships with other men during her marriage to Leclerc, she had never expressed the least dissatisfaction with him as a husband and father. Their ties had been very strong, for they shared an ambition to shine (with a love of domestic comfort and with a love of their son) in which Leclerc had led and Pauline, imperious though she was, had followed. Now Pauline was left to fashion a life for herself and Dermide without Leclerc.

Leclerc's mother at Pontoise received an official letter from the minister of marine and colonies: "It is with great regret, madame, that I inform you of the death of your son, General Leclerc. . . . He was taken from a glorious career on 11 Brumaire last by a sickness of ten days, during which the last moments were given to the care of his army." Decrès wrote of Leclerc's "noble and courageous spouse" and of the arrangements for burial at Montgobert—arrangements that may not have pleased Leclerc's mother. But first there was a period of state mourning to observe. General Rochambeau and Hector d'Aure, the prefect of Le Cap, had been anxious that no news of Leclerc's calamitous death should become public before the first consul knew it and could decide how the matter should be handled. In the event Napoleon decided that this death in his Consular family should form a first occasion for official mourning at his court at the Tuileries, and so his minister Talleyrand informed the foreign ambassadors in Paris.

While Pauline completed fifteen days of quarantine off Toulon, Leclerc's coffin was transferred from the *Swiftsure* to another frigate, the *Cornélie,* and landed at Marseille to be greeted by a guard of honor and conveyed to a resting place overnight in the cathedral there. Stage by stage, church by church, the coffin progressed northward, toward Villers-Cotterêts, where it would lie in the church before committal to the earth at nearby Montgobert. At Lyon the officiating archbishop was Pauline's uncle Fesch, who had been present only six years earlier in Milan at the wedding of Leclerc to his niece. The clergy everywhere, rejoicing in Napoleon's new Concordat, which had reestablished the Catholic faith in France, seized the opportunity to deliver sermons extolling the virtues of the consul and his brother-in-law, whom more than one likened to David and Jonathan. Alternatively they praised Napoleon as a new Constantine. Leclerc's aide-de-camp Bruyères oversaw the troops who accompanied the cortege and guarded it with pomp and ceremony at each staging place. Finally, at the end of February, the coffin reached Villers-Cotterêts, and for twelve days Leclerc's embalmed body was exposed to view in the church there, before he was privately buried in a tomb at the end of one of the allées he had laid out with such enthusiasm.

But the honors Napoleon was determined to heap on his brother-in-law after his death were not concluded. The first consul commissioned not one but two statues of Leclerc. One, sculpted in Italy, in which the general appeared heroically nude and more than life size, was destined for Versailles. The other, where Leclerc wore his general's uniform, was destined for the Panthéon, the Church of Saint Geneviève, which since the Revolution had acquired a new role as a mausoleum. These attentions were only just. Much later, Napoleon, reflecting on all those who had served him over a long career, was to single out Leclerc as the man above all those he had commanded who had combined administrative and military skills. But, more than that, Leclerc had, through thick and thin in Saint-Domingue and elsewhere, never questioned the decisions or orders of Napoleon. His sense of duty to the republic, his admiration for the first consul, had been absolute. Had he returned alive to France from Saint-Domingue, as he had hoped to do, and joined the theater of war elsewhere, a bright future would no doubt have lain ahead of him. Had he become, as one may posit, a marshal of France, Pauline would have made a charming *madame la maréchale*. But the destiny of this talented young member of the petty bourgeoisie turned revolutionary officer had been otherwise, and so Pauline Bonaparte's own path now took a new turn.

PAULINE COMMISSIONED from Fontaine a stele, nearly ten feet high, to stand sentinel over her husband's burial chamber in the park at Montgobert. At a cost of 850 francs a retired officer then worked for six months, under the architect's direction, to embellish it with a Roman helmet, a laurel wreath, and a sword on each face. She was not present, however, when the coffin lay open in Villers-Cotterêts or when Leclerc was buried at Montgobert. From Saint-Cloud Napoleon had written to her while she was still in quarantine in January at Toulon, giving notice that he was sending his equerry Lauriston to Toulon to bring her to Paris: "You have been worthy of Leclerc and of me. Return here soon. You will find in the friendship of your family consolation for your unhappiness."

At the end of January, Pauline and Dermide duly arrived in Paris and, with no home in Paris to go to—it would appear that Jean Louis Leclerc had not rented the house that his brother had requested—they became the guests of Pauline's brother Joseph and his wife, Julie, in the Hôtel Marboeuf in the rue du Faubourg Saint-Honoré. Here and elsewhere in Paris there were additions to the Bonaparte family for Pauline and Dermide to encounter. In the first place, in a most incestuous court alliance her elder brother Louis had taken as his bride Josephine's daughter, Hortense de Beauharnais, and they had had a son, Napoléon Charles. (The child was at once Napoleon's nephew and his stepgrandson.) Then, while Pauline was away, her sister Caroline Murat had given birth to two children, Achille and Letizia. At the Hôtel Marboeuf, moreover, Dermide had the company of two further cousins, Charlotte and Zenaïde. But still the union of Napoleon and Josephine proved frustratingly barren. Pauline did not hesitate to express her dissatisfaction with her sister-in-law, and Josephine was blamed within the Bonaparte family for this sorry situation. Despite the self-evident proof that Josephine had once been fertile, in the shape of her children, Eugène and Hortense de Beauharnais, she was now in her late thirties. It was easier for all to suggest she was no longer fertile than to hint that the first consul was sterile.

At the Hôtel Marboeuf, Pauline slowly recovered her health, which had been badly affected during the voyage from Saint-Domingue, and set about reclaiming a place in Parisian society. Her mother was, as ever, a source of comfort to her, and Pauline's spirits were restored sufficiently by April to make a visit from Norvins, her husband's former secretary, an entertaining occasion.

Norvins had brought disastrous news to the first consul and to Decrès, the minister of marine and colonies, from Saint-Domingue. Of the fourteen thousand men who had been sent out to General Rochambeau since Leclerc's death, most were now dead. (Together, black troops in revolt and the arrival of British regiments were to force the evacuation of the island in November. In 1804 Toussaint Louverture's lieutenant Henri Christophe anointed his fellow general Dessalines, who had once carried out Leclerc's butchery, emperor of Haiti, as the new independent state was named.) But in his interview with Decrès, Norvins had been so infuriated by the other's lack of interest in his tale that he had ended by abusing the minister. Jumping onto a silk-upholstered armchair, above which hung a large map of Saint-Domingue, he indicated the extent of the rebels' hold on the island and said angrily: "We wrote to you of this, Leclerc and d'Aure and I, day after day."

Pauline laughed at Norvins's anxieties about the outcome of his interview with Decrès. "I will calm him down," she said. "He is madly in love with me and pursues me night and day. He wants to marry me." Now it was Norvins's turn to laugh, along with Pauline. "He disgusts me, that great rough sailor," she went on. "But, as he is so enamored, I listen to his declarations." Norvins replied, "He wouldn't be so keen if you weren't the first consul's sister." "Oh, he wouldn't look at me," replied Pauline, not a whit disconcerted, and promised to put all right for Norvins with her suitor.

"By the way," Norvins added, "did you get a better carriage than your sister Murat?" "Oh yes, indeed," said Pauline and smiled, remembering the dinner at the Habitation d'Estaing. "Imagine, Norvins, I asked my brother for money, and he sent me eighty thousand francs." "That's not bad," the other replied, no doubt remembering that Pauline had asked her husband in vain for one hundred thousand francs. "Yes. Well, I sent it back and got what I wanted, which was three hundred thousand francs." Thus, early in her widowhood, Pauline Bonaparte Leclerc had established a supply of suitors for her hand, as well as a direct line to the coffers of her brother Napoleon. It remained to be seen whether she preferred the independent life of a rich widow or whether she would once more seek the commitment of marriage.

CHAPTER SEVEN

Union with a Roman Prince, 1803

I F PAULINE HAD NOT BEEN THE MODEL of a republican general's wife, she had loved Victor Emmanuel Leclerc and had respected his principles. But now, upon returning to Paris, she was quick to see how changed the capital was since she and Leclerc had left for Saint-Domingue, and how changed was her status and that of her other brothers and sisters since her brother Napoleon had become consul for life in 1802. The Bonapartes, who had grown up in that modest street running down to the port in Ajaccio, now had all but the status of a royal family.

Being practical as well as independent by nature, Pauline Leclerc made it her business, while staying at her brother Joseph's *hôtel* in the rue du Faubourg Saint-Honoré, to find a suitable home for herself and Dermide and their household. Before his death Leclerc had written of acquiring a house between the Tuileries Palace, where Napoleon and Josephine held Consular court, and the Italian theater. But now the stakes were higher. Pauline's sister Caroline, with Murat, was about to move into the Élysée Palace, which had belonged to the Bourbon kings. Close by, Joseph's house on the rue du Faubourg Saint-Honoré, in which she was staying, had formerly been home to the Marquis de Marboeuf, governor of Corsica and Letizia Bonaparte's protector. Pauline, widow though she might be, wanted a residence as splendid as those of her siblings.

Guided as ever by the spirit of emulation, Pauline's choice fell in the summer of 1803 on the Hôtel Charost, a delightful mansion two doors down from Joseph's *hôtel,* close to Caroline's, and quite as large as either of theirs. Two pretty pavilions framed the main entrance to the property on the rue du Faubourg Saint-Honoré. Across the courtyard inside, the ground floor and first floor of the *hôtel* were connected by a splendid staircase. Meanwhile, on the garden front, three principal salons gave onto expansive gardens running down to the Champs-Élysées. Much of the original early-eighteenth-century decoration was intact, and the house was all long mirrors and glittering enfilades of gilding, glass, and light.

Pauline was quick to see the advantages of acquiring a house that preserved its original character and had a ducal pedigree but had been recently renovated. (The owner, widow of the Duc de Charost, who lived elsewhere, had rented the *hôtel* a year earlier to the diplomat Lord Whitworth, who had repaired and restored it and filled it with furniture to serve as the British Embassy. With the Peace of Amiens foundering, however, he was recalled to London in May 1803, his furniture dispatched after him, and the property lay once again empty.) The only problem was that the Duchesse de Charost had no wish to sell the property. Pauline was not a woman to let such objections defeat her, and with three hundred thousand francs supplied by Napoleon, she wore the reluctant vendor down. But the negotiations took most of the summer of 1803, and the purchase was not effected until November.

In the meantime news of the negotiations circulated in Paris, as did rumors that Pauline had brought home with her from Saint-Domingue untold treasure, with which she proposed to purchase the *hôtel.* Some even said these ill-gotten gains had been hidden on the voyage home in Leclerc's coffin and had made their way to Paris in that sad cortege that passed through France, en route for Montgobert, in January. Pauline was, at any rate, popularly imagined to be now the richest of Napoleon's siblings. In fact she had inherited from Leclerc only seven hundred thousand francs in capital, and Lucien, who inhabited the Hôtel Brienne in the rue de Grenelle and who had made a fortune as ambassador to Madrid, was many times richer. But around the widow Leclerc, secluded in the Hôtel Marboeuf, and "veiled in black, as beautiful as any angel," these and other myths now began to wreathe. Indeed, when Laure Junot visited and noticed an unsightly abscess on Pauline's hand, souvenir of a tropical infection, she had no hesitation in assuming it to be the legacy of a venereal disease.

Officers returning to Paris from the bloody mess that had become the French position in Saint-Domingue contributed to the legend. Some hailed Pauline's devotion to her husband, her patriotism, and her courage. Others added their mite to rumors of her licentious behavior with the natives of the island. Meanwhile Pauline tired of the regulations governing mourning in the Civil Code that her brother had so recently and inconveniently produced. She told Laure Junot, when she visited, "I am so bored. I will die here, and if my brother wants to forbid me seeing company for ever, I will kill myself." Pauline was twenty-two years old, and she had done for the moment with mourning Leclerc. Her brother was the ruler of France, and she was acknowledged to be the most beautiful woman in Paris. Like a caged tigress, she waited to take her place in society, while those about her grew nervous at the thought of it.

Among those who thought to remove Pauline from Consular society altogether was her brother Napoleon. He wrote to Francesco Melzi d'Eril, a Milanese nobleman with estates in Spain and a fine villa on Lake Como, suggesting that he and Madame Leclerc should wed. Melzi had recently and reluctantly agreed to become vice president of the Italian republic, comprising Lombardy and other parts of northern Italy, which Napoleon had founded during Pauline's absence in Saint-Domingue. (Napoleon had reserved the title of president for himself.) This further request, however, Melzi declined, protesting that he was a fifty-year-old bachelor and set in his ways. (These, incidentally, included a mistress of long standing.)

If Napoleon had thought that Pauline's marriage to Melzi would consolidate French Consular ties with the Italian peninsula, so badly ruptured during the Revolution when the republic had first cast off religion and then employed its army to occupy the Papal States and make new republics elsewhere, he was disappointed. Nevertheless he still had useful channels at his disposal, including that of Uncle Fesch, who had recently become cardinal and whom Napoleon had dispatched from Lyon to Rome to serve as ambassador to the Holy See. Through Fesch and through Cardinal Consalvi, the papal secretary of state, honeyed words passed between the first consul and Pope Pius VII. (On all sides there was tacit agreement not to refer to the death of the pope's predecessor, Pius VI, while in French captivity.)

In Paris, meanwhile, Napoleon cultivated the company of Cardinal Caprara, Pius VII's legate. It was Caprara who presented to the first consul in April 1803 Prince Camillo Borghese, a Roman citizen of high birth and great wealth, whose arrival in the French capital had already made a great stir the previous month. Although he was not tall, Prince Borghese had a neat figure, a handsome face, and exotic Mediterranean looks. "This head with coal black eyes and mane of jet black hair, it seemed to me, must contain not only passionate but great and noble ideas," Laure Junot wrote soulfully of her first encounter with the prince. To add to his attractions, Prince Borghese paid great attention to his dress, and still more to his horses, eclipsing with his coach and four even the equipage of the Russian count Demidov, which had till then been the showiest in Paris. But then Camillo Borghese had the advantage, as excited Parisians turned accountants estimated, of possessing a rent roll of two million francs a year.

He also had most distinguished ancestors. Paul V, the Borghese pope, had been patron of the Baroque sculptor Bernini, and His Holiness's nephew Cardinal Scipione Borghese had filled the sumptuous Villa Borghese on the Pincio hill in Rome with paintings, objects, and ancient art. Since those exalted seventeenth-century days Borghese intermarriage with the Aldobrandini family, among others in Rome, had brought estates at Frascati, lands in the Roman Campagna, and further wealth. With Camillo's own mother, Donna Anna, came the Palazzo Borghese in Florence and lands in Tuscany. In Rome, while the Villa Borghese showcased the family art collection, the family resided in the vast Palazzo Borghese, which backed onto the Tiber and was known as the *cembalo,* or keyboard, from its trapezoidal shape resembling that of a harpsichord.

The twenty-eight-year-old prince had impeccable, if unusual, revolutionary credentials too. For when the French forces took control of Rome in 1798, Camillo and his younger brother, Prince Francesco Aldobrandini, despite their family's papal associations, embraced the republican cause. They pulled the vast Borghese family crest off the facade of the Palazzo Borghese in that city and added it to a bonfire of cardinals' hats and Inquisition decrees burning in the Piazza di Spagna. Then they danced wildly around the blaze before compounding their sins, in the eyes of their father and of the pope, by fighting briefly for General Championnet and his French forces and against the papal army. This was the stuff of heroes, or of revolutionaries anyway.

But the first consul does not appear to have taken any interest in Camillo Borghese, despite his wealth, papal connections, and revolutionary exploits. Indeed there was a fatal flaw, evident to anyone upon closer acquaintance with the prince and not overawed by his antecedents. He was, to put it plainly, a booby, if a harmless one. It was this quality that had enabled his father to get him pardoned by the pope for his acts of rebellion. (For penance, it was decided, he must live in exile from Rome for a number of years, upon which Camillo settled in the very comfortable Palazzo Borghese in Florence.) After a time the Parisians noticed this and disillusion set in. "He had nothing to say, although a lively manner of saying it" and "No one was more capable than he of driving a four-in-hand, but no one was less capable of carrying on a conversation" were among their comments. Indeed Camillo could barely write Italian correctly, let alone speak or write French, and it was said that he preferred the company of the concierge at the Hôtel d'Oigny, in the rue de la Grange-Batelière in Paris, which he was renting, to that of anyone more demanding in Paris.

Camillo's father, Prince Marcantonio Borghese, a noted patron of the arts and a man of culture, had, it was said, deliberately neglected his sons' education, believing that, as vassals of the pope, they would do better to remain ignorant than chafe, as educated men, at the restrictions of Roman life. Or then again, it was suggested, he believed that an "incomplete" education would spare his sons, whose spectacular wealth and titles would inevitably attract envy, further resentment. Whatever the explanation, Don Cecco—as Camillo's younger brother was known—if ill educated, was no booby. It was Camillo Borghese's misfortune to be both ignorant and lacking in intellect—and an innocent abroad, who fell into the traps laid by men far more sophisticated than he. For, while the first consul took no interest in the Roman prince's presence in Paris, this was not true of his brothers Joseph and Lucien. It was with Joseph Bonaparte, who had served in Rome as ambassador in 1798, and with Lucien that an Italian diplomat and friend of Cardinal Caprara, the Chevalier Luigi Angiolini, concerted a "great project"—namely, Camillo Borghese's marriage to Pauline Bonaparte Leclerc.

As Pauline emerged from the confines of widowhood in the late spring of 1803, there was occasion for her and Camillo Borghese to meet, even to flirt, no more. But then in June, fatefully for the house of Borghese, Camillo accepted an invitation from Joseph Bonaparte to spend a few days at Mortefontaine, the latter's country house twenty miles north of Paris. The company, with whom the Roman prince innocently drove and walked about the gardens and grounds of the château, included, besides his hosts, the Bonapartes' mother, Letizia; Louis's wife, Hortense; the matchmaker Angiolini; and Cardinal Caprara. Unaware that most of the above were, or became during these few days, resolved that he should marry Pauline—Angiolini having numerous conversations with Letizia on the subject—Borghese returned contentedly to Paris. It was not long, however, before he received a late-night visit from Angiolini at the Hôtel d'Oigny. The Italian diplomat, come on Joseph's urging, to unveil to Borghese the glorious prospect they had in mind, utterly destroyed the Roman prince's peace of mind.

Borghese was "as much frightened as astonished at the prospect, so great did it seem to him," Angiolini wrote to Joseph. "It didn't seem possible to him that it could be achieved." Angiolini said he had let Camillo think the idea was only his own, but he hinted at "favorable circumstances that authorize me to hope for a happy outcome"—in other words, the approval of the Bonaparte family. Their conference was long, but did not suffice to "decide" Borghese. Nevertheless the Italian diplomat did not lose heart. "I have discovered the essential object exists," he wrote coyly. "The person [Pauline] pleases him. We have promised to speak of it more."

By the following day Camillo had ceased to flounder and had been safely landed. Angiolini wrote to Joseph, "The affair is concluded. Prince Borghese would believe himself too happy if the First Consul would accord him the honor of having as his wife our very amiable sister Madame Paulette." Angiolini hoped, however, that they could accommodate Camillo in his plea to keep the news private for the moment—"until he has informed the Princess Dowager, his mother, for whom he feels both tenderness and respect." An answer from Rome should be forthcoming in three weeks, and then the prince "would be happy to share in public his satisfaction in an event which, for all his titles, will be the happiest of his life."

The plea was duly granted, and letters containing the unlooked-for news sent to the princess dowager and to Cardinal Consalvi on June 27. At no point does the question of Pauline's ability to produce an heir seem to have been canvassed, although the fact that she had borne only one child in five years of marriage might have sent warning signals to the prince. Meanwhile, as Pauline later recorded, her brothers Joseph and Lucien urged on her marriage to Camillo as her best course of action. She seems to have been easy to persuade. At any rate, or so Josephine Bonaparte told her daughter, Hortense, she informed Napoleon that "she wanted him [Borghese] for her husband, and that she felt she would be happy with him. She asks Bonaparte's permission for Prince Borghese to write to him to ask for her hand."

Napoleon's reaction to the proposed marriage of his sister and Camillo Borghese seems to have been complex. On the one hand he told his sister that what dazzled her now might seem modest in years to come, and she might repent of remarrying so quickly. On the other hand he was, and remained, to some degree mesmerized by the splendor of Pauline's match. Much later he said, "My origins made me regarded by all the Italians as a compatriot. . . . When there was question of the marriage of my sister Pauline with Prince Borghese, there was only one voice at Rome and in Tuscany, in this family and in all their allied families—'It's good,' they all said. 'It's *entre nous,* it's one of our families.'"

Although the Borgheses would have been startled to hear the Bonapartes claim kinship, the first consul was correct in saying that Camillo's family in Rome approved the match. In mid-July, Don Cecco arrived in Paris to embrace his brother. Cardinal Fesch, moreover, wrote to Napoleon from Rome: "His Holiness is enchanted, the Roman nobility have marked their satisfaction." He called the princess dowager, his niece's future mother-in-law, "an excellent woman who will make life happy for Pauline. It is a family that has a revenue of 100,000 piastres." And the ambitious cleric ended by crowing: "You see me related now to the first family in Rome."

Even the old aristocracy of Paris, which traditionally inhabited the Faubourg Saint-Germain and which had now been assimilated into Consular society, was impressed. In the heat of the moment, when Camillo appeared at the Consular court in his new guise as Pauline's fiancé, the first consul declared, "Prince, my sister Pauline seems destined to marry a Roman, for from her head to her toes she is all Roman." Angiolini told Prince Vincenzo Giustiniani, "The fiancés are already very amorous, and by God, they are right to be so. I am convinced they will be happy." His information from Pauline's mother at the end of July was that the marriage would be celebrated "in the intimacy of Mortefontaine," where the couple would stay for about two months, "to wait out the mourning period of Madame Leclerc." The marriage would then be officially celebrated in Paris.

Matters proceeded apace, with Joseph and Borghese between them managing the details of the marriage contract, in which Pauline brought her husband a dowry of five hundred thousand francs, supplied by Napoleon, while Camillo undertook to buy for her three hundred thousand francs' worth of diamonds. She would also have the use of the celebrated Borghese jewels. She was to keep her Leclerc inheritance, while, in the event of Camillo's death, she would receive a jointure of fifty thousand francs a year, and the right to apartments in the different Borghese residences, as well as two carriages. The contract was duly signed on August 25 at the Hôtel Charost, by which time the banns had been read twice in the parish of Mortefontaine. But an impediment to the marriage itself had arisen: "I cannot tell you when the marriage will take place," Angiolini wrote to Prince Giustiniani, the day before the contract was signed. "The First Consul has decided that he wishes it to be put off until the end of Madame Leclerc's mourning, which is perfectly reasonable. The fiancés must suffer a little longer."

According to the Civil Code, under which a widow could remarry within ten months of her husband's death, Pauline was free to marry from early September. Napoleon, however, ignoring his own code, wished Pauline to defer her marriage until November, when she would have completed a full year of mourning, more in line with French tradition. But Pauline and Camillo had no intention of obeying any such edict. Three days after the contract was signed, early in the morning of August 28 and before Pauline had completed even ten months of mourning, she went through a cloak-and-dagger marriage with Borghese in the chapel at Mortefontaine. Her brothers were present, as was the ubiquitous Angiolini, and the ceremony, conducted by a priest put forward by Cardinal Caprara, apparently had the blessing of Pauline's mother as well as of the cardinal himself. Although the civil marriage was not due to take place until November, from now on Pauline could consider herself Princess Borghese.

And the motive for the early marriage, which was kept hidden from Napoleon as well as the rest of society? Pauline was not known for her patience, and she had a history of disobeying her brother. Furthermore, she and Borghese had already been "amorous" in July, and had certainly not grown less so since. Her mother and brothers, as well as the cardinal, probably endorsed the early marriage in order to bestow a measure of respectability on the couple's unbridled appetites. The only mystery is that Napoleon's army of spies, headed by chief of police Joseph Fouché, learned nothing of the matter. At any rate the couple honeymooned at Mortefontaine, apparently completely content, driving about the pretty estate with its Chinese pavilions, obelisks, and streams, until the demands of the autumn season and of their coming journey to Rome brought them back to Paris.

At the Hôtel Charost, of which she now took possession, Pauline set aside indolence and instructed Monsieur Michelot, whom she appointed steward of the house, in all the improvements she wished to have made. (Another woman might have thought of selling the *hôtel,* though she had so recently acquired it, on going to live in another country and in still greater splendor there. But Pauline was not such a woman.) There were, besides, arrangements to be made for the upkeep of Montgobert, which would one day belong to Dermide. And there was a deed to be signed—by Pauline and her new husband and by members of the Leclerc family—the day before the civil marriage, making the Borghese couple joint guardians to the child. Meanwhile, with Madame Michelot and her other amanuenses, Pauline began a welter of appointments, fittings, and correspondence with dressmakers and haberdashers, with jewelers whom she commissioned to set her new diamonds, and with others whom she ordered to reset the Borghese jewels, which she had had brought from Rome.

BUT IT REMAINED to tell Napoleon that she had disobeyed his wishes. Apparently all unknowing of his sister's marriage, Napoleon ordered Pauline—without Borghese—in September to stay at Saint-Cloud, and there he toasted her coming glory. This passed without incident. But in October, at a gala dinner that he gave at the Tuileries to celebrate the couple's engagement, shortly before they went through the brief civil marriage in the *mairie* in Mortefontaine on November 6, he learned the truth and was furious at having been duped. He showed his displeasure to brilliant effect when Pauline made one of her last appearances at the Tuileries before she left with her new husband for Rome.

Her toilette was "most remarkable," one Jenny Saint-Maur, a new attendant of the princess's, records. Pauline had had her Paris dressmaker sew onto "a dress of green velvet" a great quantity of "white diamonds." Bodice, skirt, bandeau, neckline, belt were all ablaze with jewels, and Jenny Saint-Maur tells us that Pauline "had contributed to the effect all the jewels of the Borghese house." (It is more likely that these were the new diamonds that Borghese had bought for her.) The effect was tremendous, and Pauline was delighted with herself and with the other Bonaparte women's chagrin. Seating herself by Laure Junot, she said, "Look at them, Laurette, do look. They are dying of jealousy, for I am a princess, a real princess."

But, unfortunately for the success of the soiree, Pauline had had herself announced as "Princess Borghese." And now the first consul seized his opportunity. Going up to his sister, he rebuked her in these words: "Please understand, Madame, that there is no princess where I am. Have more modesty and do not take a title that your sisters do not possess." All the women of the family, according to Jenny Saint-Maur, were "charmed by the Consul's egalitarianism, and each one enjoyed maliciously the lesson doled out to pretty Paulette." To drive the lesson further home that evening, and noticing that a general's lady had the words "Liberté, egalité, république ou la mort" embroidered on the train of her dress, Napoleon read and reread aloud the words. "Republic or death. Yes, Madame, you are right," he asserted, while Pauline tried to control her tears. "The Republic. Without it, life is not worth living." Enchanted with the first consul's endorsement, the general's lady looked proudly at the assembly and indeed named the couturier who had created the design that had attracted such attention.

Napoleon's displeasure with Pauline never lasted long, whatever she did to offend him. In a softened mood he wrote to her in early November from Brussels, where he was inspecting troops. "I shall be away for a few more days," he told her. "However, the bad season is approaching and the Alps will be covered with ice. So start on your journey to Rome. Be sure to show sweetness and kindness to everyone, and great consideration for the ladies of your husband's family. More will be expected from you than from anyone. Above all, see that you conform to the customs of Rome. Never criticize anything or say, 'We do this or that better in Paris,'" he instructed her. "Show respect and devotion toward the Holy Father. . . . What I would most like to hear about you is that you are well behaved." With the admonition that Pauline should never receive any English visitors, enemies of the French, at the Palazzo Borghese, he ended, "Love your husband, make your household happy, and above all do not be frivolous or capricious. You are twenty-four years old and ought to be mature and sensible by now. I love you."

PAULINE MIGHT NOT have brought treasure home from Saint-Domingue, but when she set out on the journey from Paris to Rome on November 14, 1803, with her went incontestable treasure. Besides her dowry of five hundred thousand francs—converted into gold and transported in little boxes of white iron, each containing a thousand louis—went her new diamonds and the Borghese jewels, as well as a vast wardrobe of costly dresses, lace, and shawls. On the long journey, which included an ascent over the Alps, Camillo, still "very amorous," and Pauline traveled tête-à-tête. Meanwhile, six-year-old Dermide followed at a slower pace, in a berlin drawn by six horses, with his governess, Madame Ducluzel, and with the young Jenny Saint-Maur, who had recently been appointed *lectrice* (reader) to Pauline. When they entered one of the many French and Italian cities through which they passed en route to Rome, one of the gendarmes asked who they were. "Messieurs," replied Dermide, "it is the son of General Leclerc traveling with his suite." Saint-Maur corrected Dermide and said that, as at his age he had only protectors, this expression was ridiculous coming from him. But she had to admire his spirit.

It was not a spirit that Camillo Borghese liked, however, and his view that the child was an inconvenient legacy from Pauline's first marriage was to have a disastrous outcome. For the moment, however, everyone was relieved to reach Rome, which they did in early December 1803. And though Pauline told Madame Michelot, "I find myself so isolated," she was sufficiently herself to keep the pope waiting several days after he had offered her an audience at the Quirinale, until the dress she required had arrived from Paris. At the deferred audience, however, Pius VII and Princess Borghese greatly took to each other, as Cardinal Consalvi was happy to report to Napoleon. But Pauline did not endear herself to her mother-in-law when she failed to show at a *cercle,* or assembly, at the Palazzo Borghese held in her honor, to which half Rome had been bidden. Pauline had dined amicably and in apparent good health earlier in the day with the dowager princess, before going off to dress. Her excuse that she had a violent headache—forthcoming only after two times of asking—was in consequence ill received.

Such sins were magnified and reverberated in the small aristocratic society of Rome. But the dowager princess forgave Pauline, took great interest in her daughter-in-law's dress, and even had her seamstress make copies of Pauline's Parisian trousseau (though the flimsy, low-cut creations hung oddly on the dowager's shrunken, elderly frame). Still, Pauline would not "conform to the customs of Rome," as her brother had ordered her to do. On the grounds of economy, she even found fault with her mother-in-law's housekeeping of thirty years' standing. The gatehouse of the Palazzo Borghese was in some measure open to the public, who went there to drink coffee or liqueurs or eat an ice as in a café. Camillo and his mother were mortified and confused by Pauline's edict that this bounty must cease, and the habitués of the gatehouse were not less put out. Her brother-in-law Prince Aldobrandini said nothing but contrived to spend little time with his brother and his new wife.

Soon not only was Pauline turning the established practices in the Borghese household on their head, but she was failing to love and respect, as her brother had instructed her to do, the head of that household. Camillo remained in thrall to Pauline, was still "amorous" toward her, and feared her, in his timid way. But now that she had his titles and money, his jewels, his carriages, and his palaces, she had tired of the prince and saw all the defects that others had noted in Paris. Worse, she had to live with the man, and, among new traits that her husband displayed and that annoyed her, Camillo was maddeningly jealous of other men's attentions to her. He, in return, was "almost continually discontented with [her]," as he told Angiolini in March 1804.

Irritable, regretful, Pauline harked back to her marriage with Leclerc as a great loss. Writing to her brother-in-law Murat in February, she sighed for Paris: "I don't know, but I think the air in Rome may not be good for me. I always have a cold. . . . I hope we may all meet again soon in France." And, married to a great and wealthy prince of the south, she took as a lover a very poor "Prince of the North"—the hereditary prince of Mecklenburg-Strelitz, who was a man as unlike Camillo as possible, being highly educated, cultivated, and the son of an Enlightenment German duke. When her husband went to Naples, Pauline seized her opportunity. By day she picnicked with the prince out in the Borghese houses that dotted the Roman Campagna. At night she had her black servant, Paul, escort the hereditary prince, in disguise, into the palazzo and up a secret stair to her apartments.

Camillo was beside himself with jealousy and rage when he discovered the truth, catching Pauline red-handed with a letter he would have "given the world not to have seen." He wanted all her attendants, conspirators in the affair, to be dispatched back to Paris. Pauline refused, and when Borghese appealed to her uncle Fesch it was clear that the cardinal had no influence with his headstrong niece. Angiolini, when consulted, counseled tolerance: "Women, my friend, especially before they reach a certain age, are determined to have what they want, and neither force nor a show of authority will deter them." Napoleon, however, was not of this opinion. When informed by Cardinal Fesch in April of the Borgheses' quarrels, he wrote to Pauline with the clear intention of frightening her into obedience:

> Madame and dear Sister, I learn to my sorrow that you have not
> had the good sense to conform to the manners and customs of

the city of Rome, that you have shown disdain for its people, and that your eyes are constantly turned towards Paris. . . . Do not count on me to help, if at your age you let yourself be governed by bad advice. As for Paris, be assured you will find no support here, for I shall never receive you without your husband. If you fall out with him, it will be entirely your own fault, and then France will be forbidden you. You will lose your happiness and my friendship.

The departure northward of the hereditary prince coincided with the arrival of Napoleon's letter. Pauline had often defied her brother's rule, but his letter—this "show of authority," with its threat that Paris would be closed to her—was enough to make anyone reconsider. In a private letter to Fesch, Napoleon showed himself more understanding of Pauline's behavior than he had been in his official reprimand. He recommended that Camillo remember that women in Paris lived differently.

Meanwhile Pauline's mother, who had been known to reason with her daughter, had arrived in Rome in Holy Week, to be feted by the pope. Letizia Bonaparte was also hoping to broker a peace between Napoleon and her younger son Lucien, who—against Napoleon's wishes—had married Madame Alexandrine Jouberthon, a French merchant's widow, the previous year and had now settled with her in Rome. Declaring that he would henceforward live as a private citizen, Lucien refused to countenance divorcing Alexandrine and abandoning the children whom the union soon produced—they were to number ten in all—in favor of the dynastic marriage his brother sought for him. Letizia now took Lucien's part, estranging her, too, from Napoleon.

Would the first consul's sister be more tractable? Would the Borghese couple now settle down, would Camillo follow the advice provided by Angiolini and "give Paulette a child"—a half sibling for Dermide, a cousin for Lucien's children, and an heir to the great fortunes of the Roman family? Or was a child in fact out of the question and Pauline all but infertile owing to salpingitis? Did the ability to have sex without danger of pregnancy mean that Pauline was all the more hell-bent on trying out different partners? At any rate hers was a *non-conformista* life that appalled the Romans. They were used to discretion and propriety in the affairs that many of them—including, for many years, Pauline's own mother-in-law—conducted. It was Pauline's Parisian openness about her liaison with the hereditary prince as much as the liaison itself that had so tormented Camillo.

As Camillo anxiously waited in Rome to see if there would be more liaisons, as Angiolini counseled him to be "less the lover, more a loving husband," momentous news came from Paris in May. Napoleon had been declared by the Senate emperor of the French, a plebiscite had approved the title as a hereditary one, and his brothers Joseph and Louis and their wives, Julie and Hortense, were made imperial highnesses. Lucien, who remained in his Roman retreat, received no title. Nor did Jérôme, who had married, while in Baltimore, Maryland, the previous year, an American girl, Elizabeth Patterson, to the outrage of his brother Napoleon. The emperor was no better pleased when a nephew, Jérôme-Napoléon Bonaparte-Patterson, appeared.

Days later, following angry representations from Elisa and Caroline in Paris, came a further announcement: All three of the emperor's sisters were to have the rank of imperial highness. At the Palazzo Borghese, where quarrels continued between Camillo and Pauline, the prince, who had not received the rank of imperial highness, received the news of his wife's elevation in silence, "not knowing whether to laugh or cry." Prince Aldobrandini offered his congratulations coldly. And Pauline was not entirely pleased that her sisters now shared the rank of princess and imperial highness with her. (Their mother was to become known as Madame Mère.) But she had further thoughts to offer. Upon reading letters from her family full of pride and joy, she said, "I may be wrong, but I think my brother might have done better to remain First Consul. How astonished, how angry my poor Leclerc would have been to see it. He had such democratic ideas, he so hated despots and grand airs. I promise you, there would have been harsh words between him and my brother."

Pauline had no expectation that Camillo would make any such

protest. Although some in Rome might scoff at her brother's titles, on one point she and Camillo were in accord: They both had the highest admiration and respect for Napoleon. And together, in the summer of 1804, and with the sculptor Antonio Canova, they embarked upon a commission that was both to mark that love and respect and to become one of the most potent emblems of Napoleon's Empire—the *Venus Victrix.*

CHAPTER EIGHT

Bitter Summer, 1804

S O FAMOUS IS THE VERY TILT OF PAULINE'S HEAD, to say nothing of the tilt of her breasts and of her haunch in the near-life-size reclining statue that now adorns the gallery of the Villa Borghese in Rome, it is astonishing to think that this pink and pearly emblem of the Napoleonic Empire might never have existed. It was not that Pauline was reluctant to be portrayed in marble—and "nearly naked"—as Venus Victorious. Napoleon had written of Pauline to Uncle Fesch in April 1804, "Tell her from me she is no longer beautiful, and she will be still less so in a few years, and it is more important to be good and esteemed." To have herself represented with her torso, arms, and abdomen unclothed might not bring her esteem, but Pauline was, as ever, unconcerned for her reputation. And, whatever Napoleon might say, she knew she was beautiful and likely to remain so, evoking admiration in all who looked upon her.

Even the writer Chateaubriand, who was acting as Fesch's secretary in Rome, fell under the spell of "la diva Paolina" when he was deputed to bring her some slippers that had arrived in the diplomatic bag from Paris. Chateaubriand did not generally relish the menial duties Fesch assigned him, but, on being shown into the apartment at the Palazzo Borghese where the princess was at her toilette, the bagman forgot his resentment. His description of their meeting was lyrical: "The virgin shoe that she put on her foot grazed only for an instant this tired old earth." Later he recalled that "she shone with all the glory of her brother. . . . If she had lived in the time of Raphael, he would have painted her as one of those amours who lie so voluptuously on lions at the Farnesina." Extravagant as Chateaubriand's language is, it may have been the case that a modern Raphael was required to paint Pauline. None of the portraits we have of her by artists of the day, with the possible exception of a beguiling half-length by Lefebvre, captures the mix of classic beauty and allure that so seduced those who saw the princess.

Pauline prized her supple, milk white body, her bosom and hips, her exquisite hands and feet, as much as Chateaubriand and everyone else admired them. They were, as she well knew, perfectly to the taste of her time, and she spoke of them matter-of-factly as "advantages of nature." In Paris the earlier rosy and lusty images of Fragonard and Boucher had now been succeeded in popularity by languorous, long-limbed bodies—on show clothed in David's paintings and unclothed in those of Girodet. In Rome, Pauline's slim figure and small breasts recalled those of the nymphs and naiads of antiquity in the Borghese collection, even those of the *Sleeping Hermaphrodite,* which aroused the admiration of papal subjects and tourists alike. She could have been a model for the sculptures of the seventeenth-century master Bernini, who had reinterpreted in marble for Cardinal Scipione Borghese's collection to erotic effect the stories of Ovid: Persephone, being borne off by Pluto; Daphne, under Apollo's touch, metamorphosing into a laurel tree.

What more suitable, given the wonders of Pauline's body and of the Borghese inheritance, than for Prince Camillo to commission Canova, the internationally celebrated sculptor resident in Rome since the 1780s, and incorporate her image into the family collection? Canova had already depicted Psyche being awakened with a kiss by Cupid, a sculpture group that Murat had bought and that showed the artist's skill in handling mythological subject matter and lissome bodies alike. Later Pauline stressed, in a letter to Camillo, that "the statue was created for your pleasure." It was a commission on which they were both agreed, to which they were both committed, and for which Camillo was happy to pay.

But there was a hitch. Canova was initially reluctant to oblige the couple, as he had been similarly reluctant to go to Paris two years earlier to sculpt the colossal nude statue of Napoleon as Mars the Peacemaker. (Canova came from the Veneto and deplored the French pillage of artifacts from Venice and other Italian cities.) According to Pauline's attendant Jenny Saint-Maur, Canova protested at first that he had a long list of commissions he must honor. But upon seeing Pauline, she attests, he was so excited by her appearance that he agreed to begin work after only a month. And so, just as he had obeyed Napoleon's orders, now Canova bowed to Pauline's commanding beauty.

Once the commission was agreed, Pauline apparently declared that she wished to be depicted as Venus, the goddess of love. Canova demurred and suggested as model Diana, virgin huntress and goddess of the moon. But Pauline laughed and said, "Nobody would believe in my chastity." Besides, the Borgheses, like many still more ancient families in Rome, claimed descent from Romulus, founder of Rome and son of Mars, and hence kinship with Venus, the god of war's sister. (In eighteenth-century Rome such genealogical leaps of faith were not uncommon.) Accordingly it was decided that Pauline should be depicted as Venus. Furthermore the sculpture should bear an apple in one hand in allusion to the famous judgment of Paris in antiquity, when that Trojan eschewed the charms of Hera and Athena and awarded to Aphrodite or Venus the golden fruit, inscribed "to the fairest one of all."

Aphrodite's sister goddesses Athena and Hera, who failed to win the prize for beauty in ancient times, had been suitably disconsolate and had subsequently sided with the Greeks in the Trojan War. Did it occur to Pauline that her own sisters, Elisa and Caroline, would be no better pleased now by this statue in which her beauty was celebrated for eternity? The idea that she had again eclipsed the rest of her family can only have added to her mischievous pleasure in a work of art that scandalized those who in the summer of 1804 saw its plaster model in

Canova's studio. (The full-size version was not to be finished and dispatched to Camillo Borghese until 1808.) For *La Paolina,* as the statue was to become known in Rome, showed Princess Borghese reclining against pillows heaped in lifelike fashion on a divan, naked to the waist. There were only loose draperies around her pelvis and hips, and her lower legs and feet were on display. With one hand the princess supported her head on the pillows behind her; the other, on her thigh, curled around the apple, and drew attention to the drapery plunging to her lower abdomen.

Pauline's reported remarks on the sittings for this celebrated statue are entertaining if not informative. To enquiries about how she had borne posing so lightly clothed for the artist, she variously—but always contemptuously—replied, "Oh, Canova is not a real man," "There was a good fire in the room so I did not take cold," and "Every veil must fall before Canova." A grand saloon in the Palazzo Borghese, with coffered ceiling, blue and gilded walls, and a vast fireplace is today pointed out as the site of the sessions. But Jenny Saint-Maur tells us that the sessions took place both in the Palazzo Borghese and in the artist's studio, which lay close by, behind the Hospital for Incurables. Canova habitually first made sketches at his client's home and worked with clay and plaster at his studio when working on marble portrait statues, and one may assume this was his method here. The sessions were finished by June, and the plaster model in Canova's studio by July 1804. Pauline's brother Lucien, who had recently come to live in the city, apparently took pleasure in visiting the studio and conversing with Canova about the ancient statues of Rome and the environs, in which he was beginning to interest himself. Standing between the models for portrait statues of his sister and of his brother Napoleon as Mars the Peacemaker, Lucien observed, "He looks more belligerent than pacific." His remarks on his sister's near-naked body are not recorded, nor are those of Napoleon, who would have heard of his sister's latest exploit from his spies.

The arrival in Rome of Lucien and his family in February had pleased Pauline, not least because, with her brother and his second

wife, Alexandrine, came Lucien's children by Christine—ten-year-old
Charlotte and six-year-old Christine—as well as Lucien and
Alexandrine's two-year-old son Charles. Pauline, being family minded
like all the Bonapartes, welcomed her nieces and nephew but especially
valued them as playmates for their cousin Dermide. Lucien had not yet
made up his quarrel with Napoleon, but Pauline was expert at remain-
ing friends with her more quarrelsome siblings and did not take sides.
When Lucien settled on a country house, the Villa Rufinella, close to
the Borghese and Aldobrandini villas at Frascati, she was delighted that
Dermide, Charlotte, and Christine would see one another there.
Meanwhile, between bouts of illness that kept her in her bed during
March, she was arranging for the decoration of a new apartment in the
Palazzo Borghese in Rome, which she believed would be very pretty.
But she reassured her friend Madame Michelot, "Don't worry, my dear
Poulotte, the Rome season doesn't please me enough to make me for-
get Paris, or the friends I have left there." Nor did the fashions in
Rome satisfy her. She continued to requisition them from Madame
Michelot—even ribbons and accessories—in Paris. "Dermide is very
well and talks often of your dear children." With her letter she sent
miniatures to be mounted on a little mother-of-pearl box for Der-
mide's grandmother in Pontoise. "It's an age since I promised them to
Madame Leclerc."

PAULINE, IT SEEMED, was adjusting to life in Rome as Princess
Borghese. At her husband's request she had received communion at
Easter in the ornate Borghese chapel, beneath which lay the tombs of
Pope Paul V and Cardinal Scipione, in the basilica of Santa Maria
Maggiore. Pauline, baptized in the small cathedral of Ajaccio, with an
archdeacon for a great-uncle and now a cardinal for an uncle, found
nothing odd in maintaining a religious belief while disregarding many
of the provisions of the Catholic creed. For her additional pleasure,
Madame Mère, as we have seen, arrived to stay with Cardinal Fesch
in Holy Week. "You know my fondness for her," Pauline wrote to

Madame Michelot and claimed to have won Letizia's approval. "My mother, who is quite severe," she wrote triumphantly to Napoleon, "both praises my conduct and repeats often that I have changed to my advantage."

Pauline was responding to rumors that had reached Napoleon's ears that she and Camillo were on the point of separating, and that such fission would already have occurred if her brother had not forbidden France to her. "Since I have lived in Rome," she replied, "despite the difference in customs, and, I will say frankly, despite the difficult and disputatious character of Prince Camillo, our household is the picture of peace and happiness. For I have made sacrifices you would not have believed me capable of." She surmised, "People jealous of advantages that I have received by nature and fearing my return to Paris invent these black words to encourage you to abandon me. But write to Prince Camillo and his family, for their responses will convince you that my accusers play false."

There was a measure of truth in what Pauline wrote. Although she and Camillo were prone to quarreling—she flustered him with her demands and angered him by flouting his wishes—they shared an aesthetic sensibility and a love of good living, so that the detail of their domestic life was not without its pleasures. Camillo continued to admire his wife's beauty, and she appears to have been content to allow him the privileges of a husband, once the Mecklenburg prince had left for Germany.

By the early summer, at any rate, Pauline's divine body was in need of rest and a cure, and she and Camillo had formed a plan. "We leave," she wrote to Madame Michelot in May, "for Florence in two months, and from there we go to the waters." She had taken the waters at Frascati already with her mother, but to little avail. "I suffer all the time in this climate," she complained. It was hoped that the baths at Pisa would have a better effect. "Please, my dear Poulotte," Pauline added, "have the goodness to send me four or five summer hats, in pale colors, and another straw one." They were to be well made and in the latest fashion, and she required them to be sent to the Palazzo Borghese in

Florence, where they would stop first. "I will be happy to abide by your taste," she ended as usual.

According to Jenny Saint-Maur, "At the moment of arranging the departure, an altercation arose between husband and wife." Pauline wished her son to come with them. But the prince advised leaving young Dermide at Rome. "If you fear the fetid summer air, send him to Frascati," he said. "My brother . . . can supervise him." The boy's uncle Lucien would be nearby, at the Villa Rufinella. "Think too that your entourage is already very considerable," said the prince, who was not overfond of Dermide, "that the lodgings at the waters are very small, and that the fatigue of the road could well hurt his health." Pauline, as she later explained to Napoleon, was swayed by her husband's arguments. "I thought of him surrounded by his little cousins whom he loved, under the care of my brother-in-law, who behaved very well, and of Madame Ducluzel, who loved him and paid the greatest attention to him." She was therefore "without worry" when Dermide, his governess, and his tutor, Monsieur de la Ronde, were installed at the Villa Mondragone in Frascati under the aegis of Camillo's brother, Don Cecco. She and Camillo, meanwhile, took the road for Florence with a caravan of attendants.

"Mon Dieu, what a journey," remembered Jenny Saint-Maur:

> You might say that caprice traveled with us. Every instant some real or imaginary suffering of the Princess's stopped the carriages. Two maids then had to get down into a ditch, or crouch behind a hedge, or just stand in the middle of the road with Her Highness to make some adjustment or other. Her corset needed unlacing, or her hair restyling. . . . Out came all the packages, they opened all the traveling cases and necessaires to find some eau de cologne. . . . The Prince fumed, the suite grew irritable . . . and the postilions did what they could to see the Princess undressed.

But Pauline was all smiles at their first port of call. "I am very content with the town of Pisa," she wrote in Napoleonic fashion to her brother-in-law Murat, now a marshal of the Empire and governor of Paris. With Don Cecco, her brother-in-law, she and Camillo attended the annual regatta held on the feast day of San Ranieri, when night-lights floated on the Arno and candles burned in every window of the town. The widowed Queen of Etruria, Maria Luisa di Borbone, was present and singled Pauline out, paying her attentions in public and making her private visits. Pauline took these favors from the King of Spain's daughter as her right. (When they had first met in Florence the previous year, she had scoffed at the queen's appearance, disfigured by smallpox, but politics now fostered the Bourbon-Bonaparte alliance.) The baths at Pisa did not suit Pauline, however, or her mother, who joined them, and soon they were off to Florence, to mark the feast of Saint John the Baptist on June 24. At nightfall, as fireworks lit up the river, and grandees of the town, bearing candles, proceeded on horse-back from the Piazza Signoria to the Duomo, Pauline sat with her friend the queen, resplendent in the royal box.

In early July the Prussian minister at Rome informed his wife, "Princess Borghese is still at Florence and enjoys the greatest honors possible." But as suddenly as she had appeared in the city, Pauline left it, for the baths of Lucca. On the night of July 7 Signor Raffaello Mansi, a rich merchant in that walled town, was unceremoniously awakened and asked to provide dinner for Pauline and Camillo, who had that moment arrived. Admittedly, while in Florence, he had offered the Borgheses hospitality—both when they were to break their journey in Lucca and at the baths themselves, where he owned a house. But he had not expected his invitation to be taken up at such an hour and without any notice. Following an impromptu midnight feast, the next day Mansi prepared a more orderly dinner and invited a select company. But the Borgheses, it turned out, had already left for his house in Bagni di Lucca, as the bathing station high in the hills above the town was known, and the Lucchese nobility sat down in their fin-ery without the promised guests of honor.

Bagni di Lucca was in great vogue, both for the supposed efficacy of its curative waters and for the beauty of its location, a gorge several miles long. Sulfuric springs, bathhouses, and vertiginous residences with balconies occupied three different levels on one steep side of the gorge. Below, meanwhile, rushed the Lima river, whose eddies visitors could inspect from the safety of a wide path cut along its bank for promenades.

The noise of the torrent and the picturesque form of the mountains above, the fresh air that circulated and was cooled by the river, pleased most invalids. Pauline, however, immediately found fault with the bathhouse facilities, and a new bath had to be made for her. That settled, she and her mother, who now joined her, bathed, douched, and drank glass after glass of acrid water. But then there were the lodgings to consider. Pauline felt that Mansi's house, although large, was poorly laid out and too simply furnished, and its owner was summoned to be rebuked and ordered to remedy the matter.

It was not that Pauline sought to entertain at the Casa Mansi, although such was the general practice in the resort. "There is an enormous crowd of people there, practicing luxury without restraint," wrote one observer, Conte Averardo Serristori, of the scene this summer. "They game all the time, give dinners continually, and often balls." Pauline, her mother, and Camillo, however, appeared rarely in public and they received only a few, if regular, visitors. A local priest said mass every morning, and later in the day came Dr. Rossi, director of the baths. Whether Pauline had a cure for particular ailments in mind or whether she hoped that her visit to this bathing station would act as a general tonic is not known. In addition to the long-lasting problems Dermide's birth had caused, her health had been weakened by bouts of yellow fever in Saint-Domingue. And there was always the possibility, increasing with every lover she took, that she was suffering from one or more venereal infections. At Bagni di Lucca a wide range of cures was offered.

Not only were Pauline and her mother eager to rest and restore their health. There was also the troubling matter of Letizia Bonaparte's status. While Napoleon had made his brothers and sisters imperial highnesses, he had not yet settled on a title for his mother, and, no one knowing quite what to call her, some settled on "Empress Mother," others on "Imperial Highness." As Cardinal Fesch wrote to his nephew the emperor, this caused Letizia great distress, and she wished the matter to be settled before she went about in society. Ultimately, the title of Madame Mère was settled on.

In part, too, it is plain that Pauline and Letizia adopted at Bagni di Lucca, in the shady depths of the Casa Mansi, an almost peasant and penny-pinching existence. It resembled, in a way, the life they had known when they had lived hand-to-mouth, following Pauline's father's death, in the Strada Malerba in Ajaccio, and in I Milleli, their summer house in the hills above that Corsican harbor town. Letizia apparently got the village baker to agree that, of each day's order, she could trade a quantity of stale leftover bread for fresh bread the following morning. Meanwhile Pauline was relentless in the daily tally with her cook of provisions and preserves, demanding that leftovers be recycled the following day and giving orders that dinner should consist of no more than seven or, at most, nine dishes.

Letizia was, by nature, parsimonious to an obsessive degree. In Rome she had forbidden her suite to drink tea or coffee on grounds of expense, and they had had to buy it themselves and brew it in secret. Now Pauline's commands to Madame Michelot betray her mother's influence: "Madame Verdière, who leaves at the end of the month for Paris, will give you my embroidered tunics. I add to them three bonnets of lace. Please have the two dresses embroidered with all economy possible." But Pauline had anyway, with her brother Napoleon, inherited from her mother a belief that the devil was in the detail. Secluded with Madame Mère at Bagni in the months of July and August, adding up her accounts, and with Camillo in attendance, she was not unhappy. From Frascati, Madame Ducluzel sent cheerful accounts of Dermide's health, and at the end of August, Pauline would be reunited with him in Rome. Even with Camillo she could indulge in a "more or less sweet tête-à-tête." She wrote to Madame Michelot, "I am certain I must have some secret enemy who harms me about my brother. None of my conduct merits the least reproach, and their hate must be active and their character truly false to invent all the absurdities they lay at my door. All Italy must be aware that my dear Prince adores me and that I cannot live without him." If this was not entirely true, it was a narrative that could at least pass muster with those at a distance from her.

But while Pauline was recovering her health in Tuscany—Conte Serristori maintained on August 18 that her douches had had a good effect—in Frascati events were unfolding that were to drive a near-indissoluble wedge between husband and wife. In the third week of August, Jenny Saint-Maur was at Pauline's bedside, reading a historical romance to her mistress, when Camillo came in and, out of sight of his wife, made frantic signs to the attendant. "A gesture that he made gave me to understand," Jenny writes, "that a terrible secret weighed on his heart and that he wished me to know it." The princess, however, would not allow the reading to be interrupted.

The prince wriggled around on an armchair, ever more imploring, his wife's calm contrasting with his distress. It was four long hours before the implacable Pauline would let Jenny stop, and the attendant was no sooner in her own quarters and preparing to make her toilette for dinner than the prince entered and threw himself into a chair, his face wet with tears.

"You see me in despair," he said. "Dermide, my wife's son, is dead." A lightning strike could not have convulsed Jenny more. "Dead!" she cried. "It's impossible. We had news yesterday, he is wonderfully well." "That letter was delayed," sighed Camillo. "My brother arrived two hours ago with this cruel news."

Apparently, a few days earlier at the Villa Mondragone in Frascati, Dermide had taken a fever. The doctors had been called in and to begin with had not considered that there was cause for alarm. However, the climate of Frascati, usually so beneficial, had that summer been perni-cious. Lucien Bonaparte and the boy's cousins had had bouts of fever and had recovered. But despite the doctors' best efforts, Dermide did not. (His mother was later to believe that his blood had been thinned by the months he had spent in Saint-Domingue and by the bouts of yellow fever he had suffered there.) At the Villa Mondragone, despite the anxious care of his attendants, the little boy's fever worsened, and on August 14 Dermide died.

Jenny burst into tears on hearing this account, but Camillo was focused on his own unfortunate position. "You alone can be the comforter," he told the weeping woman. "Pauline will regard me with horror. Wasn't it I who wanted her to leave her son in Rome? No doubt he would have died anyway, but she is bound to accuse me of his death. For I have given her the right to be unjust." With these words the prince crushed Jenny to his heart, while begging her not to abandon him. "Certainly never was embrace so pure as that," she recorded.

They decided at length to conceal the fact of Dermide's death until Pauline's health should be better established, and resolved that Don Cecco, who had brought the fateful news, should not appear at the house. He was to return to Frascati to deal with the sad obsequies, but before he left he was to write three letters. The first should announce the onset of Dermide's illness, the second its crescendo, and the third the sad and fatal truth. The dinner hour approached, and Madame Pauline had already asked for Jenny twice. The prince, seeing the attendant's pinched and pale face, said, "She will see something is wrong. Find some cause to justify it."

"Be calm," replied Jenny. "I will have received some news from France that a member of my family is very ill." And she adopted a somber crepe redingote to lend credence to a lie, which the princess accepted. She merely observed that Jenny's family was thoughtless in worrying her when she was so far from home, and when her relative might well by now be recovered. Dinner was nevertheless a tense affair. Jenny had given orders that no one was to approach the princess without talking to the prince or to her first, in case they let slip the awful news. But at one point Jenny was called out to receive a courier, dressed in the livery of mourning, who came with a note of condolence from the Queen of Etruria for the princess. Jenny immediately dispatched the messenger back with a message of acknowledgment, before his presence could come to the attention of her mistress.

The next day Jenny went early to Madame Bonaparte, who received her, although she was still in bed. Thanking the girl for her attentions to her daughter, Letizia approved the plan to keep the news of Dermide's death a secret for some days. But when Jenny declared that the princess's "active imagination" would no doubt force them soon to tell her the truth, Letizia refused to agree that the task should fall to her. When Jenny said that "a mother would, better than anyone, use words to soften such a rude blow," Letizia said "very forcefully" that she would not be drawn into any such arrangement. She had no wish to charge herself, she said, with such a sad commission. She knew her daughter's mercurial personality and did not wish to expose herself to it. She was, besides, careful, she said, to ward off painful emotions and in short refused to reveal the truth.

Over the next few days, knowing nothing of her son's death, Pauline displayed an almost eerie "softness and calm. She had even a kind of gaiety that confounded us," wrote Jenny, who was obliged to hide half of the letters that arrived for the princess, as they expressed regret for her loss. "She talked of her approaching recovery, of the pleasure that the latest news of her son had given her, reproached the Prince for his preoccupied air and Jenny for her sadness." Pauline, while continuing to blame Jenny's relations for worrying her with bad news, even complained that her attendant's melancholy bored her mortally. Jenny would have had her mistress "chagrined, capricious, even unjust; I would have pardoned all, except this calm which tore at my heart."

One day Pauline called on Jenny to take up her pen, saying she had decided to hire a governor, or male preceptor, for Dermide. "Dermide now being six years old, it is no longer suitable that his education is in the hands of a woman. . . . I want him to receive early on the education that befits the son of General Leclerc. Come on, Jenny, sit down and write what I want you to say." Jenny was overcome and wished to excuse herself, but her mistress would brook no argument. The letter, listing the manly virtues this paragon must exhibit, was three pages long, as Jenny had no presence of mind to edit Pauline's thoughts, and the princess, never doubting her powers of dictation, repeated her ideas a dozen times at least.

More than ten days had elapsed since Don Cecco had brought the dreadful news, and since Pauline had had reports from Madame Ducluzel of Dermide's well-being. The governess's silence suddenly seemed inconceivable to Pauline. It was no longer possible to put off the moment when she should learn the truth, and Dermide's tutor was summoned from Frascati so that he could give the princess an account of her son's last days. Jenny meanwhile took Pauline the first letter from Don Cecco, announcing that Dermide was ill.

Pauline's first reaction appears to have been to set out for Frascati immediately. She wrote to Madame Michelot, "My little angel Dermide is ill. I fly to Rome. My baths are not finished, but my heart suffers so much that nothing in the world could hold me here." Jenny added a postscript: "You see by this letter, which your unhappy friend has just dictated, that we have told her half. We leave tomorrow at ten for Rome, she will find there her family who will do all to sustain her in this terrible blow."

However, before they could depart, what the attendant had foreseen occurred. Pauline's "devouring imagination" led her swiftly to review Jenny's earlier tears and other incidents. She called in her attendant for questioning, and the prince, entering at that moment, was similarly interrogated. He lost himself in vague excuses, while Jenny said that Monsieur de la Ronde, Dermide's tutor, who had arrived from Rome that instant, could best tell the truth.

On seeing her son's tutor, Pauline said, "Be truthful, Monsieur de la Ronde, my son is dead." He bowed his head and said nothing. "Oh, I understand this silence," she said. "I have been deceived for a long time . . . my son is dead far from me." After the tutor, under Pauline's questioning, had narrated the painful facts of his pupil's death and had been allowed to withdraw, the princess immediately turned on Camillo. "It's you, Monsieur, who has been the cause of my son's death. Without you I would never have been separated from him, and he would still be alive." As he cowered, Pauline continued: "What will the Emperor have to say? And my family? Leave, Monsieur, I cannot bear the sight of you. You, the butcher of my son!"

The wretched Camillo left, and, alone with Jenny and her women, Pauline said that the death of her son had destroyed all her happiness. While all about her wept, she maintained dry eyes and a calm born of desolation. Of Rome and of Italy, she said, she now had a horror, and nothing on earth would make her stay there. She spoke of the unhappiness that pursued her and of her poignant feelings for General Leclerc. The death of their son now doubled her sorrow, she lamented, and, taking a big pair of scissors that lay to hand, she sheared off her hair. Having cut it in Saint-Domingue for the father, she said, she must pay the same homage to her son. Then, gathering up the tresses, she gave them to Jenny, whom she instructed to leave next day for Rome and see that they were placed in Dermide's coffin, which was to be transported to Montgobert in due course.

As for Pauline herself, on the understanding that Camillo would take her to France, so that she could attend the burial of Dermide beside his father, she agreed to a rapprochement with her husband. Camillo "conducted himself in the most touching manner," Jenny tells us, "and made no objection except to say that the Emperor seemed to want her to stay in Italy." Pauline's reply was magnificent: "What do his wishes matter? It's not Paris I wish to go to, it's Montgobert, where the general lies, and where my son will join him. Is my brother God? Does he have the right to decide my fate? I care no more for the trappings of his court than for his crown. And as you will be accompanying me, there is no more to be said." Camillo, "to have peace, to be pardoned, to have this pretty face that he still loved accord him again a smile," agreed to everything.

Jenny was instructed, therefore, while at Rome, to pack up all the princess's effects at the Palazzo Borghese and dispatch them to Montgobert. While Pauline and Camillo awaited Napoleon's permission to travel, they settled at a villa outside Florence, and, to console the princess, her friend the Queen of Etruria came every evening to dine with her. When Napoleon sent no word, Pauline took matters into her own hands. The Michelots were alerted in early September to her plans: "We will go to Montgobert and not return to Paris until after the coronation." Pauline then wrote to the emperor, toward the end of September:

> This blow has been so severe. Despite summoning all my courage, I find no strength to withstand it. My health is altered visibly, and my husband is so alarmed he wants to take me to France, hoping that the change of air, and the pleasure of being near you, will be beneficial. . . . We leave in four or five days. And I dare to hope that my dear brother will receive me with his usual kindness. We go to Montgobert. . . . Paris at this moment, where all is rejoicing, is not the place for a soul as sad as mine. In all other circumstances it would have been a great pleasure for me to witness your coronation, but fate pursues me in too cruel a manner to allow me such enjoyment.

Pauline's letter was bound to irritate her brother. First, he had not given her permission for her journey to France. Second, if he were to overlook that lèse-majesté, she was now refusing in advance to appear at the December ceremony to which he had devoted much thought and time, and at which he expected all his family, except the recalcitrant Lucien, to play a supporting role. But Pauline was not only grief-stricken and thinking ahead to the inhumation of her son in the tomb with his father at Montgobert. She was also revolted by the role Napoleon's sisters were destined to play at the coronation. They were to be their sister-in-law Josephine's trainbearers, as she bowed her head to be crowned—by her husband, it had been decreed.

AS THE BORGHESES and their suite journeyed north to Montgobert, Pauline had much to say, according to her faithful attendant, on the subject of the coronation: "Believe me, dear Jenny, all these grandeurs do not touch me. I have suffered too much. I am determined to live out of the way and cultivate my brother's friendship, but only so that I can be left alone in France, where I am truly better than anywhere else. I leave it to my sisters to shine. I have no ambition, except for a comfortable existence, a small number of good friends, and freedom of action." Pauline persisted with her disapproval of her brother's coronation even after arriving at Montgobert and receiving orders from Napoleon to appear at the ceremony. When her brother Joseph came to remonstrate with her, she told him dramatically and without sparing Camillo's feelings that she wished to bury herself at Montgobert to mourn the deaths of Leclerc and Dermide. She was still awaiting the arrival of Dermide's body, which had been embalmed, like his father's, and was traveling by slow stages from Rome. Dermide's heart, she had determined, was to join that of his father in the gilded urn she guarded so jealously.

Disdaining Joseph's compliance with his brother's imperial wishes, Pauline said angrily, "What do I care for his coronation? Do I have to be there to swell his wife's court? . . . Oh, honorable indeed, Bonapartes in the suite of a Beauharnais. Truly, my sisters make me sick with their submission. We ought to detest her, for the Emperor would betray us all for his dear Josephine." Joseph attempted reason: "But, my dear Paulette, why did you come back at this moment, since you didn't wish to take part in the coronation?" "Why?" Pauline was swift in her reply. "To escape the tyranny of my husband. Because, since my son's death, Italy is insupportable for me. Besides, I needed to breathe the air of France. Every time I leave it, I suffer."

On went the diatribe: "What I suffered in America! And it was the Emperor who forced me to go there. It was the cause of my poor general's death and in consequence the cause of my marriage to the most insupportable of men. Don't talk to me more of going to Paris. I want to stay here. And if I am persecuted further, I declare," she ended, "I will receive my family no more, not even you, Joseph, whom I love dearly."

Pauline had instructed Jenny exactly how to proceed when the corpse of her child should arrive, and on the morning after the cortege had entered the park at nightfall, Jenny, dressed in mourning, approached her mistress's bed in silence. Pauline took her hand, keeping silent too. She rose, dressed herself, and added a hat with a great veil. Leaning on Jenny's arm, she descended to the vestibule, where the small coffin was laid. Members of the suite shouldered it and began the long walk to the tomb in the allée that Fontaine had designed and where Dermide's father had been laid less than two years earlier. Pauline and Jenny walked, too, the princess saying not a word, but Jenny heard her weep. When they arrived at the door of the tomb, Pauline had the coffin set down inside beside the larger one, and she sent away her people. Then she prostrated herself before the two tombs, watering them with her tears and addressing to her husband's and son's shades the most bitter regrets. Later that day, abandoning her usual carefulness with money, she ordered twenty-five louis to be distributed to each of a hundred poor families in the area.

The inhumation of Dermide proved a cathartic event, and the renaissance of Pauline's feeling for Leclerc, and her wish to live secluded, seemed to die. More adroit courtiers than Prince Joseph appeared at Montgobert and talked of the fashions in Paris and of the pleasures that would follow the coronation. In the middle of a very scientific discussion of the form court dress would now take, a lady appeared—an emissary from one of Pauline's imperial sisters. She had a hat and gown made in the latest mode to present to the princess, and Pauline pronounced them delicious. "You know, Jenny," she said pensively to her attendant, when they were alone once more, "I must conciliate the Emperor. He is my protector, he will defend me against the evil designs of my husband. I am determined, in short, to attend his coronation."

And Pauline began to consider her choice of robe for the ceremony. "I need to know first what my sisters have chosen. I don't want to copy them or choose a color they are wearing." On leaving the princess that night, Jenny took with her orders to write to the many couturiers, milliners, haberdashers, and other merchants of Paris who were to help embellish Princess Pauline's appearance in Notre-Dame in the first week of December.

CHAPTER NINE

The Borgheses at War, 1804–1807

PAULINE'S RETURN TO PARIS came at a tense family moment. With the approaching coronation had resurfaced the emperor's resentment that his wife had borne him no children. According to the rather histrionic memoirs of her lady-in-waiting Claire de Rémusat, Josephine wailed: "It is a great misfortune for me, not to have given a son to Bonaparte. It will always be a means by which vicious tongues can trouble my peace of mind." Certainly Pauline was among those who urged on her brother divorce and remarriage to a younger woman. "His family takes advantage of his weaknesses to make him break off little by little his intimacy with me, and abandon all relations with me," Josephine lamented.

Meanwhile, in default of a son and heir of his own, Napoleon had done what he could to secure his legacy, and, in so doing, had managed to aggrieve all four of his brothers. Originally he had thought that the succession should follow the so-called Salic law, which forbade female inheritance. However, given that Napoleon had quarreled with Lucien and Jérôme over their marriages, he wished to exclude those brothers— and Lucien's son, Charles—from the succession. And even should Joseph, Napoleon's natural heir, survive the emperor, the eldest of the Bonapartes had as heirs himself only daughters. So, following Salic law, the imperial mantle must fall next on Lucien, and then on his son,

Charles. To this the emperor was unconditionally opposed, and indeed Lucien, increasingly absorbed in excavations of republican and imperial Rome, disdained his brother Napoleon's modern pursuit of imperium.

The emperor meditated declaring as his heir his brother Louis's elder child, the two-year-old Napoléon Charles Bonaparte. (In Bonaparte birth order, Louis came after Joseph, Napoleon, Lucien, and Elisa and before Pauline, Caroline, and Jérôme.) He even thought of adopting the child in due course, leaving to Louis and his wife, Hortense—Josephine's daughter—their second son, Napoléon Louis, who had been born in October. The question of the imperial succession would then be resolved, even if Joseph was affronted at being passed over, Lucien scornful, and Jérôme no better pleased than Joseph.

But the matter was not to be so easily concluded, so serpentine were the relationships of the Bonapartes and the de Beauharnais, who seem to have been designed by nature to feed off each other's suspicions. Josephine supposedly told Claire de Rémusat that grumbling, reclusive Louis was not happy with the glorious future envisaged for his son and that he doubted the child's paternity. Louis believed, Hortense's mother added, not only that his wife had been adulterous but, to twist the knife further, that she had been so with Napoleon himself. His own family, confided Josephine further, had brought these rumors to Louis's attention. As a result, the empress said, her son-in-law—who was also her brother-in-law—was furious with Napoleon and Hortense, and was resisting the proposed elevation of his elder son as imperial heir.

Josephine's candor, when in private with her women, was renowned and was thought to be a legacy of her colonial upbringing in Martinique. But Claire declared herself amazed by this foray into the interior of the Bonaparte family, and she had been no less astonished by some earlier remarks. The empress, Claire said, had given full rein to her feelings about her husband: "He has no moral principle, he hides his vicious leanings . . . but, if one left him alone to pursue them . . . bit by bit he would give himself up to the most shameful passions. Has he not seduced his own sisters?" Josephine concluded bitterly that her husband believed himself, as emperor, licensed to satisfy "every fantasy."

Even allowing for the empress's anguish—the coronation was drawing nearer, and her husband had as yet assigned her no firm role—these were extraordinary claims that de Rémusat recounts. But other, more trustworthy sources agree that the indolence and tolerance that generally distinguished Josephine in her dealings with her husband had deserted her. For once she did not turn a blind eye to the sexual appetite for her ladies that periodically beset Napoleon. She followed him and one unlucky quarry of the moment into the bedroom to which they had absconded. There she was hot in her denunciation of their conduct. Her husband was predictably furious, and Josephine more miserable than ever.

Are de Rémusat's claims to be believed? She burned her memoirs once, and reconstituted them with the aid of Chateaubriand, no supporter of the Bonapartes. But stories that different members of the close-knit Corsican family were incestuous—Lucien with Caroline, Lucien with Elisa—circulated in Paris. And, rather than being a serious accusation, the empress's denunciation of her husband appears more to have provided an opportunity for her to fulminate against the whole Bonaparte tribe. Other sources would in due course attribute to Josephine more precise allegations of incest, centered on the relations between Napoleon and Pauline, who, according to Count Metternich, Austrian ambassador in Paris from 1806, was "as beautiful as it is possible to be." Opponents of Napoleon's regime and enemy pamphleteers would adopt the accusations wholesale and add, for good measure, that Pauline had been a prostitute at the age of fourteen in a brothel her mother kept in Marseille. For the time being, however, this was invective aired, nothing more—a part of the hubbub and commotion and emotion that marked the approach to the coronation.

In the days before this event, which was to take place on December 2, 1804, Louis Bonaparte agreed to his elder son being named the imperial heir presumptive. But Napoleon and Josephine came nearly to the point of divorce once more over the detail of the coronation ceremony itself. Josephine wanted to be crowned as empress, but Napoleon was reluctant to allow her this dignity. They were both aware that, once she was crowned, the road to divorce would be, though not impassable, less easy. The French people would be reluctant to see a crowned empress cast aside, and the pope, who was coming from Rome to attend the ceremony, less willing to grant the divorce. Pauline, of course, argued fervently that her sister-in-law should not be crowned.

The arguments shifted back and forth in the private apartments of the Tuileries. Napoleon could be objective about the pursuit of rank and title around him, as during the hysterics exhibited by his sisters Elisa and Caroline earlier in the year, after their brothers Joseph and Louis had been elevated to imperial rank. While their sisters-in-law Julie and Hortense were henceforth to be addressed as "Altesse," they remained Mesdames Bacciochi and Murat. Napoleon gave way, as we have seen, and bestowed imperial rank on all his sisters, but he was sardonic: "One would think I was sharing out the patrimony of our father the king."

Now, however, Napoleon was endeavoring to create a coronation ceremony based on that of the Frankish emperor Charlemagne and to add substance to the appearance of empire by appeal to the Julio-Claudian precedents of ancient Rome—prompting Foreign Minister Talleyrand to grumble in private, "The combination of Charlemagne and the Roman empire has quite turned his head." (Napoleon linked his empire to that of Rome by adopting Jupiter's bird, the eagle, as an emblem of military might. Likewise, he revived the use of Merovingian golden bees to link his reign to that of earlier rulers of France.) The emperor was riled that Josephine insisted on being crowned, and the Bonaparte women—Pauline adding her voice to those of Elisa and Caroline—when not seeing to the details of their costume for coronation day, fanned the flames of his discontent. (Napoleon had decided that the court dress of the Renaissance French king François I should be the model, and the painters David and Isabey designed the individual dresses.)

But Pauline went too far. Intercepting a triumphant look that his sister shot at Josephine during one particular battle, Napoleon was seized by remorse for his treatment of his wife. Gathering the empress in his arms, he said tenderly, "Indeed you shall be crowned." Pauline and the other Bonaparte women, he decreed, should bear her imperial train—yards of heavy crimson velvet embroidered with golden bees and lined with ermine. And although Napoleon and Josephine had to go through a hurried nuptial mass, because the pope refused point-blank to consecrate a couple who, owing to the rigors of revolutionary times, had only ever gone through a civil marriage, crowned she was.

THE MOMENT THAT CHILLY DAY in Notre-Dame when Napoleon crowned himself emperor was for many surpassed in felicity by what came next. Josephine knelt at her husband's feet, bowed her head, and clasped her hands together. The emperor raised her up and placed her crown lightly on her head while they exchanged radiant glances. This moment David later captured when he produced a vast painting of the coronation, at Napoleon's request. The graceful incline of Josephine's neck beneath her stiff lace collar and the puffed sleeves of her dress are no doubt perfectly true to life. (Less true to life is his inclusion of Madame Mère in the picture. She had remained with Lucien in Rome and, when asked her opinion of her son's exalted position, said, "Let's hope it lasts.")

But Pauline and her sisters were not going to endure the central part their sister-in-law played at the coronation without complaint. Napoleon's injunction that his sisters bear Josephine's train had already been the subject of argument. The Bonaparte sisters had demanded that the trains of their own dresses be carried, if they must bear that of the empress. Julie and Hortense were also to walk behind Josephine with the three sisters. When Napoleon deputed Gérard Duroc, grand marshal of the Tuileries Palace, to find five chamberlains to carry out this task, Pauline's choice fell on Montbreton, her neighbor at Montgobert, brother of Leclerc's secretary and long-standing friend Norvins and, it was said, her lover when no one else offered. He and the other chamberlains carrying the Bonaparte women's trains were brought to an abrupt halt as Napoleon and Josephine moved from the altar where their unconventional crowning had taken place and up the flight of twenty-odd steps to the thrones awaiting them. For Pauline and her sisters had simply pulled back on Josephine's train—all twenty-five yards of heavy velvet—and the empress was unable to move forward.

Napoleon fixed his sisters with a look that, for once, quelled even Pauline. They slackened their hold on the train, and the rest of the coronation continued without incident. "What a mummery" was one general's opinion of the long ceremony. "Nothing is missing but the 100,000 men who sacrificed themselves to do away with all this." At the banquet that followed a triumphant Napoleon whispered to his brother Joseph, "If our father could see us now"—a sentiment with which Pauline, with her distrust of her brother's imperial pretensions, might not have wholly concurred. It would certainly have made her furious to know that at supper much later that night her brother asked his wife to keep on her crown while they ate. In his opinion no woman had ever worn a crown with more grace, and he forgot her failure to provide him with an heir. Indeed, for all his lust for a son, there were moments when the emperor accepted that it was his destiny to shine alone, rather than father a dynasty, and leave "a name that should have no equal and glory that would not be surpassed." Reviewing the day's events, he confided to his wife, "I believe I am destined to change the face of the world."

THE CORONATION CONCLUDED, arrangements were made in the new year for the imperial family to sustain Napoleon's dignity by their attendance at numerous court functions, both in Paris and at Saint-Cloud. At the latter country residence, once decorated by Marie Antoinette and now preferred by the emperor, Pauline found her husband no less irksome than before—and showed it. From Saint-Cloud, displaying a sagacity beyond his normal range, Camillo Borghese wrote to his confidant, the Chevalier Angiolini, that he found a morning bath essential, so that he could preserve his equanimity. "It has the gift of calming me and permits me to bear with patience all the rest of the day which passes always in the same manner." Like many, he found the atmosphere of the emperor's court enervating, and indeed, when taxed with the criticism that life at the Tuileries was melancholy, Napoleon agreed. "Yes, so is greatness," he replied. "My mistress is power, but it is as an artist that I love it, as a musician loves his violin."

Pauline apparently punctured the numinous atmosphere when she burst out laughing one evening while the imperial family, including Cardinal Fesch and the pope, were gathered together. When asked what was the cause of her hilarity, the princess replied: "I was just thinking how it would edify our contemporaries, and astonish posterity, had the Holy Father, who sits there so grave, been so fortunate as to convert me to Christianity, or if I possessed the wiles to pervert him into infidelity." When Fesch responded intemperately, Napoleon condemned both his uncle and his sister. Only the pope was calm, pardoning Fesch and Pauline, and telling the latter that he was certain of one thing, that "you, before your death, will become one of my flock." "Then, Holy Father," retorted Pauline, "you must live to a great age."

Discontented, blaming her husband for her continued ill health—his presence preyed on her nerves—Pauline determined that the Borghese ménage should shift to Le Petit Trianon at Versailles, memorably another haunt of the executed queen, which the emperor now made available. While at Versailles, Camillo had an interview with Madame Mère, who had returned to Paris and had healed the breach in her relations with Napoleon that Lucien's second marriage had brought about. She counseled further patience. Her daughter's health continued precarious, she warned, and for the prince to act other than generously would be to put himself in the wrong. Camillo, who though not clever was certainly not unkind, accepted for the moment the supporting role allotted him at the imperial court.

Pauline was instructed by Duroc, the grand marshal of the Tuileries, that she should host a weekly reception at the Hôtel Charost every Wednesday. Other days were allotted to her brothers and sisters. This enforced entertaining Pauline found less to her taste than life at Saint-Cloud or at Versailles, where, as her brother's guest, she could spend all day, should she wish it, in bed or attending to her wardrobe in order to outshine all at night. (Claire de Rémusat tells us that Pauline and her sister Caroline spent hundreds of louis on their court dress and then covered the costly material with a further layer of jewelry.) According to Laure Junot, when Duroc furnished Pauline with a list of guests the emperor wished her to invite to the Hôtel Charost, she crossed out the names of all the pretty women.

Laure added that, although Pauline appeared every Wednesday evening in a concoction of finery that had given infinite trouble for days to her milliner and silk merchant, her haberdasher and jeweler, she had made no effort to prepare her house for the weekly deluge of guests. Their comfort gave her pause for thought, according to Laure, only on the Wednesday morning. The lack of forethought showed in the slapdash nature of the entertainment, the hasty arrangements of flowers, and the insufficient food and drink. The distracted expressions of the sorely tried household and the inadequate service were further evidence that Pauline disliked the role of official hostess. Despite remonstrance from her brother, this was not a way in which she would serve him.

Napoleon was soon gone again. "In Paris nothing is remembered for long," he remarked. "If I remain doing nothing for long, I am lost." In April 1805, Russia, Austria, and England formed what became known as the Third Coalition against France. They had very different aims. The czar Alexander wanted to obtain Constantinople and the Dardanelles and Poland, Austria wanted to reoccupy its former territories in Italy, and Britain wanted to defeat France and recover the colonies that it had lost since entering the War of the First Coalition in 1793. Napoleon was occupied massing an invasion force at Boulogne, which he intended to transport to Dover once his admirals had wrested command of the English Channel. He planned to move against Russia and Austria thereafter, and was transferring further regiments to positions close to the Rhine. The doings of Pauline in Paris, as a result, escaped his notice, although his chief of police, Fouché, kept detailed reports on the activities of the emperor's brothers and sisters.

A vignette of this period shows Pauline in a familiar role, seducing with her beauty and allure a famous mulatto officer from Saint-Domingue. General Thomas Dumas, the officer in question, had been born on the island, and had served with Napoleon in Italy and Egypt. He was now an inhabitant of Villers-Cotterêts and husband of the innkeeper's daughter there. With his small son, Alexandre, the handsome general paid Princess Borghese a visit at Montgobert in the course of 1805, and much later that son, Alexandre Dumas *père* the writer, noted his impressions of that visit, a "luminous" memory of his childhood in which we see the scene through the child's "astonished" eyes.

Father and son were first ushered upstairs by servants in green livery, then led through a long sequence of apartments to a boudoir lined with cashmere. Their hostess was there, lying on a sofa. "It was a charming creature who offered herself to our sight," remembered Alexandre Dumas, "a petite and graceful being who wore little embroidered slippers, such as Cinderella's fairy godmother might have given her." The princess was so young and beautiful, he added, that, though only a child, he was quite dumbfounded.

Pauline didn't get up when they entered, only extended a hand to Dumas's father and lifted her head. Burly General Dumas wanted to take a chair at the princess's side, but she made him rather sit on the sofa at her feet. These she then placed on the officer's knees, toying with the buttons of his coat with the toe of one slipper.

"This foot, this hand, this delicious little woman, milk white and shapely, next to this mulatto Hercules . . . it was the most marvelous picture," enthused Alexandre. The child's sense of wonder only increased when Pauline called him over and gave him a tortoiseshell bonbon box, encrusted with gold. (To his dismay, however, she first emptied out the bonbons.) Pauline then leaned forward to whisper in the general's ear. "Her pink and white cheek grazed my father's dark skin," recorded Alexandre. "Maybe I saw them with the eyes of a child—an astonished child—but if I were a painter, I could make a fine portrait of those two."

The sound of a horn interrupted matters. It was the princess's chamberlain and neighbor Montbreton, out hunting in the park. Over to the window went the general, full of enthusiasm: "Look, here comes the hunt. And the quarry is going to come right down this allée. Come and see, Altesse."

"No, no," replied Pauline. "I am very well where I am, and it tires me to walk. You can carry me, if you like."

And so the general picked up the princess in his big hands, "as a nurse might a child," and took her over to the window that commanded a view of the allées and lawns that Leclerc had so painstakingly laid out before his death. There they waited, for the animal did not break cover for some minutes. At length appeared a stag that flashed across the allée. In hot pursuit came hounds, huntsmen, and gentlemen riders. From above the princess signaled with a handkerchief, and the riders responded, touching their hats, before she allowed the general to carry her back to her sofa.

"I do not know what went on behind me," wrote Alexandre, who remained at the window. "I was so absorbed in the stag . . . the hounds, the hunt. All this was more interesting for me than the princess. My memory of her stops entirely with that signal she made with her white hand and that white handkerchief. . . . Did we stay at Montgobert or did we return to Villers-Cotterêts that same day? I don't recall."

Pauline did not feel constrained in her relationships with other men by her ties to Camillo. Nevertheless she was gratified when her brother the emperor returned in the summer of 1805 from Milan, where he had been crowned King of Italy, and addressed her complaints against the prince. There was also Camillo's list of injuries done him by Pauline for the emperor to consider. Napoleon had already deflected Camillo's threat the previous year to return to Rome unless he was suitably honored and decorated, like his brother-in-law Murat. Knowing that Pauline would refuse to accompany her husband back to Rome, and determined not to have his volatile sister resident in Paris without her husband, Napoleon had conferred on his brother-in-law the Grand Cordon of the Légion d'Honneur. (This honor, created in 1802, conveniently resembled in shape and color the aristocratic Order of Saint Louis.) Waiving the usual law requiring ten years' residence in France before an alien could take French citizenship, Napoleon had also created Prince Borghese a French citizen and a prince of the imperial house.

Satisfied, Camillo had remained, but now he and Pauline were at each other's throats. Providing the makings of a peace with honor for the Borghese couple, Napoleon named Camillo head of his squadrons of mounted grenadiers, a formation of heavy cavalry then encamped at Boulogne and primed to invade Britain. From Munich, en route to survey the troops drawn up against the Austrians in Germany, Napoleon gave orders for Camillo to join his men. The prince was delighted with himself, Pauline could breathe freely in the Hôtel Charost, and only the grenadiers were the losers. Not for nothing did Napoleon say, "It is because the nation believes I possess the civil qualities for a ruler that I govern."

Napoleon was not happy when, after his Channel fleet suffered a reverse at the beginning of August, his plans for an invasion of England foundered. Pauline was delighted, however, by her brother's decision to remove from Boulogne the forces constituting the Army of England and send them to reinforce the Army of the Rhine and combat the Austrian threat. For to Strasbourg went Camillo, now a colonel of carabiniers—another heavy cavalry formation. "I could have come to Paris and not accompanied my troops," Camillo told Angiolini, "but I prefer to go with them, which I'm sure you would agree is the right thing to do. I can tell you," he wrote with a flourish, "that I don't care how much powder flies, I'm not going to make for my carriage. If I'd wanted to be in my carriage, I would have come to Paris." (Fortunately for the honor of the Borghese family, Camillo's brother, Don Cecco, was a gifted soldier and, after Napoleon offered him a command in a cuirassier regiment, ultimately became a general of brigade.) Pauline meanwhile was minded to be gracious. She wrote to her brother-in-law

Murat in August 1805, "Camillo works hard, the Emperor is content, and I am charmed. I never doubted his aptitude." And her health improved—she did not so much eat her dinner, wrote the ever-assiduous Angiolini in October, as "devour" it.

THE BATTLE OF TRAFALGAR, which the French and Spanish fleets fought against the British in October 1805 and which the latter won so convincingly that it effectively ended Napoleon's dream of "colonies, ships, commerce," meant that the emperor had to confine his imperial ambitions to Continental Europe. But the details of her brother's campaigns did not interest Pauline, so long as the emperor was safe and well and her husband was a long way away. "I am charmed by the Emperor's arrangements for Camillo," she wrote, on hearing that her husband had been posted to distant Poland. "I have just received letters from him." News in mid-November that the emperor had entered Vienna and, in December, that he had crushed Austrian and Russian forces at the Battle of Austerlitz were for his sister harbingers of his return to Paris, an event to which she looked forward, even though her health had again deteriorated. "For some days," Angiolini wrote to Camillo in November, "the doctor has forbidden any visits. Her nerves are so feeble that her door has been shut, even to her mother." Her condition was only marginally better in December. Pauline wrote to Murat, "What will contribute to my complete recovery is the presence of those I love, for I do not fear to tell you I lead a sad and monotonous life that doesn't suit me."

The peace between France and Austria that was signed at Pressburg and that greatly enlarged French territories in Europe unfortunately brought back to Paris Pauline's husband as well as the emperor. But before the princess could sulk or upbraid him, Camillo, ever obliging, paid a diplomatic visit to his mother in Rome. Pauline, meanwhile, with her brother's triumphant return to Paris, came back to life. Although she was no more inclined than ever to bow to imperial etiquette, and when the order of the day was for court dresses was likely to appear in a negligee that revealed her figure, she dazzled Paris during the official imperial celebrations to mark the new enlarged empire. Only when Napoleon tried to bend her to his will did she revolt.

The emperor wished his family to act as trustworthy suzerains or satraps, who would, in exchange for the grant of territories and titles, execute only his bidding. A year earlier, in an exchange of territories with Spanish Bourbons, Elisa and Felice Bacciochi had departed for the newly created principality of Lucca and Piombino. At that time Pauline had said, "Our brother loves only Elisa, and forgets us all." Now Napoleon's notable victories over the Austrians and Russians at Austerlitz in the winter of 1805 had brought France as prizes not only Austrian territories in northern Italy but also Naples. The emperor might once have thought of appointing as overseer of the first his Borghese sister and brother-in-law, but Pauline's disinclination for court life as much as Borghese's lack of intellect and their marital discord deterred him. In the event he appointed his stepson Eugène de Beauharnais Viceroy of Italy.

Paris, recently so full of the Bonaparte tribe, was emptying fast. Upon Joseph, Napoleon bestowed the Kingdom of Naples, and off he went southward with his wife, Julie, and two daughters. Meanwhile the Holy Roman Empire, over which Francis II had reigned as emperor, was dissolved, and that ruler became Emperor Francis I of Austria. Of a conglomeration of German states named the Confederation of the Rhine, Napoleon became protector. Caroline departed with Murat and their four children for Düsseldorf in Germany, where they were invested as Grand Duke and Duchess of Berg, a part of the new confederation. With Louis, to whom was apportioned the Kingdom of Holland, northward went Hortense and their two sons, Napoléon Charles and Napoléon Louis.

There remained, therefore, Pauline to consider, in the general apportioning of honors and lands. The Grand Empire was conceived of as a kind of federation of "brother kingdoms." And in addition to the Confederation of the Rhine, a Saxon Duchy of Warsaw sprang into being. In March 1806 Napoleon informed Pauline that she was to be

Above: Pauline's parents, Charles and Letizia Bonaparte

Below: Pauline's childhood home in the Strada Malerba, Ajaccio, Corsica

Above: Pauline's love of cameo jewelry is on show in these portraits by Robert Lefèvre

Below: A drawing by Jean-Baptiste Wicar of an older Pauline

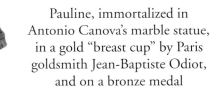

Pauline, immortalized in
Antonio Canova's marble statue,
in a gold "breast cup" by Paris
goldsmith Jean-Baptiste Odiot,
and on a bronze medal

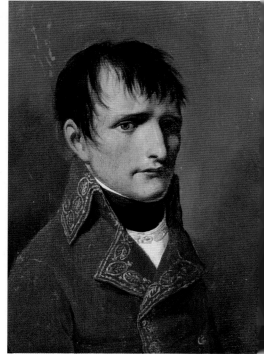

Napoleon as revolutionary general
and as first consul

A portrait by Anne-Louis Girodet de Roussy-Trioson of Napoleon
as Emperor of the French, in his coronation robe

A British cartoon showing Pauline and her sisters bare-breasted and with face patches, denoting blemished reputations

A French cartoon showing Pauline and her brother Napoleon surprised in bed together. Pauline paid little attention to such accusations of incest—or to those who branded her a modern Messalina. See the banner above the bed

Pauline's chiselled beauty, seen in a detail from Canova's statue of her as Venus

Pauline, with emerald *parure*, to the left of her sisters at their brother's coronation in Notre-Dame, 1804, as shown in a detail from Jacques-Louis David's painting

The Empress Josephine, by Pierre-Paul Prud'hon. Napoleon divorced his
wife reluctantly when she failed to give him an heir

Above: Pauline's first and second husbands,
General Victor Emmanuel Leclerc and Prince Camillo Borghese

Below: An idealized portrait of Dermide, her son by Leclerc, who died young

Forbin

Blangini

Tchernycheff

Poniatowski

Canouville

Talma

Six of Pauline's many reputed lovers, among them soldiers, a musician, an artist,
and the great actor Talma

While Pauline is buried in a Borghese vault elsewhere in Rome,
it is her marble image housed in this room in the Villa Borghese
that attracts thousands of visitors every year

Duchess of Guastalla. By the Peace of Pressburg this small principality, barely four miles square, had been ceded to France, with the Duchies of Parma and Piacenza, while the Bourbons of Parma had received Tuscany under the name of Etruria.

Pauline was apparently at first delighted with the idea of being joint sovereign, with Camillo, of this new French territory, but then thought to enquire further. "What is Guastalla, dear brother?" she asked. "Is it a fine great town, with a palace and subjects?"

"Guastalla is a village, a borough," replied Napoleon incautiously. "In the states of Parma and Piacenza."

"A village, a borough!" spat Pauline. "What do you expect me to do with that?"

"Whatever you like," came the answer.

"What I like!" And Pauline began to cry. "'Nunziata [Caroline] is a grand duchess and she's younger than me. Why should I have less than her? She has a government and ministers. Napoleon, I warn you I will scratch out your eyes if I'm not better treated. And my poor Camillo, how can you do nothing for him?"

"He's an imbecile," her brother responded.

"True, but so what?" answered Pauline, who had apparently taken to styling her husband "His Serene Idiot."

The emperor shrugged, the spitfire princess wept. And the result of this scene? The principality of Guastalla was ceded to the Kingdom of Italy (a collection of northern states, including Piedmont, Lombardy, the Emilia and the Veneto, that was a dependency of the French Empire), and Pauline, who kept the title of duchess, received six million francs as a sale price. This sum she invested in French government bonds, which gave her an annual income of 400,000 francs. Moreover she kept the feudal lands that went with the duchy, which gave her a revenue of 150,000 francs. With this arrangement Pauline was extremely satisfied. Her inheritance from Leclerc was still the subject of dispute with his family. (Following Dermide's death, the child's share had reverted to them.) Nevertheless, the Hôtel Charost and Montgobert were her own property. Pauline had, besides, by virtue of her second marriage contract, rights to apartments in the Palazzo Borghese in Rome and elsewhere, carriages, and jewels. With the addition of the Guastalla rents she had become, by any standards, a wealthy woman and an independent one. In celebration she extended her house in the rue du Faubourg Saint-Honoré on the garden front and required Camillo to bring paintings from the Borghese collection in Rome to adorn one of the wings she created, while the other she designed to be a banqueting room.

Titles and lands she did not crave, but for the power of money Pauline always had considerable respect. Napoleon, from whom all patronage flowed, continued to give proof of his strong affection for her. (By contrast, his other sisters annoyed him. Elisa he regarded as a shrew. With Caroline, he said, "I have always had to fight a pitched battle.") So Pauline could count herself in one respect a happy woman. But there is no doubt that, in these years following her disenchantment with Camillo and the death of Dermide, she was not at her best. She was querulous, in poor health, and, though as lovely as ever, inclined to quarrel with those around her. A contemporary but anonymous account of Napoleon's court published in England, *The Secret History of the Cabinet of Bonaparte,* had these sly remarks to make: "She is very witty; and very frequently, in her sallies, tells her imperial family some bold truths, and very often mocks them. She thinks, I suppose, that, as she is married to a genuine prince, such liberties are permitted." When Camillo was about to set off for Germany following the resumption of war, this time with Prussia, Pauline supposedly begged her brother, in full hearing of fifty people assembled in Josephine's drawing room, to procure her husband, "after a useless life, a glorious death." "You always go too far," Napoleon replied.

Pauline being Pauline, there were of course lovers, and the frequent visits of a Comte de L——, for instance, vexed Prince Borghese. Defying Pauline's cruel declaration that "to give oneself to Camillo was to give oneself to no one," and despite his alleged impotence, the prince attempted to begin a liaison with one of his wife's ladies in revenge. What was particularly galling to Camillo was Pauline's flaunting of her affairs. She "gave herself carte blanche with her favorites and took a kind of pride in making her preferences public property," wrote a lady at court. "People talked of nothing but Pauline's intrigues," the Polish countess Anna Potocka recorded in her memoirs, "and they certainly did provide material for lengthy discussion." But there is no evidence that Pauline felt much for the lovers she took. That was soon to change, however, as she embarked in the summer of 1806 on a journey to Plombières, the bathing station in the Vosges where she had recovered her health while married to Leclerc, and where she now hoped to do so again. There, in most unseasonable rainstorms that rendered her journeys to and from the baths hazardous, Princess Borghese was to begin a whirlwind romance.

CHAPTER TEN

Messalina of the Empire, 1807

A s Madame Leclerc, Pauline had traveled to Plombières with few attendants. Matters were very different now when Princess Borghese undertook one of her imperial journeys. She sent runners ahead to secure her board and lodging in houses of distinction along the route. In addition she chose to make at least part of the journey to Plombières in a litter, borne by porters in the imperial green-and-gold livery. And finally she took with her what was becoming a fixture on these journeys—a bathtub.

When the need to stop at Bar-le-Duc in Lorraine arose, Pauline's former brother-in-law, Jean Louis Leclerc, who was prefect of the Meuse, was selected to be her host. He was informed that his guest required for her health to bathe in milk, and he accordingly sent detachments into the neighboring villages, armed with milk cans and with orders to bring them back full. Well content with his arrangements, the prefect welcomed Pauline. "Carry me as you used to do," she demanded, and Jean Louis Leclerc obliged, bearing her into the principal salon.

When she asked if her bath was ready, he was able to respond in the affirmative.

"And my shower? I take a shower after my bath," she informed him.

"Ah, that I cannot arrange. I have no equipment," he replied.

"My dear man, don't concern yourself. Nothing so easy," came the answer. "Just make a hole in the ceiling above my bath, and have your servants pour the milk through when I am ready. It's a slight inconvenience to you, I know, but think of the consequences to my health."

Jean Louis Leclerc had, like so many before and after him, no answer to Pauline's airy confidence that her every wish was his command. He had his servants follow the princess's directions, and Pauline, well bathed and showered, went on her way. She left the disconsolate prefect to make good his wrecked rooms in a house pervaded by the smell of sour milk for months to come.

The milk bath and shower on which Pauline insisted may have been intended primarily to whiten her skin. Her journey to Plombières, deep in the Vosges country westward of the Black Forest, however, was in search of a cure for deeper-seated ills. The hot springs had had the reputation since antiquity of being particularly beneficial for women. Indeed, they enjoyed the specific renown of curing sterility, and Pauline's sister-in-law Josephine had visited the spa on numerous occasions since her marriage to Bonaparte, in hopes, destined to be dashed, that the waters would promote a fruit of their union. Even now that the empress, aged forty-four, was apparently undergoing erratic menstrual cycles, Napoleon hoped that a visit to Plombières would bring on a "little red sea."

As Madame Leclerc, Pauline might have been happy to have become pregnant with a sibling for Dermide. But now she was not interested in providing an heir for Camillo Borghese, and, as we have speculated, she may have been unable to give him one, if her fallopian tubes were severely infected. Indeed, it was about this time that it suited her to announce to Laure Junot that to "give oneself" to the prince was to give oneself to no one, meaning that he was impotent. (She had evidently forgotten the two months the couple had spent at Mortefontaine enraptured with each other following their church marriage and before she had tired of him.) At any rate, her visit to Plombières appears to have been occasioned by gynecological worries. She was, as so often before, suffering from lower abdominal pain and intermittent lower back pain. There is frequent mention of days spent prostrated, her family was in a state of anxiety about her health, and her expressions of distress when traveling over rough roads suggest that she was almost permanently in this invalid state at this time. As noted earlier, even her coquettish demands to be carried from place to place may have had their source in suffering, with a weakened pelvis the cause. Certainly she gave detailed instructions for the manufacture of a girdle or belt for her pelvis around this time, no fashion accessory but a practical aid to living. But Dr. Peyre, the army surgeon who had attended Leclerc during his last illness in Saint-Domingue and who had now been Pauline's personal physician for five years, was convinced that at least some of her current troubles stemmed from inflammation and infection of her reproductive organs, specifically her fallopian tubes. The hot springs at Plombières were a logical remedy for such trouble.

As already mentioned, this putative infection may have dated from 1798, when Pauline gave birth to Dermide. During the process of childbirth, bacteria, entering via the vagina and womb, can penetrate the upper genital tract and cause disease. In that case the problems associated with Dermide's birth that had sent Pauline to Plombières five years earlier still lingered. But it is at least conceivable that she had contracted chlamydia, gonorrhea, or another sexually transmitted disease, which can also give rise to infected and inflamed fallopian tubes. An abscess on her hand that took time to heal on her return to Paris from Saint-Domingue had already led Laure Junot to surmise as much. And then there were the reports of her uninhibited displays of sexuality in the former colony. Josephine's former lover Barras, who encountered Pauline shortly after a visit that she made to Gréoux, another bathing station about this time, was forthright in his diagnosis: "Excessive sexual activity, in consequence of *furor uterinus*"—Latin for nymphomania—"had given her an incurable ill. Too weak to walk, she was in such a state she had to be carried everywhere."

Nymphomania, or an obsession with sex and an insatiable appetite for genital stimulation, was not the only infirmity of which Pauline was to be accused in these years. Josephine apparently continued to maintain, when distressed, that her husband, Napoleon, was "too intimate" with Pauline. One Sunday evening at Malmaison during this winter of 1805–6, Volney, one of Josephine's confidants, had been chatting by the fire to Hochet, secretary of the Council of State. The empress suddenly appeared, haggard and in tears, and rushed over to them. "Oh dear, oh Volney, I am wretched indeed!" she cried. Philosopher Volney was used to the empress's laments when she was upset by some new infidelity of her husband's: "Be calm, Madame, it is you the Emperor loves. I am sure you are mistaken. . . . Very well, I believe you, but this is a mere fancy, an enchantment of an hour." Josephine replied grimly: "You don't know what I've just seen. The Emperor is a scoundrel. I have just caught him in Pauline's arms. Do you hear! In his sister Pauline's arms!" And, apparently feeling better for sharing this astonishing confidence, she rushed again from the room.

The rumor that Napoleon was incestuous with Pauline was certainly in circulation around this time. Gouverneur Morris, earlier American minister to France, heard a year later in New York from General Moreau that Josephine had made the latter her confidant in Paris. "Madame Leclerc, as all the world knows, the present Princess Borghese," Morris recorded in his journal, "is a Messalina." This Roman empress, the wife of the Emperor Claudius, had been notably cruel, avaricious, and hungry for power. But she had also had an insatiable sexual appetite and kept a brothel under an assumed name where she competed with prostitutes to see who could satisfy more lovers in a night. Josephine had, according to Moreau, alleged that Pauline had been "too intimate" with Napoleon. When Moreau repeated this to Pauline herself, Morris goes on, the princess denied it at first, "saying the Empress was no better than she should be herself. At length she acknowledged it."

It is a good story that Moreau told Morris, and possibly one that he himself believed. However, having been put on trial and banished by the emperor, Morris was probably willing to smear Napoleon. And both ladies had reason to lie to the general—Josephine to express her distress, Pauline to emphasize her power over her brother. Is Hochet's story any more credible? The truth is, it seems almost inevitable, given the strong sex drive for which Pauline and Napoleon were both renowned, given, too, their mutual affection, their clannish affinity, that they should have experimented sexually together. Perhaps neither of them considered such sexual congress, if it took place, of great importance. Growing up in Corsica, they had been surrounded by examples of intermarriage among relations, even of technically incestuous unions such as those between uncles and nieces prohibited by the church. Marrying within the immediate community thus remained the norm on the island well into the nineteenth century.

The Bonapartes imported these customs into France, Napoleon giving careful consideration at one point, when contemplating divorce from Josephine, to the project of marrying a niece. And of course Louis Bonaparte married Josephine's daughter, Hortense, who was also his stepniece. Not for nothing did Bernadotte say in disgust that the couplings of the Bonaparte clan resembled those in a *chiennerie,* or kennel. In Paris, Pauline plainly liked to shock—and titillate—her contemporaries by alluding to a supposed incestuous relationship with her brother. But much of the time she played to an audience who expected nothing less from Corsicans, regarding them as bandits and as scarcely French. It was a sophisticated riddle that Pauline posed, and one to which only she and her brother knew the answer.

If Pauline had indeed been "too intimate" with Napoleon, if she indeed did have venereal disease, he was at first sight as good a candidate as any for the distasteful role of having supplied it. Indeed, it has been argued, from traces of arsenic in his hair and from his documented use of a "blue pill" containing mercury, that Napoleon suffered from gonorrhea or syphilis, in the treatment of which both were used. But these are deep waters. Arsenic and mercury were also used to treat stomach problems. And besides Napoleon, there were, as we have seen, many other candidates who could have infected Pauline with venereal disease, including of course Moreau himself when he formed part of that trio of generals who first romanced and then renounced Pauline in 1799.

WHATEVER PAULINE'S MALAISE, she and her doctor judged the small spa of Plombières, situated above the rushing Augronne River, ideal for the treatment of her condition. The mountain air gave patients "the color of health," the river trout made for an excellent dinner, and the views of rock, forest, and meadow were picturesque. The lodgings were admittedly rudimentary, rough wooden houses with balconies overhanging riverside promenades below, but, according to one contemporary visitor, the atmosphere in the little spa community was companionable: "No one thinks of anything but their health, and so no one talks of anything but illness."

Every morning two imposing lackeys, dressed in the imperial livery of gold and green, carried Pauline in her litter or in her chair to and from the baths. She then spent the rest of the day in seclusion—or she intended to, as she had done at other spas. When in pursuit of a cure, she was as tireless a huntress as when at other times seeking pleasure. But at Plombières the princess's eye was caught by a fellow patient at the spa, and her languor gave way to animation. The Comte de Forbin was the object of her attention—the handsome scion of a seigneurial family from the south, whose ancestral residence was the Château La Barben outside Aix-en-Provence. While unseasonable tempests swept the Vosges, Pauline and Auguste de Forbin began a passionate relationship, the strength of which appears to have disconcerted and delighted her. With him she lingered at Plombierès, writing to the empress, "Forgive me, Madame, I have had to sacrifice for my health the pleasure of being near you at Saint-Cloud. I am most conscious of your regard for me, and I hear that Camillo is very happy. My regret at being separated from him increases greatly my chagrin." With such duplicitous sentiments, credited neither by writer nor by addressee, did the imperial couriers hasten from Bonaparte to Beauharnais and back again.

Forbin was by inclination an artist who had taken lessons as a boy at the famous school of drawing in Aix-en-Provence and thereafter watercolor lessons while living with his parents in Lyon. Although he had no pronounced aptitude for his chosen career, he pursued it even after his father, Gaspard, was guillotined and his mother settled in Grasse. Auguste, adapting to changing times, moved to Paris and entered the atelier of the revolutionary artist David, exhibiting in 1796. Thereafter, following a year's conscription in the chasseurs and dragoons and a marriage that did not endure, he traveled to Rome to expand his artistic horizons, and dabbled in poetry and architecture as well as painting. Possibly he encountered Pauline during her few months of residence in the Eternal City. It was, however, at Plombières, when Forbin was aged thirty and in his physical prime, that he took the invalid princess's fancy.

The French novelist Stendhal, who served in the Napoleonic army, said of Pauline's brother, "Napoleon made the mistake of all parvenus—that of estimating too highly the class into which he had risen." The same could have been said of her. As we have seen, Pauline had admired the aristocratic airs of Fréron in Marseille. The hereditary prince of Mecklenburg-Strelitz in Rome had attracted her with his brand of Enlightenment culture. And even Camillo Borghese, whose taste in outfits and equipages could not be faulted, had appealed to her before his other failings outweighed his lineage. Auguste de Forbin was the current head of a family that had been of note since they traded at Marseille in coral, corn, and slaves in the fourteenth century. The Forbins of Provence had contributed grand seneschals, cardinals, and ambassadors to the annals of France. Even their home, the Château La Barben, on its rocky eminence, had been the gift of the illustrious King René to a fifteenth-century forebear. Pauline felt the glamour of this accomplished *gentilhomme* and ignored for the moment his lack of income and considerable expenditure.

Princess Borghese was not always so forgiving. In the suite that had followed her to Plombières and that had been assembled prior to the coronation were a number of ladies and gentlemen of the Faubourg Saint-Germain, where the former nobility of France resided in a state of grand disrepair. The Duc de Clermont-Tonnerre, Pauline's chamberlain, had once been famous for his witty epigrams. Now he was grateful for his salary. Madame de Chambaudoin and Madame de Bréhan, Pauline's ladies-in-waiting, were also denizens of the Faubourg Saint-Germain. But Pauline made few friends among these aristocrats, who had been visited upon her by Napoleon. (He sought, by arranging grand households for all his siblings, to make of his imperial court

something rich and fine.) Knowing that these noble employees felt little loyalty to her, with her brother Napoleon she might have said, "A
prince who in the first year of his reign is considered to be kind is
mocked in his second year." Montbreton, alone of her household, was
someone she could rely upon—as did her mother, to whom this chamberlain forwarded reports of the princess's health.

Pauline could claim that her salon in Paris was not as brilliant as it
might have been, given that the caliber of her upper household was not
superior. She therefore asked her brother if Auguste might join her
household as an additional chamberlain. Napoleon, preoccupied,
failed to suspect that his sister had an ulterior motive and agreed.
Forbin duly traveled back to Paris in September with the Borghese
suite—including the litter, the chair, and the bathtub—and was formally appointed her chamberlain in early October. Of Pauline's health
we hear no more this year, and we may conclude that her Provençal
gentilhomme had succeeded in sating her "*furor uterinus,*" with no
anatomical ill effects.

In Paris to plague Pauline was, of course, her husband, but Camillo
was not at the Hôtel Charost long to disturb her or indeed remonstrate
with her about the clear partiality she showed for her new chamberlain.
For Napoleon was going to war again, and Camillo at the head of his
carabiniers was going with him. During negotiations in the summer of
1806 with Britain and Russia, Napoleon had secretly offered to return
to Britain the Electorate of Hanover, which had fallen to France during
the Peace of Pressburg earlier that year and which Napoleon had at that
time bestowed on Prussia. Upon discovering that Napoleon had this
betrayal in mind, Prussia had rashly issued an ultimatum to France.

Napoleon, seizing his moment, took his forces, Borghese's regiment
among them, into Germany, where he crushed the Prussians first at the
Battle of Jena and then at Auerstadt in October 1806. Later that month
he entered Berlin, and in November, flushed with victory, he declared a
Continental blockade, closing French ports to British ships and forbidding his allies and conquered powers from trading with the enemy
kingdom. With Forbin, meanwhile, Pauline had spent an idyllic

autumn at Saint-Leu, her brother Louis's country residence in the Val-d'Oise, which had previously belonged to the princes de Condé.

Napoleon's ambitions were not ended. Pressing eastward across the Vistula, he headed toward a confrontation with Russia. As autumn progressed into winter, Borghese and his regiment moved into Poland. Pauline's husband might not be Napoleon's most distinguished soldier, but at least he was absent from France. "The good news we received from the army contributes not a little to the improvement in my health," she wrote.

In the winter, upon Pauline's return to Paris, her devotion to Forbin was obvious. People could not fail to note "the elegant equipage of the chamberlain and his pretty white horses." In addition Pauline had paid Forbin's debts. He was, in consequence, no longer vacillating among the métiers of poet, writer, and artist, but was assiduous in her service, as Laure d'Abrantès reveals.

During Josephine's absence at Mainz, where the empress took up residence during Napoleon's German campaign, it had been decreed that Princess Borghese should receive on a Monday. For the first time Pauline appears to have taken these duties seriously and, having now spent a good deal on the house, wished to make effective display of her taste. Guests at the Hôtel Charost admired in succession the yellow salon, the *salon d'honneur,* which was decorated in a vivid red velvet, and a grand dining room, lit by two chandeliers draped with gossamer fabrics. A state bedroom, decorated in pale blue satin—bed hangings included—lay beyond a violet antechamber. Where Pauline had previously been a lax hostess, now she was fastidious. Every Monday before the guests arrived, she made her rounds "with an implacable eye, noting all the faults, the apprentices who dare to cross from the kitchen, the dogs whom the concierge has let enter the courtyard." Flowers, candelabra, her members of household and their dress, the servants and their livery—all came in for careful scrutiny.

On one of these Mondays, Laure d'Abrantès tells us that "the princess was astonishing, she was so beautiful." Pauline wore a dress of pink tulle, lined with pink satin; diamond brooches nestled amid downy marabou feathers at her neckline, and pink satin ribbons floated at her waist. Her bodice was satin "strewn with diamonds of the first water . . . her headdress consisted of marabou feathers fixed with dazzling diamonds."

Although, like everyone else, Laure admired the princess's appearance, she was not displeased with her own. She had on a dress of yellow tulle, lined with yellow satin and embellished with double violets that were infused with a Florentine concoction, powder of iris. In consequence they gave off a heady perfume when she danced. But her hostess was not happy and dispatched Forbin to call Madame Junot, as Laure then was, to her.

The chamberlain approached Laure with a serious face. "The princess wants to talk to you immediately."

Laure replied, "Well, you're very serious. What is it?"

"It's a serious matter. Come quickly," he replied.

Laure made sure to take her time going over to Pauline, and was vexed when she reached her.

"My dear Laurette, how could you have chosen so ill the flowers of your headdress?" her hostess asked.

"Madame, they match the ones on my dress," Laure replied.

"I can see that," was Pauline's uncompromising reply. "But you must never do that. Use scabious [another violet-hued flower], for instance, instead. For artificial violets in black hair like yours make your curls look triple the size. That gives you a hard air. Now please, promise me to change those flowers."

"Yes, madame," said Laure, highly amused at Pauline's air of gravity. "What she told me, however, was true," she recorded. "Violets look terrible in black hair."

With this perfectionist eye for detail and Forbin her willing assistant, with the aid of Paris couturiers and milliners and of her Borghese jewel box, Pauline made her person as exquisite as her salons. She was moreover as energetic and lively a hostess as she had previously been reluctant, and her reputation for beauty and taste redoubled as fashionable society flocked to her assemblies. Camillo Borghese, whose presence might have sullied her mood, was happily still absent with Napoleon on the Polish campaign that ended temporarily with the inconclusive Battle of Eylau in East Prussia against the Russians in February 1807. (She had dedicated to him and his suite rooms on the first floor of the Hôtel Charost, while she occupied the ground floor.)

The gates of the Hôtel Charost were not always open to guests on Mondays. At times the concierge turned guests away, claiming that the princess was in poor health. Although this may not always have been the case, in April 1807 she twice consulted the imperial doctor, Halle, who examined her internally. Pauline's doctor, Peyre, was present on both occasions. Halle's findings, which he wrote up on the twentieth of that month for Peyre, make interesting reading, although a gloss is naturally often necessary, given the delicate subject matter of his letter:

"I have continued to reflect upon the spasmodic state in which I found Her Highness, and in which we saw her yesterday. The womb was less sensitive yesterday, but was still so in some measure. The ligaments still showed that irritation for which we recommended her to bathe last Thursday. The spasms I saw while she was in the bath were hysterical in origin, her headache also." (It is unclear whether these were uterine or other spasms.) "The general picture is one of weakness and exhaustion. It's not an ordinary inflammation [of the ligaments]. The inflammatory state we saw is temporary. The underlying condition is an overstimulated uterus. If this continues, I can't answer for the consequences." In other words, Pauline's sexual activity was, in his opinion, proving her undoing.

Halle had skirted round this matter when he examined the princess the previous week, choosing his words carefully when he gave her his opinion of her case. He had attributed the aroused state of her uterus to "internal douches," and had spoken "in a general manner" of all that could "irritate the womb." He thought that his admonitions had been heard—"but, I fear, not enough."

He went on, in his letter to Peyre, "I know nothing, I can only conjecture. What I have said of the nature of the symptoms that you and I have seen, and that you have seen more often than me, is more than sufficient to give us the key to the enigma. The douche and the hose cannot be held responsible for everything. One must suppose that there is a more substantial cause for the exhaustion this young and pretty woman, who is so susceptible, so alone, displays." (Indeed, Auguste de Forbin was a very substantial presence in the Hôtel Charost.) "It is high time to forbid the cause, for it is evident that, if we do not make haste, we will be too late. I cannot say anything more than this, because I know nothing," Halle claimed once more, "but I must all the same save this woman from destruction. And if there is someone who has preyed on her weakness and is complicit, this person, whoever he may be, could accuse not himself . . . but us—of having seen nothing, or having permitted everything.

"I am not ready," the doctor concluded, "to be treated as an imbecile, nor to be accused of being lax and complaisant. But more than that, we must save this excellent and unhappy woman, whose fate affects me. Hurry, my dear colleague, for there is no time to lose. Make of my letter any use you like, and be open with me when you reply."

Halle had insisted as vigorously as was consonant with delicacy that Pauline's health required a period of medicinal baths and sexual abstinence. Her chamberlain Montbreton appears now to have been instrumental in securing that period, for she was to write to Forbin in June from the bathing station where she was pursuing a cure, "You know better than anyone how he has behaved. He has been the cause of our separation and of many evils besides. He has betrayed my confidence."

Pauline formed the plan to visit Aix-les-Bains in the Haute Savoie—and without Forbin. Grudging approval came from Napoleon in Poland, in a letter to Archchancellor Cambacérès: "I am not opposed to the plan, only that I see that all the doctors recommend waters to their patients when they want to get rid of them, and I thought it preferable that she tend her health in Paris without running off in all directions to seek a cure." It was a permission of sorts, and Pauline took it, making arrangements to embark with a limited household at Neuilly and travel down the Seine to Auxerre, from where she would travel to her uncle Fesch's archbishopric of Lyon and on to Aix-les-Bains.

But she also made arrangements, which she did not share with the rest of her household, for Forbin to follow her down to the south of France and join her in his native Provence. She had privately determined not to linger long in the fashionable watering hole of Aix-les-Bains but to base herself rather in the Southwest, at Aix-en-Provence. There the Forbin town mansion would be available to her, and from there she could visit his ancestral home, the Château La Barben.

Madame Mère wrote to her brother Fesch in advance of Pauline's journey: "Her departure made me sad. To see her distanced from all the family, in a chronic state of suffering, tears my soul. I see in her suite only one person who merits my confidence, M. Montbreton, and I have recommended him to give me his news with the greatest exactitude and leave me in ignorance of nothing that passes. I must tell you, I am anxious about her situation, and I hear various reports I don't like."

When Pauline arrived at Lyon in mid-May, from these "reports" ensued tremendous scenes. Dr. Peyre, "through fear and stupidity," in Pauline's words, shared his belief with Fesch that Forbin was to join Pauline. "Maman, my uncle, know all," she wrote angrily to Forbin at the beginning of June. "You have no idea how I suffered at Lyon, the tears I shed to discover we were found out." Madame de Bréhan, one of Pauline's ladies, stoked the fire further when she burst out that "it was disgusting how I behaved in front of her, how we forgot ourselves in front of her in Paris." Pauline was outraged, but with tears and caresses she persuaded her uncle that she was penitent. Soothed, he accompanied her for several days down the Rhône and even bestowed upon her as a—not especially welcome—avuncular gift, when they parted, one of his clerics, Monsignor d'Isoard, as traveling confessor.

There was to be much to confess, not that Pauline showed any inclination to do so, merely an appetite to hoodwink and outwit. At Aix-les-Bains she paused only long enough to persuade a council of eminent doctors, some from Lyon, others from Geneva, that her case would be best answered by a sojourn at the little-known spa of Gréoux-les-Bains, some way from Aix-en-Provence. On the other hand, she assured Montbreton and Madame de Bréhan that they would most benefit from the waters of Aix-les-Bains and she could not think of taking them with her. Space was anyway at a premium in the only house inhabitable at Gréoux-les-Bains. It belonged to Monsieur Gravier, the proprietor of the spring, and adjoined the source. Otherwise Gréoux was a sunbaked rocky eminence devoid of trees and with village houses winding up toward a Templar castle.

In high spirits Pauline wrote at the end of May to Madame Michelot from Aix-en-Provence, where she broke her journey to Gréoux: "I have been a little tired by the journey, as you thought I would be, but for the four days I have been here, I am much better than since leaving Paris. I have no more fever. . . . I am lodged at the sister-in-law of M. Forbin in the most beautiful *hôtel*." Two days later she wrote: "Please buy me a pretty gauze muslin to your taste." The summer heat of Provence was proving to Pauline's taste.

The sudden appearance of the emperor's sister at the Forbin mansion in the main thoroughfare, the Cours Mirabeau, had delighted the Aixois. The princess charged herself with the expenses of the Fête-Dieu (Corpus Christi) celebrations on May 22 and watched as revelers followed tradition and threw oranges at one another below her balcony, and troubadours and knights on chargers paraded by. One student was so overcome by her beauty that he spent four thousand francs on a court dress and asked to be allowed to present a bouquet to the object of his admiration. But Princess Borghese, he was told, was indisposed, and his expenditure was for nothing.

Monsieur Thibaudeau, the prefect of Marseille, and his wife, she did receive, however. Pauline had a healthy respect for the power of the prefects in whose territory she traveled, not least because they were responsible for the upkeep and repair of the roads she took. In fact, showing her usual indifference to the needs of others, she proposed that Madame Thibaudeau accompany her to Gréoux. The prefect protesting that he needed his wife at his side in Marseille, Pauline turned to another matter and said that she wanted the road to remote and arid Gréoux to be smoothed and cleared of stones.

"Princess and pretty woman," wrote Thibaudeau in his memoirs, "she believed that she had only to wish for something and that nothing was easier than to satisfy her wishes." There were no funds available for such an extraordinary expense. However, "so as not to disappoint the princess," Thibaudeau had engineers labor "to hastily fill some holes and above all to clear the rolling stones that were all too common. Luckily it was the fine season, but there remained the great hazard for travelers—dust. "He reflected that perhaps a courtier of Louis XIV or Louis XV would have found "a way to water the route." He, however, gave up the challenge at that point and left Pauline to take her chances.

In mid-June she wrote to Madame Michelot from Gréoux, content with her cure: "I am taking the waters and am on my sixth bath. The waters suit me fairly well, they heat me and agitate me a little." But what heated and agitated her much more was the proposed arrival of Forbin. She had sent an express to Paris, bidding him join her. At the same time she enjoined upon him: "Those who surround us must be persuaded that all is at an end between us, so that we can be undisturbed." With Montbreton and Madame de Bréhan at Aix-les-Bains, there were now only Dr. Peyre and Monsignor Isoard and the lower servants to tell tales on them, and she held them of no account. "How this solitude will please me when you are here," she had written on June 10. "If only it could last forever, but we will never, never be separated. With prudence, we can always be happy. . . . Bring what you need for painting, you can make delightful things for me. My modest house"— the Gravier property—"begins to take shape. I am filling it with flowers and furnishing it as quickly as possible so that all is to my well-beloved's satisfaction."

PRINCESS BORGHESE had hidden away in this remote spot. She was awaiting her cavalier. News from the outer world hardly penetrated her cocoon of infatuation: "By the way, I forgot to mention that my husband has been made a general." Napoleon also appointed Borghese his messenger with news of a June victory over the Russians. Unfortunately the prince proved too slow, and Paris heard the glad tidings from

Napoleon's courier Moustache. "He writes me charming letters full of sentiments of love. I can't think what he's up to," Pauline continued. "But I must end because I am tired from writing so much."

Was she destined to break completely with Borghese and live in the south a Provençal idyll with her handsome troubadour, the Chevalier Forbin, as in some medieval romance? There was no doubt that Pauline was thrilled by her love affair. "You are my real husband," she told Forbin. "Mine [Camillo] doesn't merit so sweet, so sacred a title." She called her chamberlain "dear idol," as she had once called Fréron. "I send you flowers that have been at my breast, I have covered them with kisses. I love you, you alone."

But would the emperor permit this loose living? For, however Pauline might pull the wool over her suite's eyes, Forbin's movements did not evade the watchful eyes of Fouché and his army of spies. Upon being informed from Paris by Archchancellor Cambacérès that his sister's chamberlain had headed south to Aix, Napoleon replied: "I am very cross that you didn't tell me that there was disagreement about the good that the journey to Provence would do the Princess Pauline. You know that I was at first opposed to it, but when I was told the whole of the [medical] faculty wished it, I consented. If I had received this letter sooner, I would never have authorized it."

CHAPTER ELEVEN

Southern Belle, 1807–1808

DESPITE ALL OF PAULINE'S amorous preparations, Forbin had still not reached Gréoux when she decided to leave in September 1807. "The princess is tired, fed up with it here," one of her suite informed Prefect Thibaudeau, who had just toiled up the long hot road from Marseille with his wife to pay his respects. Her Royal Highness was done with her cure, whether cured or not. "She can't put up with it anymore," Thibaudeau now heard. "She is going to go to La Mignarde, the prince is expected there."

La Mignarde was an elegant stuccoed château built in the previous century by an Aixois confectioner as a summer home outside the town. With its spacious gardens, ornamented with statues and basins, it was a residence in complete contrast to the Gravier property at Gréoux, where there was not a scrap of shade. La Mignarde had the additional virtue of being extremely close to Forbin's home, the medieval Château La Barben, and within the latter stronghold charming apartments had been prepared for Pauline's use. For, though illness apparently delayed Forbin's departure from Paris, in the meantime his Aixois friend and fellow artist François Marius Granet had been at work. Images of the Four Seasons adorned bathroom walls. A boudoir commanding views of the gardens laid out by Le Nôtre in the previous century had been fitted out with a dressing table and other necessaries, and in the bedroom the violet wallpaper was hand-painted. All that was lacking was the count himself to play host to Her Royal Highness.

Although the princess had determined to leave Gréoux, as her suite had told the Thibaudeaus, no one was expecting her to leave the very evening they arrived. But after dinner, as the newcomers were walking in the garden with Montbreton, who had at last been allowed to join the party, a screen door opened, and out came Pauline in a white peignoir, her hair undressed. Her air was animated, her step quick. "Ladies, I leave tonight," she said. "Make haste, Montbreton, and arrange it." When her chamberlain objected that nothing was ready, that there were no horses available, she said, "I'll take the Thibaudeaus'." And she vanished back into her apartments, "like an actor, who has played her part, and retires into the wings." Behind her the suite exclaimed, "It's caprice, it's madness. . . . She will go alone. . . . Let her arrange it herself." But go the princess did, and everyone became involved in her complicated arrangements, although she reached a compromise with the prefect. He kept his horses but promised to go ahead to La Mignarde to warn them of the princess's imminent arrival.

One can only assume that a letter from Forbin announcing his imminent arrival in Aix-en-Provence was the catalyst for the princess's sudden haste. Certainly the proposed arrival of the prince at La Mignarde was unlikely to have made her hurry. But for her haste she paid a price. She "took nothing and found nothing" at the miserable house en route to Aix where she passed the night. When her path crossed with that of the Thibaudeaus in the forest of Cadarache next morning, she told them she was the "unhappiest woman alive, and had been eaten by every kind of insect."

The prefect was already, despite himself, bewitched by Pauline. During a short airing at Gréoux the evening before, she had wished to be carried over the dry bed of a stream, and he had discovered that she weighed no more than a feather. Now, in the dappled light of the forest, as Her Royal Highness lay back in her open calèche and enjoyed the shade of the trees and the cool breeze, he considered that a "voluptuous languor animated her gaze." Thibaudeau found her charming—

and, notwithstanding his wife's presence in the carriage beside him, told the princess so. "Are you being gallant?" Pauline teased him. Thibaudeau replied that she had only one defect in his eyes—that she was the emperor's sister. "A smile showed that she had understood."

At La Mignarde, where gaiety prevailed, and where the Aixois and the Marseillais gathered in circles, at assemblies, and at fetes in the grounds, Camillo Borghese took a different view of Pauline's relationship to Napoleon. "His Borghese blood revolted in secret against the supremacy of this Bonaparte female," Thibaudeau declares. All homage, all attention was reserved for the princess, and Camillo was "on the footing of a consort of a queen of England, or even less than that." Moreover, the presence of Forbin, who at last arrived, was a daily irritant to the prince. Walking early one morning beneath the windows of his wife's apartments, and knowing that she was "in the arms of another than Morpheus," Camillo said that his wife was indeed lucky to be the emperor's sister. Had she not been, he would have administered a punishment she would remember.

BUT CAMILLO BORGHESE had only to wait. For, as Pauline had tired of Gréoux, so she tired of the Comte de Forbin. Never one to resist a sudden impulse, one day she threw a book at his head. The count apparently bore the public insult with equanimity, but the love affair was over. In October 1807 we find Forbin at Fontainebleau offering his military services to Napoleon. Later that month he was named lieutenant adjutant in the Army of the Gironde under Junot, which was being sent to invade Portugal. (Following French victories over the Russians, Napoleon and Czar Alexander had met at Tilsit to settle the terms of an alliance between the two empires. As part of those terms, and in pursuance of the Continental blockade of British trade, the Russians agreed to secure the Baltic coast, while the French secured the Iberian coast.) The invasion was in response to the refusal of Prince John, regent of Portugal, to join the blockade. The regent's court fled to Brazil, while Spain helped the French occupy his country, on the understanding that it would receive a share of Portuguese territories. Junot duly took Lisbon in late 1807 and was created Duc d'Abrantès.

Passionate lover though she had been earlier, Pauline was not especially disturbed by the break with Forbin. While he headed north, she traveled farther south to Marseille, with the aim of spending the winter in the Midi for her health, and installed herself in La Capelette, at the country house of the military commander General Jean-Baptiste Cervoni. In the harbor town of Marseille she and her sisters and Madame Mère had sheltered as refugees, following their escape from Corsica in 1793. Just behind the port was the house in the rue Royale where she and her sister Caroline had perhaps acted as maids to the Clary family. Up the hill was the house where the Bonaparte women had lodged. Did curiosity drive Pauline to seek out these places, to recall her earlier passion for Fréron, who had occupied the mansion that was now the prefecture, outside whose gates had flamed torches as he and his fellow commissioner Barras partied inside? Even to recall her first meetings with Victor Emmanuel Leclerc, her brother Napoleon's close friend and fellow officer?

So much had passed since Madame Mère and her daughters had made an exiguous living there, accepting the town's charity and even taking in washing. Perhaps Princess Borghese preferred not to recall these scenes of ignominy but to remain the haughty lady at La Capelette, whose wish was the command of an entire household— besides that of the many hapless authorities whom she ordered to make available their homes, repair roads, furnish banquets, and much else. (En route to Marseille she had not only had her household lay down their cloaks and coats on the ground when she wished to rest in a meadow, she had had a subprefect from Grasse provide his back for her to lean against, while an unfortunate general was told to lie down and proffer his stomach as a footrest.) But we shall see that being near these scenes of her youth awakened in Pauline at least once the desire to revisit a past that had been at once stirring and trepidatious.

The princess continued to dazzle and to disappoint when in mid-October 1807 she reached the harbor town of Nice, which had been

annexed by France from the house of Savoy and marked the southeast-
ern extreme of French territory. Her arrival caused great excitement,
and the ladies and gentlemen who represented the upper tier of society
prepared for a season of festivities. "They say that, since the Phoeni-
cians founded Nice, they have not sold so many dresses," wrote the
Duchesse d'Escars, a resident of the town.

Apparently Pauline's first act upon arrival was to call for all the dogs
in the neighborhood of the *hôtel* where she lodged to be shut up, as
their barking disturbed her rest. She further distressed the Niçois by
departing for Grasse on a day that had been fixed for the ladies of the
town—splendidly attired—to be presented to her. Her object in traveling to Grasse was to visit the Comtesse de Forbin, her discarded lover's
mother, who lived there. Pauline was not one to hold a grudge, and in
fact she took the countess a quantity of dresses as presents. But it was
not the season to admire the roses, jasmine, and other fragrant flowers
of which the town's renowned perfume factories made use. Indeed,
during Pauline's return to Nice, it rained such torrents that she had to
take refuge in the upper story of a mill and wait for the owner to rescue
her. Smitten, he immediately offered her the use of his nearby château,
which she naturally accepted.

Upon Pauline's return to Nice in mid-November, she settled down
to winter in a sumptuous villa belonging to a Monsieur Vinaille, with
vast tropical gardens extending to the beach. Views from the villa
looked westward to crenellated fortifications; eastward, the coast
stretched away to Monaco. With the prefect of Nice, the Duchesse
d'Escars visited Pauline at the Villa Vinaille in December and found
her "dressed with extreme elegance." But the princess's dress was less
remarkable than the pose she had adopted. Her lady in waiting,
Madame de Chambaudoin, was lying spread-eagled on the floor, and
the princess had placed both feet on the good lady's throat. In the
duchess's opinion, the woman seemed "so visibly born for this ignominious situation that she felt no shame in it." But the prefect expostulated, "Madame, surely this position is tiring for you." "Oh no,
monsieur, I am well used to it," came the strangled answer.

The duchess was meanwhile mesmerized by the sight of her hostess's restless feet perambulating her victim's exposed gorge. Furthermore, during an exchange of civilities, Pauline asked if her visitor liked the theater, and, if so, whether she preferred tragedy or comedy. The duchess replied in the affirmative, adding, "I prefer tragedy." "Me too," piped up Madame de Chambaudoin from the floor. "Her voice, altered by the pressure of Princess Borghese's foot, made the sentence infinitely ridiculous," the duchess tells us, and, stifling her strong urge to laugh, she cut short her visit and hurried away. But she returned several times to visit the princess, for Pauline had offered to intercede with Napoleon, who had exiled the duchess to Nice, disliking the royalist sympathies she publicly expressed. On those occasions the princess had "other women under her feet."

Away from Paris, living separately from Camillo, Pauline was becoming distinctly eccentric. There was no precedent in the history of French court etiquette for such behavior, let alone in ordinary social intercourse. But over and over again she persuaded her entourage and others to yield to her outrageous demands. Although she was not one to invoke such language, it is plain that Pauline believed that, as she was the sister of the emperor of the French, for them to do otherwise would be lèse-majesté. There were few who were prepared, in those years in which Napoleon dominated Europe, to argue with her.

During her stay at Nice, Pauline took as her lover a young musician from Turin, Felice Blangini, who played violin in an orchestra in Paris, and who was almost more supine than Madame de Chambaudoin and the other ladies. Blangini had originally attracted the attention of Pauline's sister Caroline Murat with some Italian nocturnes and romances that he composed while in Paris. Pauline then offered him the post of *chef d'orchestre* at 750 francs a month, although she had no orchestra. Now she called him to Nice, ostensibly so that she could study duets with him. (The Bonapartes were renowned for having corncrake voices, but they did not on this account renounce musical endeavor.) And indeed study they did. "The princess liked so much to sing duets," Blangini writes, "and I to accompany her, that the hours flew by. . . . Not every throat is made of iron, however, and sometimes I had no voice left at all."

There were other encounters—"hidden within the interior of the house"—between Blangini and Pauline, where no vocal talent was required. But Blangini took fright when the princess wanted him to go out on an airing with her in her open calèche. "I knew the history of M. de Forbin, the chamberlain of whom the princess made a favorite," Blangini writes. "I knew that the Emperor was kept informed of what his sister did, the names of her intimates." Pauline took malicious pleasure in confirming to him that, wherever she went, there followed spies who dispatched detailed reports to Fouché, her brother's chief of police in Paris. Blangini begged again to be spared the public outing. "I had no wish to go and sing my nocturnes in Spain, to a chorus of cannon-balls and gunfire." (On Napoleon's orders French troops in Portugal had filtered into Spain, abandoning the pretense of an alliance with that country, and seized key fortresses and cities.) But Pauline's will, of course, prevailed, and the musician cowered throughout the carriage ride.

There were times, however, that winter when Princess Borghese exerted the magical power that kept men willingly in thrall to her. Daily life at the villa was, on the whole, regular and unexceptionable, comprising luncheon, visits from notables, a cruise at sea or an outing in a carriage, music, dinner, and more music. Upon occasion, however, in the evening, Blangini tells us, "the instruments and voices were stilled. Then the princess alone spoke. . . . She passed in review, not without malice, all the living gallery of the imperial court."

On one occasion a member of that exalted congregation—the grand almoner or chaplain assigned to Pauline, Cardinal Spina—was announced at the Villa Vinaille. He was passing through Nice on his way to the Vatican. Pauline, in mid-duet with Blangini, gave orders for the prelate to return at a time more convenient to her. In general Pauline's casual attitude toward the Catholic faith into which she had been baptized was enough to make her devotee mother and uncle Cardinal Fesch despair. Nevertheless she was at heart a believer and had made a good impression on Pope Pius VII when part of his flock in Rome. In Nice—in her own way—she observed the imperial decree that mass be said on a Sunday. "A table was dressed as an altar in the salon," Blangini relates, "as one sets a table in the dining room."

One can detect in some of Princess Borghese's habits remnants of customs that she and her mother and sisters had observed during their penurious years in Corsica and then in Marseille and elsewhere in the south of France, before Napoleon made the family's name and fortune. Proof that that past was still vivid to Pauline in her prosperity comes from a pilgrimage she made by water from Nice to Antibes. Her objective was to revisit the Château-Sallé, a "bourgeois house, quite pretty, but modest," above Antibes, which Napoleon had rented for his mother and sisters in the summer of 1794, when they were living at Marseille and he was based with the army at Nice.

Blangini accompanied the princess on her odyssey, and states, "I do not know how to give an idea of the joy the princess manifested in finding herself once more there. She ran around like a child and explained the division of rooms. 'That was my mother's room. I slept in this little cabinet next to her. My sisters were on the other side. That was the room my brother Napoleon occupied when he came to surprise us and spent two days with us.'" Although Pauline did not mention it, the months at the Château-Sallé had not been without tension. It was at Nice, during the time of the Terror, that Napoleon had fallen under suspicion and had been kept under house arrest, before exculpating himself and being released.

The Midi was to yield up no more souvenirs of Pauline's youth, and Blangini's days as her favorite were numbered. Forbin might have preempted disgrace by volunteering for the army, but Napoleon had determined to put an end to his sister's irregular liaisons. One project, to assign to her and Camillo a portion of Portugal under a secret treaty agreed with Charles IV of Spain, had foundered when France's relations with Spain deteriorated. But Pauline's plea that she must winter in southern climes was no longer acceptable to her brother, when his agents reported that basking in the sunshine with her at Nice was her young music master from Turin. And when Napoleon passed rapidly through Milan, Venice, and Turin, it occurred to him that he could bring order to what he saw as a fragmented northern Italy, and at the same time reunite the Borghese couple.

NOT LONG AFTER Pauline returned from her visit to Antibes word came that Camillo had been made governor-general of the Transalpine Department of the French Empire, embodying the five Piedmontese regions that had previously belonged to the Kingdom of Savoy. (Louis Bonaparte had previously been the region's titular head.) Turin was the seat of government, and to Turin, Pauline received orders, she should proceed with her husband, to act there as governor's lady. She was forced to give credence to these unpalatable instructions when Camillo arrived in Nice, accompanied by a secretary, Maxime de Villemarest, who was in no way inclined to allow Pauline's caprices to stand in the way of his own task, to act as guide and counselor to the inexperienced prince.

A vast gubernatorial household was assembling to swell the Borgheses' dignity in Turin, where the Palazzo Chiablese, a wing of the enormous former Savoy palace, was to be their residence. Camillo was "enchanted" with the splendor of the arrangements, de Villemarest writes. To the new governor-general were assigned six chamberlains, four equerries, and four aides-de-camp. Pauline, meanwhile, was to enjoy the attentions of twelve ladies-in-waiting, besides a mistress of the robes, six chamberlains, and four equerries. And while the catalog of attendants on the imperial payroll allowed for a director of music, Blangini's was not the name there inscribed.

But Pauline had tired of her songbird and his nocturnes, and now in Nice she gave her attention to assembling a wardrobe to fit her new dignity. She might not relish the prospect of official life at her husband's side in a provincial backwater, but she would not compromise the honor of France by appearing in anything less than the most fashionable finery. Madame Michelot in Paris had a slew of instructions for the couturiers of the capital: toilettes in shiny satin for galas, light tulle robes for less formal receptions, gowns in embroidered cotton *à la cosaque* for airings. Hats, gloves, artificial feathers: The princess believed herself in dire need of everything.

Among the truly useful items that were dispatched to Nice was the splendid berlin, or large traveling carriage, in which Pauline was to travel. The saddler Braidy, de Villemarest reports, had made it "as soft as possible, expressly for this journey." But when, in April 1808, it was judged that the worst of the winter weather was over, when the princess at last pronounced herself ready to depart and the Borghese caravan set out, the luxurious vehicle was found wanting. Every time they encountered a steep incline, Pauline insisted on dismounting and being carried in her litter. "The prince could hardly contain his irritation and impatience," writes de Villemarest.

Even when Pauline remained in the berlin, she sometimes complained of the cold, though there were four or five pillows placed in the carriage for her comfort. The indignity Madame de Chambaudoin had suffered when the princess had used her throat as a footrest was as nothing compared to the poor woman's plight now. For when the princess's feet grew chilled, seeking a place of warmth, she would thrust them indecently under the skirts of her lady-in-waiting seated opposite. At other times the princess felt too warm, and then she piled all the pillows in the coach on the Duc de Clermont-Tonnerre's knees. Not being very tall, he was obliged to sit stiffly upright, so as to be able to breathe over the rampart of feathers.

In short Pauline was at her most tyrannical, and, during the journey over the Alps and down into the plain of Piedmont, she developed her grudge against Camillo into an argument. First she reminded him that, following a recent Senate ruling, not only her brothers but also her sisters' husbands, by virtue of being French-born, took precedence over him. Hence, she asserted, she too, being a French-born princess, took precedence over him. That being the case, she concluded triumphantly, it was for her to reply to the harangues and other addresses they would receive from the authorities upon their arrival in their new domain.

In vain the prince objected that it was he who was the governor-general, not she. "She did not wish to give up her point," de Ville-marest recounts, "and told him in a not very amiable fashion that he was only governor-general by virtue of being her husband, and that he would be nothing if he had not married the Emperor's sister. Which," the governor's secretary admitted, "had some truth in it." Then the prince cried, "Paulette! Paulette!" in what de Villemarest describes as "the most piteous manner." But the princess was intractable, and she was undeterred by the vicious weather that swirled around them as they passed over the heights of the Col de Tende. The snow fell densely around them, and the carriage wheels sank into deep drifts. At the very first village they reached in Piedmont, the princess made good her threats. And the mayor's cordial expressions of welcome were suc-ceeded by an unseemly altercation between husband and wife as they both attempted to reply to his address.

When they arrived at the next port of call, de Villemarest took the liberty of approaching the princess and observing that, should the emperor hear of these doings, His Majesty would be very displeased. "The invocation of the Emperor's name could sometimes have its effect, although not always," the secretary had already learned. Cer-tainly there was no other recourse available to those who wished to deflect Pauline from a proposed course of action. On this occasion the "invocation" had its effect. Next day the prince alone replied to the rep-resentations of the bishop of Coni, on behalf of the Stura region. He and de Villemarest could only hope that Pauline would prove equally biddable in Turin.

Upon arrival in Turin the princess took a surprising liking to two of the ladies appointed to serve her. Philippine de Sales, Comtesse de Cavour, was a worldly-wise French aristocrat who had come from Savoy to Turin on marriage twenty years before, and so escaped the guillotine. Her son acted as lord-in-waiting to Camillo. The Baronne de Mathis, on the other hand, was young, pretty, and fashionable. "I am pleased that you like your Piedmontese suite," Napoleon addressed Pauline from Bayonne, a month after she had arrived in the city. "Make yourself beloved, be affable to the world, try to be good-humored, and please the prince," he instructed her, in language similar to that he had employed when Pauline left Paris for Rome as Camillo's bride.

One evening, just a few days after the Borgheses' arrival in Turin, Pauline did indeed make herself beloved—with careful coaching beforehand from de Villemarest. The authorities of the city had resolved to hold a ball at the opera house, the Teatro Carignano, in honor of the new governor and his lady. Pauline was to open the ball. "Madame," said de Villemarest to the princess, "as you know, little attentions can sometimes reap dividends. . . . The Piedmontese take great pride in their traditions . . . why not have the ball begin with a monferrine?" This was a country dance—originally from Monferrina in Piedmont—that had become popular in the ballrooms of Europe. "It's a childish device, I agree, but it will undoubtedly give pleasure."

Pauline was delighted with the plan and followed directions admirably, rising from her chair in the opera house with a blaze of diamonds to take her place in the dance. To produce the maximum effect, suggested the secretary, the orchestra should first strike up the refrain of a French country dance. This was duly initiated. The princess then theatrically commanded silence and made known her preference for a monferrine. As the musicians broached the lively air and the princess began to dance, the opera house exploded with huzzahs and acclamations: "A monferrine! Vive l'empereur, vive le prince, vive la princesse!"

But Pauline tired quickly of a routine that included a small party every Sunday, reviews of troops, and gala dinners. She found relief from these duties in the sylvan setting of Stupinigi, a sumptuous hunting lodge outside the city that she first visited when her brother Lucien came calling at Turin. She was reluctant for Napoleon to know that she had seen their brother, as he surely would if she received him at the Palazzo Chiablese. (The emperor had still not resumed relations with Lucien.) "There is no order that can stop me giving you my news," Pauline had written to Lucien from Gréoux. "But you must know that I owe much to the head of our family and must respect his intentions in all other things." Napoleon might have been surprised to hear this description of Pauline's relationship with him, especially as Lucien's visit was succeeded by the visit to Stupinigi of a young violinist, Niccolò Paganini. According to local legend Pauline and Paganini, who was in the employ of the princess's sister Elisa in Tuscany, enjoyed a forest idyll together at Stupinigi.

But Pauline was more concerned to leave Turin than to tarry with another musician, however talented. Her health was bad, and the damp climate affected her, she told Napoleon. He wrote back, "I suppose you are being good, and that none of this is your fault." She wrote lyrically of the baths in the Alpine valley of Aosta, which lay between Piedmont and the French Alps: "The doctors of Turin speak of marvels at the thermal waters." Napoleon answered in early June: "What you are experiencing are the vagaries of spring weather. Stupinigi can be a bit humid, I admit. . . . I don't see why you don't go to Bagni di Lucca. Alternatively there can be no difficulty about your going to Saint-Didier"—a Piedmont spa—"as it is within the department." But he was firm: "You must not leave the department without my approval."

Napoleon, preoccupied by his Iberian campaigns, wrote too late. For in the meantime Joseph Bonaparte, whom Napoleon had called from Naples to join him in Spain, had stopped at Turin to visit Pauline and had been shocked by what he saw. "I have found Paulette here in a deplorable state of health," he informed Napoleon. "She has not eaten for eight days and can only take thin soup. The doctors have told me she must leave the humid air of Turin as soon as possible and go to the baths of Aix-les-Bains." Camillo had wanted Pauline to wait for Napoleon's permission to depart, but Joseph had overridden the prince's fears. "I have not hesitated, but told her to go, and that I would answer for it to Your Majesty who must want above all to see his sister live."

Three days after Napoleon wrote of Saint-Didier and Bagni di Lucca, Pauline was already at Chambéry. The next day she had reached Aix-les-Bains. Her mother and her uncle Fesch had hurried to join her there, alarmed by Joseph's reports of her health. But the breezes that wafted over the deep waters of Lake Bourget soon revived Pauline, and the French soil beneath her elegant feet had its effect. A little over a month after she had arrived, in mid-July 1808 she embarked for Lyon and from there continued to Paris. Her sister Elisa wrote to Lucien in Rome: "Paulette has tricked us. I said that she would trap the emperor, for her illness is nothing other than the wish for Paris."

It was a wish soon realized, and upon arrival at the Hôtel Charost, Pauline sent to Turin for her wardrobe—and for the Comtesse de Cavour and Baronne de Mathis, who had so pleased her during her brief stay in the Piedmontese capital. She had no intention of ever returning to Camillo's side there. It remained to be seen if her return to the French capital would bring her the satisfaction she anticipated. Certainly pleasure and heady power lay ahead—but, in Spain, there were indications that Napoleon's army might prove less than invincible. As Pauline said, she owed much to her brother. But her prosperity also depended on his, and, should his founder, she too would be vulnerable. What then for the princess?

CHAPTER TWELVE

Agent for Divorce, 1808–1812

F OR THE MOMENT Pauline was content. Not only was she in her beloved Paris, but when Napoleon returned from overseeing the Spanish campaign in August 1808, far from reprimanding his sister for disobeying his command to remain in Piedmont, he loaded her with largesse. "The Emperor has been charming to me," Pauline wrote blithely. "I stay in France and he is going to arrange my finances. But only after his return from Germany." Guerrilla forces were devastating the French army in Spain. However, before Napoleon committed more troops westward, he wanted Russia to help protect France's eastern frontiers from attack by Austria. He had therefore arranged to meet Czar Alexander in September at Erfurt in Germany to discuss an alliance.

Napoleon's unexpected goodwill toward his insubordinate sister that summer had a simple explanation. His thoughts had turned once more to divorce—and this was a project that had Pauline's wholehearted support and encouragement. Already in 1807 there had been signs that Napoleon still dreamed of remarriage and of fathering a son and heir. In the summer of that year, Louis and Hortense's firstborn son, Napoléon Charles, who had been declared the imperial heir, died unexpectedly at the age of eight. The emperor went to some trouble to arrange a sumptuous burial chamber where his nephew's small coffin was laid. The vault would be, he decreed, the place of interment for all members of the imperial family. However, he refused point-blank to declare the child's younger brother, Napoléon Louis, his heir.

The imperial succession was still in abeyance when Napoleon went to meet Czar Alexander at Erfurt in September 1808. In the course of that conference he secretly asked the czar for the hand in marriage of his sister, Grand Duchess Catherine. He promised that his childless union with Josephine could be swiftly terminated. The pope, who might have obstructed such a measure, was conveniently under house arrest in Rome, after refusing to block the ports of the Papal States to English trade. The emperor of the French waited anxiously in hope of an answer in the affirmative. "It will be a proof to me that Alexander is an ally," he wrote to Caulaincourt, his ambassador in St. Petersburg. "It would be a real sacrifice for me. I love Josephine. I will never be happier with anyone else, but," Napoleon, servant of the state, affirmed, "my family and Talleyrand and Fouché and all the politicians insist upon it in the name of France."

Pauline was ready to jeer at *"la vieille"* and the *"Beauharnaille,"* or the "old hag" and the "Beauharnais rabble," and gloat over a displaced Josephine. But the Russian czar foiled her brother's plans, acceding neither to a full alliance nor to the proposed marriage. The French foreign minister, Talleyrand, who had in fact reached the conclusion that Napoleon was acting against the nation's interest, was now secretly in Austria's pay and had coached Czar Alexander in his responses. Thwarted, Napoleon returned to Paris, but his desire to take a new bride only increased. Nothing that Josephine did pleased him, and the "elegant equality" of their relationship, which had struck so many in the early days of the Empire, dissolved in acrimony and recrimination.

The emperor was inclined to turn to his family for company, for comfort. But Madame Mère, although no friend to Josephine, was still opposed to divorce on religious grounds. And the other members of the extended Bonaparte family on whom he had previously relied— Caroline and Murat, Hortense and Louis, Joseph and Julie—he had dispatched to govern distant European realms. For, while Murat had forced the abdication of the Bourbon rulers of Spain in May, he had then been sent to replace Joseph Bonaparte as king of the Two Sicilies, whose capital was Naples. And Joseph, when in Turin in the spring and anxious about Pauline's health, had been en route from southern Italy to Madrid to appropriate the Spanish crown. The crowning of these brothers-in-law in Paris in October 1808 was somewhat farcical. As Chateaubriand later wrote, the emperor "rammed these crowns onto the new kings' heads, and off they went like a couple of conscripts who had exchanged caps by order of the commander." However, both Joseph and Murat considered that they were constitutional monarchs, bringing the benefits of the Revolution and abolishing feudalism.

Thus it fell to Pauline, blandishing and seductive, to play confidante to Napoleon in Paris—an asp in Josephine's bosom. The rewards for Princess Borghese's attentions to her brother were considerable. Napoleon was not long in Paris before he was off again to oversee the Spanish campaign, but in that time he bestowed upon her the Château of Neuilly, a league from Paris, which had been built by the Comte d'Argenson, Louis XV's war minister, and had formerly belonged to the Murats. They had bought it and the adjoining estate of Villiers while Joachim was governor of Paris, but, upon becoming king and queen of Naples, they had had to renounce all French property.

The emperor also resolved to increase his sister's annual income by the sum of six hundred thousand francs. This was to be hers alone, "separate property" on which Camillo could have no call, as Napoleon established in a side letter. In return he required of her that, instead of acting a lackadaisical part, as she had done in the early days of the Empire, she would continue to bring luster and style to the imperial calendar and preside over *cercles* and balls, as she had done more recently. It was a bargain that Pauline was to keep on the whole faithfully, and one that would establish her reputation, in these years when Josephine was distracted by fears about her future, as the presiding deity at the imperial court.

"Pauline Bonaparte was as beautiful as it was possible to be," the Austrian ambassador Count Metternich, who first romanced Laure

Junot and afterward Caroline Murat, later reminisced. "She was in love with herself alone, and her sole occupation was pleasure." (There appears to be no substance to claims that Metternich, who wore Caroline's hair plaited in a bracelet, was also intimate with Pauline herself.) The princess's neighbor at Montgobert, Stanislas de Girardin, confirms the Austrian diplomat's account: "Pauline Borghese was then in the full brilliance of her beauty. Men pressed about her to admire her, to pay court. And she enjoyed this homage as her due. In the glances she exchanged with some of them, indeed, there was a recognition of past favors granted or hints of romance to come. Few women," he concluded, "have savored more the pleasure of being beautiful."

At Neuilly, in the middle of a ball, Pauline would call for a basin of milk, and, when her black page brought it, she would sip from it, languishing—white and appetizing as the milk itself—on a sofa. "When she waltzes, all the other dancers stop," we are told by another Austrian observer, "so as not to hurt this delicate and gentle imperial highness. She is very pretty and says very amusing things." Consolidating this reputation as a fragile fairy princess, at her house in Paris, Pauline slept—when alone—in a little pink bed, hung with embroidered muslin and so small and low it seemed out of a dollhouse.

But of course Pauline was not always alone. "She had a habit of falling into a reverie when contemplating an affair," noted an Austrian, the diplomat Prince Clary. At Neuilly, following a *cercle,* there were generally card games till ten or eleven in the evening. But then, when the assembly dispersed, Pauline kept with her "some few elect" for the rest of the evening. "And then there was dancing, gaming, and all the pleasures of the golden age. Moreover, sometimes among these elect there was one further favored," Clary slyly adds.

One such was a young German lieutenant named Conrad Friedrich, who had formed part of the army of occupation that Napoleon sent to Rome to arrest the pope and annex the Papal States to France. The lieutenant, in Paris to beg reinforcements and the rank of marshal for his commanding officer in Rome, went to Neuilly to inquire if the princess would use her influence with her brother to secure his objectives, and he caught Pauline's fancy. Though she smiled and said she had no influence with the emperor, she asked Friedrich to walk a little with her in the gardens, and murmured to her lady that "for a German" the lieutenant had a good air. It finished with her making a rendezvous with him for the following afternoon at a grotto on the grounds.

Friedrich recites in his florid memoirs a remarkable afternoon that followed next day. When he passed into the interior of the grotto, rooms and galleries opened up to his astonished gaze, among them a magnificent salon with a large bathtub. "The adventure seemed to me out of a novel or even a fairy tale." As he wondered what would be its outcome, the princess appeared, smiling and asking him how he liked the place. As she advanced toward him, Friedrich saw that "the opulent and perfectly molded curves of her body" were only thinly veiled, and were perfectly visible with her every movement. "She gave me her hand to kiss, wished me welcome and had me sit next to her on a yielding daybed," recalls the soldier. "I was certainly not the seducer, but the one seduced, for in the cavernous twilight Pauline employed all her charms to bring my blood to boiling point and my senses to a point of frenzy. Soon the nameless emissions which marked our mutual passions were imprinted on the velvet cushions. In which Pauline revealed herself still more experienced a lover than I, having greater staying power." Afterward, "clothed in fine linen wrappers," he records, they bathed together. "We stayed nearly an hour in the azure water, after which we ate in a neighboring room an exquisite meal, and there we stayed till dusk."

Friedrich, however, disliked being prey rather than hunter: "I had to promise to come back soon, and I spent more than one afternoon like that. All the same, I never felt very proud of my conquest, for Pauline had granted the last favors to more than one before me, and was later to grant them to many more. Moreover, she was almost too routine in seeking her own pleasure, and before long, it was more aversion than anticipation that I felt in going there, despite her beauty."

Pauline might be on pleasure bent in public at her balls and in the cool privacy of the grotto at Neuilly with Friedrich and others, but she was not unaware of the ugly mood in France spawned by the unpopular war in Spain and Portugal. When Napoleon left for the front in November 1808, the princess said that she and all the Bonapartes would be assassinated if he were killed in battle. Not only were decisive victories needed to quell disaffection in France, but the war was proving increasingly costly in men as well as weaponry. When the British came to the aid of the Iberian patriots in August 1808, the French became engaged in a punishing battle for control of the peninsula. After losing the battle of Vimeiro that month, under the terms of the Cintra Convention, Junot and his army evacuated Portugal. The British, meanwhile, advanced from Portugal into Spain, where they would prove a potent foe. By 1809 more than a quarter of a million Frenchmen were under arms in the region, tens of thousands had already died in guerrilla warfare, and conscripts were deserting in quantity.

In the meantime Napoleon not only survived but took Madrid in December 1808. He had to return posthaste to Paris in the new year, however, as Austria, advised by Talleyrand, had made good its threat to arm against France. Although the French emperor was victorious in the battles that ensued, notably at Wagram in July 1809, the death toll was heavy. "This year is an inopportune time to shock public opinion by repudiating a popular Empress," Napoleon declared. Josephine had apparently won a reprieve—and Pauline, disappointed, went off with her mother to Aix-la-Chapelle that summer to take the cure, where the old lady, as usual, disputed the cost of the lodgings and food and demanded an imperial discount on the staff of life itself.

Metternich had observed of Napoleon in the autumn of 1807 that he had ceased to be "moderate." That summer, upon being dispossessed of his Vatican realm and imprisoned in northern Italy, Pope Pius VII issued a bull that, by implication, excommunicated the French emperor. But Napoleon was heedless of such disapprobation. For in September, to his great joy, the Polish Marie Walewska announced that she was pregnant and that he was beyond doubt the father. This changed everything, in Napoleon's mind. For now he had proved he could father a child, and Josephine's vaunted popularity could not be allowed to stand in the way of his clear imperial duty. Divorce and remarriage—not to the beautiful Marie but to a nubile princess of great rank—must follow.

The empress did not need her husband, all protestations and regret, to speak her fate. "I know I will be shamefully dismissed from the bed of the man who crowned me," she said, "but God is my witness that I love him more than my life and much more than the throne." An autumn of humiliation for Josephine, spent mostly at Fontainebleau, ensued. "The divorce was ordered in his head," observed Hortense of her stepfather later. "My family was a charge; his own, now important to him. He went to his sister Borghese nearly every evening, he went out without the Empress in his carriage." From her apartments the lonely empress saw the lights of late-night soirees that her sister-in-law held in her rooms and that the emperor attended. "They say a Pied-montese woman was the cause [of the estrangement]—I think," wrote Hortense accurately, "a distraction from the divorce he meditated."

Pauline, in buoyant spirits, wrote to Murat in Naples, requesting him to send her some of the fans for which the south Italian city was noted. She declared that she was plump and in good health and attended all the *cercles*. She did not mention any Piedmontese woman, but we may name her—Cristina, Baronne de Mathis, one of the ladies assigned to Pauline in Turin and for whom the princess had sent on her return to Paris. As we have seen before, when Napoleon was going through a period of emotional strain, he had invariably started a liaison with one of the ladies in Josephine's suite. The difference now was that Pauline's suite supplied the female in question.

The diarist Stanislas de Girardin gives us the details: "One of those ferrets at Court who detect the latest scandals has told me of a new La Vallière who has taken the eye of the monarch." (Louise, Duchesse de La Vallière, had been one of Louis XIV's mistresses.) "It is an Italian woman attached to Princess Borghese. She is, they tell me, petite, blond, round as a ball, and fresh as a daisy. Like Louis XIV, the lover enters by a window. And the princess, like a good little sister, arranges the rendezvous for His Majesty." Notes from Napoleon to Pauline that survive detail the pander part that the princess played this autumn. "Monday morning," wrote the emperor. "What's the news? Is she amiable or capricious this morning?" Again: "She is very lovely but quite severe. Sometimes I doubt if she loves me." Another reads: "I would be charmed if she were to come to the review, which will be very fine, with top-rate troops." And there is this too: "Tonight I'll come by the garden. Tell Madame de M. to await me."

Dalliance with a Piedmontese daisy notwithstanding, the moment of truth between Napoleon and Josephine had to come, and after dinner on November 30, 1809, he gave orders that they were to be left alone. When he had broken the news that Josephine had expected— they were to divorce—and told her that the ceremony of divorce was to take place two weeks thence, the empress lay on the floor, weeping. The confusion in the emperor's mind is best shown in his remark to Hortense, who, entering, told Josephine that she and Eugène would go away with their mother and live quietly as a family together. "You too would betray me?" Napoleon said to his stepdaughter and sister-in-law.

A few days later, on the fifth anniversary of the coronation in Notre-Dame, it was Jérôme, and not Josephine, who traveled with the emperor to the cathedral, and there was no place of honor for the empress at the banquet that followed. The divorce was pronounced by the Senate ten days later, and in the throne room, as though for a celebration, the court assembled. "The Bonapartes gloated," observed Hortense. "Try as they might not to show it, they betrayed their joy by their air of satisfaction and triumph." Josephine pronounced the words that had been assigned her, and then Napoleon led her back to her apartments. When she collapsed on her arrival there, her courage spent, Hortense came and urged the empress to remember that Marie Antoinette before her had left the Tuileries for prison and the scaffold. Josephine, on the other hand, was to go to her beloved Malmaison.

It was scant comfort, but next day the empress did indeed leave with her dogs and parrots for Malmaison, where she would live a life of retirement. Napoleon departed for Versailles and issued orders for Pauline to join him there, instructing her to bring Madame de Mathis. "I'll be with you in the garden by 9," he wrote to Pauline. "I won't come to you unless you think she will be amenable. I have need of sweetness and contentment, not headaches." But the Baronne de Mathis was not destined to occupy Napoleon's attention long, once the friction of the divorce was past. His thoughts were leaping ahead to remarriage, a project that—astonishingly—had Josephine's support. When Napoleon begged the hand in marriage of the Austrian arch-duchess Marie Louise, the empress Josephine told Metternich that she hoped he would be successful. She did not want, she said, to have made the sacrifice of her happiness for nothing. Marie Louise's father, Emperor Francis I, appears not to have considered his daughter's hap-piness, though she had been earlier taught to view Napoleon, who had occupied Vienna, as a tyrant and an ogre. The Austrian emperor's let-ter, accepting the proposal, arrived in Paris simultaneously with that of the Russian emperor, declining on his sister's behalf the separate over-tures that Napoleon had made to St. Petersburg.

Paris was ready to celebrate the arrival of Marie Louise in March 1810. Plain, ungainly, and red faced she might be, according to reports, but, at nineteen, her age was generally regarded as a delightful attribute. Pauline, however, was less sure and would have preferred her niece Charlotte—Joseph's daughter—to have become the emperor's bride. Princess Borghese did not relish the fact of the Austrian arch-duchess's high birth—and, now that Josephine's hegemony at court was over, there was the possibility, unlikely though it might seem, that Napoleon might feel affection for Marie Louise.

In the newcomer's favor right away was her appetite for sex. The emperor's report was as follows: "I took her straight to bed when she arrived at Fontainebleau, and as soon as we finished, she asked me to do it to her again." But Napoleon Bonaparte and his teenage Hapsburg bride did not otherwise prove especially congenial to each other. Pauline settled for joining her sisters, who came to Paris for the imperial wedding at Saint-Cloud in sulks mirroring those in which they had indulged at the coronation of Josephine six years earlier, and centering once more on a reluctance to bear their sister-in-law's train. "Tears, prayers, fainting fits, absolute refusals. . . . One made a moue, the other, her smelling salts under her nose, threatened illness, the third let the mantle fall and that was worst of all, for then she had to pick it up again."

The only one who apparently acted with any dignity was Josephine's daughter, Hortense, whom Napoleon, with his usual tactlessness, had appointed Marie Louise's mistress of the robes. But then, he had sent to meet Marie Louise at the French border Caroline Murat, who had appropriated the crown of the Austrian princess's great-aunt, Queen Maria Carolina of Naples. (More thoughtfully he had provided for Josephine the distant Château of Navarre, to which the slighted empress retired for the course of these nuptial celebrations.)

PAULINE'S ENERGY in these years was prodigious, and the tales of her conquests legion, featuring, among others, the wasp-waisted Russian general Prince Alexander Tchernitcheff, emissary of the czar, and the Polish veteran general Josef Anton Poniatowski, who wore the Grand Eagle of the Légion d'Honneur and was still a spry lover at fifty. The accounts of the balls and fetes that Pauline held in Paris and at Neuilly, and where the celebrated mulatto conductor Julien officiated, are likewise numerous. One fete at the latter place, however, which she planned in honor of Napoleon and his new bride and gave in June 1810, stands out. "Tell the designer, M. Bernard, that it must cost no more than 80,000 francs," she instructed Monsieur Michelot from Compiègne, where the court had taken up residence following the imperial nuptials, that April. "But I want everyone to think it cost 120,000 francs, so economize on the details." Bernard fulfilled this difficult brief, and on the evening of June 14, seven hundred guests enjoyed the gardens of Neuilly, strung with colored lights.

Sixty-five members of the corps de ballet from the Paris Opéra performed allegorical dances on the lawn. Temples of Love, Hope, and

Glory featured costumed pilgrims from the Holy Land, while guards in Austrian livery and Tyrolean dress patrolled in front of a transparency showing the Viennese palace of Schönbrunn. (To a more select audience, sitting in boxes garlanded with flowers in the little theater up at the house, actors from the Théâtre Feydeau had earlier performed a comic opera, *Le Concert Interrompu*.) As the climax to the outdoor festivities Napoleon put a match to a fire-breathing dragon and fireworks burst out on the Seine beyond the lawns, while overhead a tightrope dancer, Signora Saqui, with a torch in each hand, performed acrobatic wonders.

Three days later, at Napoleon's insistence, Pauline illumined the gardens again—this time, for the bourgeois of Neuilly and the surrounding area. Five thousand tickets were issued, and the gardens soon filled. But the visitors were discontented, despite the six dancing orchestras provided. The house, which they had hoped to see inside, was firmly closed, and Pauline was nowhere in evidence—although Napoleon and Marie Louise were there, incognito. "The court sends us its leavings" was the general complaint. "Everything seemed to suggest, 'It is good enough for the rabble,'" wrote de Girardin.

Pauline was unperturbed by the criticism. She was en route to Aix-la-Chapelle for the summer once more, and keen only to ensure that everything necessary for daily life at the Hôtel Charost in Paris was put away or removed so that Camillo could not enjoy the amenities of the place during her absence. When he had come to Paris from Turin, where he was proving a popular governor, for Napoleon's marriage to Marie Louise, Pauline had first read him the document that Napoleon had drawn up, establishing their "separate property," then refused to speak to him, though they shared the same house for days at a time. Nor would she open letters that, in desperation, he addressed to her. Last, she would not feed him and his suite and suggested they eat at a restaurant. Only upon the insistence of Napoleon, to whom her intransigence became known, did she relent.

Upon Pauline's return from her sojourn in Aix-la-Chapelle, she was to feel the weight once more of her brother's disapproval. For she was now intimate with a young hussar, Jules de Canouville, who was on General Berthier's staff, and whom she had first noticed during the carnival season earlier that year. With his close friend Achille de Septeuil, who was himself romantically involved with Princess Borghese's lady Madame de Barral, Jules had taken part in a masque that Count Ferdinando Marescalchi, representative of the Kingdom of Italy in Paris, mounted. He caracoled in a Battle of Chessmen, while his friend played a Fool in a uniform of red and gold. Shut up at Neuilly that autumn with de Canouville, Pauline lavished presents on the handsome, brash officer. He responded with ardor, and the affair appears to have been the first to trouble her mind, not just to represent the pleasures of the flesh, since her liaison with Forbin.

De Canouville's devotion was fierce, sometimes nonsensical. During a ball given by Prince Eugène, the officer approached his host, viceroy of Italy and the Empress Josephine's son. Not a whit abashed by the rank of this great personage, he demanded that the contra dance that was in progress be halted. "The princess wishes to waltz with me." Eugène, ever elegant, demurred. "A waltz, a waltz," de Canouville insisted. Eugène had his way, but Pauline was no doubt entertained by her cavalier's championing of her desires.

A comical scene ensued when the princess had toothache and the imperial dentist, Bousquet, was called to Neuilly. While he inspected the princess's mouth, de Canouville, whom he did not know, lay on another sofa in a dressing gown and gave anxious instructions: "Take good care not to harm her, monsieur. I am very fond of Her Highness's teeth, and I shall hold you responsible for any accident." Understandably Bousquet took the gentleman to be the princess's husband, and, when he had concluded his ministrations and returned to the antechamber, he said to the ladies and chamberlains assembled there: "It is sweet to see such an example of conjugal love in a couple of such great rank." The snickers and broad smiles that met his remark informed the dentist of his error.

Pauline herself now made a mistake in her dealings with de Canouville. Following the court's removal to Fontainebleau in the autumn of

1810, she had made herself agreeable to Marie Louise, entertaining the young empress with a troupe of dancing dogs on one occasion, with a magic lantern show on another. Napoleon had responded suitably and indeed had made de Canouville an imperial baron, at his sister's request. But then Pauline went too far. The Russian czar had sent Napoleon three sable pelisses, one of which the emperor had given his sister. Now she had the fur cut into wide bands and sewn on a dolman, or hussar's jacket, with diamond buttons for her lover. De Canouville wore the gift proudly at the next review in the place du Carrousel. But Napoleon had noted his sister's transgression and, when the officer's horse proved difficult to control, told him, "That hot blood will get you sent to Russia." In the event the emperor ordered Berthier to send de Canouville instead to Portugal. He was to search for Marshal André Masséna, who had now been there several weeks with a large force without sending back any dispatches.

Even in the midst of this duty, de Canouville thought only of Pauline. Knowing that, with her, to be absent was to be soon forgotten, he covered 170 relays at a gallop, a distance of over seven hundred miles, and arrived a few days later, covered in mud, at headquarters in Salamanca. There he learned that the supply lines to Portugal were cut and resolved to return the next day to Paris with the news, rather than pursue his quarry further. An hour without Pauline, he said, was a desert, and he whiled the evening away telling all who would listen that Napoleon had charged him with his mission only by way of vengeance. Reciting the details of his romance with Pauline from the first meeting at the ball on the final day of the carnival, he punctuated his narrative with sighs to make the candles gutter.

They say that when de Canouville reached Paris he was not admitted to the Hôtel Charost and that, as he had feared, the princess had already found another. But reconciliation followed, although he was not to be allowed to remain long in Paris. Berthier sent him back to Spain—and there, soon enough, came his friend and fellow officer Achille de Septeuil. His story was a different one. Following de Canouville's departure, Pauline had courted and been rejected by Septeuil.

"You are a flirt, madame," he said, for he was true to Pauline's lady Madame de Barral. Pauline's answer had been to go to Napoleon and engineer Septeuil's removal to Spain. In her appetite for revenge she was a true Corsican, and her brother was understanding of her need.

Together both de Canouville and Septeuil eventually beat a path to Masséna in Portugal, and in due course both, serving on his staff, took part in May 1811 in the Battle of Fuentes de Onoro, when the French marshal tried to relieve the besieged fortress of Almeida. In that battle de Canouville was wounded; Septeuil, upon charging Wellington's forces at the head of his dragoons, had his horse killed under him and his arm blown off by a shell. Pauline's reaction was cool: "He can still dance."

The princess had a new source of anxiety. On March 20, 1811, at nine in the morning, a hundred cannons had been fired to mark the birth of Marie Louise's son by Napoleon. He was christened that same morning Napoléon François Charles Joseph Bonaparte and given the title King of Rome. Napoleon was beside himself with joy, Pauline less happy, for her brother seemed to transfer the warm feelings he had for her to his baby son—and even to extend them to the mother of his child. That summer, continuing the theme of revenge, Pauline embarked at Aix-la-Chapelle on an affair with "le beau Montrond," the fashionable diplomat and confidant of Talleyrand of whom Napoleon had said, "There will never be morals in France as long as Montrond lives there."

Montrond had been banished from Paris for repeating in public criticisms of Napoleon's imperial strategy that his intimate Talleyrand had made in confidence. (Talleyrand had resigned as foreign secretary in 1807 in protest at the Franco-Russian alliance.) Montrond was living at Spa, and Pauline followed him there with a few of her suite in September. A Colonel Vladimir Kabloukoff, attached to the Russian embassy in Paris, who was convalescing at Aix, escorted her. "There is no one here. I ride and rise early," she wrote mendaciously to Cambacérès, the archchancellor of the Empire, in a letter meant for Napoleon's eyes. But the police spies were aware of both Kabloukoff's role as escort and Montrond's presence in the fine house Princess Borghese rented, and dubbed both of them Pauline's lovers. How much she cared for Montrond is unclear. But when he showed a *tendresse* for Mlle Jenny Millo, her waiting woman, who had married in Turin and was now Madame Saluzzo, the princess was furious. She sent Jenny off to her husband in Turin and demanded she repay the dowry she had given her. Meanwhile Montrond was arrested and imprisoned by French police at Antwerp. Although he escaped to England, Pauline had once again shown that it was unwise to cross her.

In Paris once more, Pauline found, to her dismay, that de Canouville was not available to dance attention on her for long. For in November, on Napoleon's orders, he ceased to be on Berthier's staff and was sent to join the Second Regiment of Cavalry in Danzig as squadron commander. At no point, his instructions ran, was he to venture to Paris. Pauline had not tired of de Canouville, but she submitted to the dictat. For, as the new year of 1812 dawned, it brought fresh troubles in its wake. Pauline's health was in decline once more, and she was thinking of heading south to a warmer climate. Meanwhile Czar Alexander, who had opened his ports to the English in defiance of the pacts made at Tilsit and Erfurt, gave the French emperor an ultimatum in April: If Napoleon did not withdraw to the west of the river Elbe, Russia would mobilize against France.

Napoleon began to amass a Grande Armée, 650,000 troops in all, while he asked for negotiations rather than war. But his hope that the show of arms would frighten the czar into backing down was misplaced. It became evident that Napoleon must indeed lead the Grande Armée in an attack on Russia, and in June, on the point of departure, he visited Josephine at Malmaison, when the empress entreated his valet Constant to keep her former husband safe. By contrast, in May, before heading south to Aix-les-Bains, Pauline had successfully begged Murat, who was to head the cavalry bound for Russia, to allow de Canouville to serve on his staff. Death or glory was a concept that appealed to Pauline.

As the French war machine rumbled into action, and as Pauline headed south to Aix-les-Bains with the intention of spending a year in the south, a ball that she and Caroline Murat had jointly held at the Tuileries during the February carnival seemed a distant memory, of a golden age before debt, loss of men, and nascent nationalism had afflicted the French Empire. At the ball Pauline, carrying a golden lance and shod in purple-laced sandals, had shone in the character of "Rome." Elegant in a golden helmet with a cloud of ostrich feathers and a golden breastplate over a tunic of Indian muslin, she looked into a mirror to see the fate of the Eternal City and discovered, behind her, the reflected face of "France."

To stern critics Caroline Murat—"France"—seemed encumbered by her helmet, and in addition her plumpness detracted from the whiteness of her hands and arms, considered her best feature. But the little drama, in which "Rome" and "France" embraced each other, pleased most of the court. Not so Napoleon. "It's a farce. Everyone knows the Romans hate being yoked to France," he complained. "These young women are more difficult to control than a regiment. I'm not a grizzly bear. They could ask me. But oh no, these women are too confident to do anything of the kind." It would perhaps prove fortunate that Pauline was indeed so confident, because during the next few years, she would have only herself on whom to rely.

CHAPTER THIRTEEN

Survival, 1812–1814

THE ALPINE BATHING RESORT of Aix-les-Bains, near Chambéry, where Pauline took up residence in June 1812, attracted that summer, among a numerous Parisian clientele, several female members of the extended Bonaparte clan and some of their intimates, among them Laure d'Abrantès. The emigration eastward of Napoleon and his enormous staff of marshals, generals, and officers had left their womenfolk in a state of anxiety and uncertainty. In consequence many of them chose, rather than go to their country estates for the summer, to gather where they could more easily glean news of the advance on Russia. Madame Mère came south in July to be with her daughter. They were joined the following month by Joseph's wife, Julie, queen of Spain, who had been suffering from an outbreak of erisypelas, and by her sister Désirée, who had once, as Désirée Clary, been courted by Napoleon Bonaparte. Her husband, Marshal Bernadotte, was now newly crown prince and regent of Sweden.

The latter royal latecomers lodged in a house in the main square, opposite that rented by Laure. Madame Mère occupied, as usual, modest rooms. But Pauline had secured the best house in the spa, the Maison Chevaley. Situated in pastureland up on the alp, it commanded views of Lake Bourget and, beyond, of the jagged mountain range dominated by the Dent du Chat. There Pauline entertained, among other suitors for her pretty hand, the great actor Talma, who had for twenty years dominated the theater in Paris and whom Napoleon had often honored with summonses to come and read from Voltaire and Molière at the Tuileries.

What had drawn together Pauline and Talma, now of a certain age and jowly, when they had been known to each other for so many years, is a mystery. It is said, however, that, for some weeks before Pauline went south, she lived secluded with the actor, and that at Aix they resumed an existing relationship. But, if so, Talma's duties were not confined to the bedroom. Just as Felice Blangini had once feared he would lose his voice, given Pauline's wish to partner him in evening duets, now the great thespian told Laure d'Abrantès that he was condemned, soiree after soiree, to read Molière scenes and did not dare to refuse. "I will have to leave Aix, which I like exceedingly," he lamented. "But I have to perform every evening. For, you know, she wants to learn the roles of Agnès [from *The School for Wives*] and Angélique [from *Le Malade imaginaire*]."

If Talma believed that he had misled Laure into thinking that his role at the spa was merely that of elocution teacher, he was himself deceived. However, he could draw comfort from the fact that he was not the only male drawn into Pauline's orbit up at the Maison Chevaley around whom rumors of a sexual relationship with the princess hung. Princess Borghese's former admirer and chamberlain the Comte de Forbin had left her impetuously five years earlier to be a soldier in Spain. But he had abandoned that career, following imprisonment in Cintra and subsequent involvement in the Austrian campaigns of 1809. Now he stopped off in Aix en route to Paris from Naples, where he had occupied his time producing Spanish history paintings. Still handsome, cultured, and in every way agreeable company, if no richer, Forbin had turned novelist as well as history painter, and gave readings in the Aix salons that summer of his novel, *The Quaker of Philadelphia*. But, although assiduous in his attentions to Pauline, he made no attempt to become intimate with her again. Once bitten, twice shy.

At the Maison Chevaley, Princess Borghese was kept informed of her brother's advance across the Neman River into Russian territory on June 23 and of Alexander's consequent declaration of a patriotic war. Her sisters wrote too—Caroline from Naples, where she was managing the kingdom's affairs during Murat's absence at the head of the cavalry in Russia. The Queen of Naples asked her sister in Aix for "a little chemise like the one I saw you wear next to your skin, with short sleeves." Thus valetudinarian Pauline in her diaphanous dresses warded off the cold. Elisa wrote from her Tuscan grand duchy, sending straw bonnets from Florence and patent remedies, and wishing Pauline and Madame Mère would join her on a visit she projected to the baths of Lucca. Even Jérôme's wife, Catherine, contributed to the family budget, writing in July from Kassel, capital of the Westphalian kingdom. She wanted new fashions, new headdresses, and she was fretting for her husband during his absence with the emperor. "If I thought my letters could charm the hours of so delightful an anchorite, I would write more often," she told Pauline. "But I would have to be gay—the danger Jérôme runs checks all levity in me. . . . From what I understand, from letters of the fourth [July], the Emperor was then at Vilna [in Russia, formerly Polish territory]. I know no more. It's precisely this uncertainty that destroys me." Catherine was by birth a princess of Württemburg. Her marriage to Jérôme in 1808 had been a dynastic alliance—quite unlike his earlier marriage to the American, Elizabeth Patterson, whom he had, without compunction, divorced in order to marry again and please Napoleon.

Pauline accepted the flood of correspondence, and contributed to it too. Her brother Jérôme, with seventy thousand men under his command, wrote to her from Warsaw, acknowledging a letter that their brother-in-law Murat had forwarded to him there, and anticipating the campaign to come: "You would be wrong to doubt my tender and constant love. But you know that being far off and very busy . . . one writes less often. I hope, my dear Pauline, that the Emperor, who is not maladroit, and who knows at least as much as another, will do great things, as is his wont."

Jérôme spoke too soon. For the emperor had not reckoned with a late summer. As July succeeded June, the grain on which he had counted to feed his troops and horses as he progressed eastward had not been forthcoming. Second, heavy rain had turned fields and roads into quagmires. And then a blistering-hot summer struck, creating new and difficult conditions; men grew parched and horses dehydrated, and thousands of both were dying daily. But Jérôme was constitutionally cheerful and wrote from Bielitz (now Bielsko-Biala, Poland) on the Neman: "We are chasing the enemy, and we are, as you see, far away. The emperor is in the best of health and forty leagues to my left. It is very hot, but everything is going well. . . . I am in good health, although on horseback from two or three in the morning till nightfall."

Pauline, in her own way, followed the action in Russia as closely as any other of the imperial women—as well she might. For Napoleon's personal safety as well as his glory and national prestige were all at risk. That her brother Jérôme and her brother-in-law Murat held crucial commands in the mighty war machine progressing eastward toward Moscow made her still more attentive. And then again—of Princess Borghese's former lovers heading for Moscow, one could indeed say, "Their name is Legion." Among them were Marshal Macdonald, General Beurnonville, General Poniatowski, who commanded the Polish army, and Lieutenant Friedrich, with whom the princess had lingered in the grotto at Neuilly. She could even claim a bedfellow among the enemy, for General Moreau had followed Talleyrand in changing sides and was even now furnishing Alexander with advice and military support. But of course, of all the soldiers in the field it was for Jules de Canouville, on Murat's staff, that Pauline retained special feeling—feeling that was given tangible form in the magnificent, jewel-encrusted sword she now commissioned from Paris for the ardent officer.

Archchancellor Cambacérès in Paris kept Pauline closely informed of the emperor's movements. For news of de Canouville's movements, however, she was indebted to his commander, Murat, who wrote to her in August, boasting of victory over the Russians two days earlier. "The Emperor has ordered me to chase them all the way to Moscow. . . . I am seizing a moment when we are rebuilding a bridge they burned to reply to you. My dear sister, it is impossible to love you more than I do. All my thoughts and those of those who love you"—by this he meant her lover—"are with you. I am saddling up, the bridge is back, and some Cossacks ahead of us need a good drubbing."

Neither Pauline's concern for Jules de Canouville, her fondness for Forbin, nor her current relationship with Talma precluded her finding a new admirer at the baths. Auguste Duchand, an oversize artillery officer who had served in Spain under Suchet and Sebastiani, was convalescing at Aix-les-Bains following wounds incurred at the Battle of Valencia. With Pauline's encouragement he became a devoted visitor to the Maison Chevaley. But for some time he remained in awe of the tiny princess and her autocratic ways. One day Laure d'Abrantès found him among the company gathered at the Maison Chevaley. As Laure tells us, the short climb from the spa to the house was steep and some of it not negotiable by horse. In consequence her footwear and hose and those of other guests were irksomely dirty upon arrival, in contrast to those of their elegant hostess—and, mysteriously, those of Lieutenant Captain Duchand. He was something of a dandy, and his unsullied knee boots were gleaming with wax.

Irritably Laure taxed the captain with this anomaly. He showed her his old servant soldier and said he made him carry him up the slope on his back. Laure looked at the large captain and at the shrunken little man and imagined the awkward journey. Such were the lengths to which men would go to please the fastidious princess, when she had not as yet done more than smile sweetly upon them.

On another occasion, after Laure had climbed up to the house, she saw to her dismay that Pauline was arrayed in a manner that boded ill. For when Princess Borghese received wearing a demi-negligée and seated in a bergère, she was ready to entertain and be entertained. There were other outfits she wore to recline on a chaise longue, and then animated conversation was still permitted. But when, as on this occasion, she languished on a sofa in a peignoir, all ribbons and ruffles, it was forbidden to remark even upon her appearance—and she was as pretty as an angel under her lace-trimmed English bonnet. The sole subject allowed was her health.

The doctors, Pauline informed the company that day, had just pre-scribed a miserable diet for her to follow. In the last eight hours she had taken nothing but soup. "And that without salt," she added. "Without salt," echoed one of the gentlemen present. "Without salt," confirmed Pauline tragically, then glared at Laure d'Abrantès as the latter let out an involuntary peal of laughter. Even Forbin raised a satirical eyebrow. Nevertheless Laure repented of her hardness when Pauline sent her a bouquet tied with a beautiful rope of pearls to which was affixed a note, "From your oldest friend at Aix."

Pauline's health remained a matter of prime concern to herself, if not to others. In August she addressed Baron Vivant Denon, master of the Mint in Paris and director of the Louvre, on this subject. (He stood high in her favor, as he had a cast of her hand by Canova in his cabinet of treasures.) "I am still extremely frail and live on asses' milk and chicken consommé," she informed him. "Eight days ago I began the waters, and although they tire me, I hope they will have a favorable outcome."

But Pauline was also always concerned to burnish her image. She was delighted with a medal featuring her classical profile that Denon had had struck from dies cut by the engraver Andrieu, as part of a series marking alleged visits by women of the imperial family to the Mint. (It was not, in fact, judged necessary for the visits to take place, nor did they.) The medal commemorating Pauline bore, on one side, her cele-brated profile *à l'antique* and the inscription in Greek, "Pauline, Sister of the Emperor." On the reverse a naked group of the Three Graces was depicted, with the inscription in Greek, "Beauty, be our Queen." "They are charming," wrote the original. "I am in your debt for the trouble you have taken. You have only to undertake something to be successful, and I have asked Mme. Cavour to beg you for more." In due course Pauline sent a medal to her sister Elisa, who pronounced the likeness exact, and indeed Canova himself could have modeled the neat and regular neoclassical features that aroused so much admiration and desire in Pauline's contemporaries.

Pauline had already that summer had a bust of herself by the sculp-tor Bosio sent from Carrara to the emperor's doctor, Corvisart, to reward him for medical advice. (He might have preferred payment in coin.) As the summer wore on, she consulted more medics—eminent doctors from Geneva as well as the spa doctor, Desmaisons, and, of course, Dr. Peyre, who had been at her side since they left Saint-Domingue together. It seems clear that by now the princess had a chronic—and painful—inflammation of her fallopian tubes. But, in addition to other remedies for her persistent problems with her reproductive organs, they advised the application of leeches to her genital area. (Enemas, as well as bleedings, douches, purgatives, decoctions of herbs, and extracts of minerals, featured as a matter of course.) Whether her original problems had been occasioned by childbirth, this new and horrific remedy suggests that she was suffering from a venereal disease, probably gonorrhea, in whose treatment leeches were widely used. Pauline appears to have accepted the diagnosis and the medicine. The advice that she would have been given, however—that she should abstain from further sexual intercourse, for fear of infecting others and being reinfected—she showed no signs of heeding, as we shall see. But, to be fair, nor did most of the other men and women of her time who suffered from the *chaude-pisse,* or "a dose of the clap." Unmentioned and unmentionable in polite society, it was nevertheless ubiquitous.

SLOWLY PAULINE APPEARS to have recovered her spirits and her health. At any rate, at the beginning of September she was well enough to propose a boating expedition to the romantically situated Abbey of Hautecombe on the far shore of Lake Bourget. Founded by Cistercian monks in the Middle Ages, it was also the burial place of the counts and, latterly, the dukes of Savoy. By 1812, however, following the French occupation of Savoy, the monks were gone and the abbey buildings lay mostly in ruins, only in part in secular use as a china manufactory. The arrangement was for the party—which included Laure d'Abrantès, Forbin, Duchand, and Talma—to meet midmorning at the dock and set off at ten. The oarsmen were at the ready, the day was fair, but tempers frayed as the princess failed to appear. At last, nearer eleven than ten, Pauline arrived, borne on a palanquin and quite unperturbed by the ruffled feelings of those she had kept waiting.

Laure d'Abrantès tells us that Pauline sported a singular costume for an excursion to the ruins. Over an embroidered skirt, embellished with Valenciennes lace, she wore a shorter, matching dress, a polonaise. Adding a dash of vibrant color to the frilly ensemble, three great red plumes and satin ribbons were secured to a little Italian straw hat that perched on her sleek head. It was hardly surprising that, with such an outfit to concoct, Princess Borghese had run a little late. "She looked like a fine lady from Málaga," recorded Laure, who had accompanied her husband, Junot, on his campaigns in the Iberian Peninsula.

Pauline had a purpose that day, it would seem. Until now she had accepted handsome Captain Duchand's admiration as her due but had contented herself with Talma's embraces alone. However, with Talma about to leave for Geneva, where he was to begin a season of performances, she had grown restive. Captain Duchand, moreover, was resplendent in the white dress uniform with which he had honored the expedition. (His more sophisticated male companions were wearing redingotes, which was the accepted day dress in the spa.)

To Talma's growing dismay, as the boat progressed across the deep waters of the lake, Pauline "declared herself for M. Duchand" in very histrionic fashion. The tragedian's eyes grew round and fearful as the princess, at the helm of the craft, recited lines from Petrarch's sonnets to Laura that Fréron had taught her years before in Marseille:

> *Che fai? che pensi? che pur dietro guardi*
> *nel tempo che tornar non pote omai,*
> *anima sconsolata? che pur vai*
> *giugnendo legno al foco ove tu ardi?*

> [What are you thinking of, looking back
> To days that can never come again?
> Miserable creature, why go on
> Stoking a fire that already consumes you?]

Not only Duchand, at whom the verses were aimed, but all members of the company held their breath on the bright September day as the princess's voice sounded over the lapping of the oars:

> *Levommi il mio penser in parte ov'era*
> *quella ch'io cerco e non ritrovo in terra . . .*

> [My thoughts led me up to where
> She was, whom I seek and find no more on earth . . .]

The picture Pauline presented was so heavenly that it was no surprise Duchand was entranced.

As Pauline continued to declaim the whole way across the lake—the crossing took an hour—Laure d'Abrantès declared herself very glad to reach the farther shore and have the opportunity to wander over the stones of the ruined abbey with erudite Forbin her guide, his strong arm her support. Meanwhile, venturing less far, Pauline continued to weave her spell over the hapless Duchand, and Talma sulked in vain, until the sun set above the chestnut groves that overhung the abbey and its reflection in the water beckoned the party back across the lake to Aix.

Pauline was, as ever, pitiless when she had done with a lover. From Geneva late in September, Talma wrote wretchedly: "A hundred times I have decided to go to Aix just to stare from afar at your windows, to offer you the sighs and sorrows of my heart, without seeing you and troubling with my presence the calm which you need. But I fear I would not be able to be so near, and not press myself on you. I dread displeasing you, and losing perhaps all your favor by an unconsidered move. So I have restrained myself." But the actor need not have held himself in check, for he had already lost all favor in Pauline's eyes. His successor, Duchand, whose convalescence still had some months to run, was at her side as the princess planned a journey to the Midi, where her doctors, hastily consulted after her health took a turn for the worse, had advised she should winter.

Pauline's latest bout of ill health had been brought on by devastating news from the Russian campaign. Her lover Jules de Canouville had fallen at the bloody Battle of Borodino, which had been fought on September 7—the very day she had led her expedition over to the Abbey of Hautecombe and entertained the ship's company with her recitation of Petrarch's sonnets. Murat and his cavalry divisions, as we have seen, had had orders in August from Napoleon to pursue "the Cossacks," who were fleeing before them, to Moscow. For some time the Russian troops adopted a policy of scorched earth as they retreated eastward, burning fields and destroying anything that might be of use to the Grande Armée that followed in their wake. But in early September, at the village of Borodino, 120 miles west of Moscow, the Russian General Kutusov stood and gave fight. Napoleon launched into the fray all the troops available to him, hoping to devastate the Russian forces in one single battle.

The day proved, rather, one of attrition, in which Russian counterattack succeeded French assault and in which an important redoubt was captured by the latter, then regained by the former. At nightfall seventy thousand combatants—marginally fewer French than Russians—lay dead on the battlefield. Among the corpses was that of Jules de Canouville, for whom Pauline had so recently commissioned a new sword. It was later adduced that the bullet that had killed him had been fired by a fellow officer, rather than by any Russian. Some said the French marksman was jealous of de Canouville's relationship with Princess Borghese, others that Napoleon, wishing to put an immediate end to his sister's liaison, had given the order to fire. In the general carnage, it was impossible to substantiate such claims. What is certain is that the Conte di Saluzzo, who formed part of the Borghese suite in Turin and who was at Borodino, discreetly removed from around de Canouville's neck the miniature, set with brilliants, that depicted the princess.

Jules de Canouville's boasting of his liaison with his imperial lover, those headlong gallops to return to her pliant arms, were over, and the news of his death was communicated to the princess at Aix toward the end of September. The blow was severe. Apparently this braggart cavalier, with his joie de vivre and optimism, had touched in Pauline some chord that her other, more sophisticated lovers had not. Weeks later Pauline's librarian and confidant Ferrand wrote: "She does nothing but cry, she doesn't eat, and her health is altered." A journey to the Midi, toward the end of October, was planned, he added, in the hope that it would bring relief. Pauline was evidently suffering in body as well as mind and may even have gone through an operation in the south of France, as she ordered two liters of sulfuric ether—an anesthetic—from Paris at this time. However, the operation that one might think could have cured some of her troubles, a hysterectomy, was at this time so dangerous as to be very often fatal. It is unlikely that her doctors would have suggested it.

Further accounts of the ill-starred Russian campaign reached the French spa community in the course of that month. A week after the Battle of Borodino, Napoleon, with a reduced force of one hundred thousand men, entered Moscow, a city in flames. Its retreating governor, Prince Rostopchin, had given orders for it to be torched, and the fires burned for four days. Meanwhile Pauline recovered her spirits enough to address her steward on the subjects of her projected journey to the Midi and of her jewels: "Send me the amethyst parure, since Friese has finished it. With the carnelian earrings and parure I ordered from Nicolas. Also some bracelets, which must be finished by now. Send them by Lavalette. Tell Nicolas to finish, as we agreed, the turquoise parure, using the stones I bought from Picot." Were these pieces of jewelry intended purely for Pauline's adornment? Or did she see clouds gathering about her brother's Empire and mean to gather about her portable items she could dispose of easily? At the very least, she wished them in her possession and not in the hands of jewelers, who might prove fickle in uncertain times.

After visiting Archbishop Fesch in his diocese of Lyon, Pauline traveled on to Marseille, where Dr. Peyre awaited her. From Paris, Madame Mère rebuked Pauline in mid-November: "Yesterday I got a letter from you at last. I don't expect you to give yourself the trouble of writing when you are not in good health, but it seems to me you could easily give orders . . . for me to be informed of your health at least once a week. . . . Not doing so shows an indifference that has to affect me." But of course what Pauline wanted from her mother was reports of the emperor, reports that were not forthcoming, despite Madame Mère's privileged access to the Empress Marie Louise and—incidentally—to Napoleon's one-year-old heir, the King of Rome. "The Empress and King, whom I've seen this morning at Saint-Cloud," wrote Madame Mère, "are in the best of health. . . . We have no news of the army beyond what you've read in the *Moniteur.*"

THE REALITY WAS HARSH and hardly comforting. After occupying the ruined city of Moscow some weeks, while failing signally to win from Alexander his agreement to capitulate, Napoleon had taken the decision in October to retreat back across the Dnieper to Europe, rather than face a winter cut off from supply lines. This time it was the Russian general, Kutusov, who forced the pace, attacking the retreating and demoralized French army where it was weakest and forcing it, in the weeks that succeeded, along the Smolensk road, which had already been stripped bare of supplies by both armies.

Following the disastrous Battle of Berezina in late November, where the pursuing enemy savaged the remnants of the Grande Armée trying to cross the river, Napoleon abandoned his troops to the Russian snow. Even the cavalry was now on foot, as the horses, without fodder, had died or been killed for meat by starving soldiers. While the survivors tramped westward, in early December the emperor made for Paris in a sleigh, accompanied only by his former ambassador to St. Petersburg, Caulaincourt. His decision was hastened by the news that, in Paris, one General Malet had nearly staged a successful coup d'état when he had announced that Napoleon had been killed in combat in Russia. But, before he left, Napoleon prepared a bulletin, dated December 3, to be sent ahead to Paris. "I shall tell everything," he told Caulaincourt. "Full details now will mitigate the effect of the disasters that have to be announced later to the nation."

That same day Pauline settled at Hyères near Toulon, where she declared she would spend the winter. In this pretty town, three miles from the sea, she had the novel idea that she could take the air best on a swing in the garden of the villa she rented. Her suite—the Duc de Clermont-Tonnerre, Madame de Cavour, and Madame de Turbie—were now inured to their mistress's caprices, some selfish, some kind. She sent "productions of the Midi"—hams and salami—to her uncle Fesch at Lyon. "I will eat them in good company," he promised her, "at the feast I give to the authorities after the Te Deum to commemorate the emperor's coronation."

Authorities might have celebrated the coronation of eight years earlier in early December, but there appeared little to celebrate when, ten days later, the Twenty-ninth Bulletin of the Grande Armée was published in the *Moniteur,* giving details of the disastrous losses suffered during the Russian campaign. Nevertheless, when the emperor reached Paris, he was optimistic. "Fortune dazzled me. . . . I thought to gain in a year what only two campaigns [Alexander's capitulation and a peace treaty] could achieve," he said with a frankness that astonished his listeners. "I made a great blunder, but I shall yet recoup." On Christmas Day, Gaudin, the finance minister, wrote loyally to Pauline: "We have enjoyed now for eight days the Emperor's presence. He is arrived from Russia, as he came back from Egypt, when it seemed least permissible to expect him. . . . His Majesty's health is admirable. Since the first day, there has not been the least trace of fatigue on his face."

Did Pauline believe these cheerful words? Although Napoleon called for festivities to greet his return to Paris, the effect of the Twenty-ninth Bulletin, the first in twenty years to acknowledge defeat, lingered on. Private letters began to filter through to Paris, too, detailing the fates of those hundreds of thousands of French soldiers, including many officers of high rank, who had gone with the Grande Armée to Russia and not returned. Comte Montesquiou-Fezensac, who had, like Napoleon, survived the Russian campaign, later reflected on the *cercles* and parties at the Tuileries, those affairs of silk and lace: "I shall always remember one of those dismal balls, at which I felt as if I were dancing on the graves of those who had died in Russia."

Meanwhile Murat, claiming jaundice, had deserted the Grande Armée soon after Napoleon left it, to return to his Kingdom of Naples and forge ties with the Allied powers. It was left to Marshal Ney and to Eugène, Josephine's son, to bring the tattered forces of the Grande Armée—now numbering barely ten thousand men—to France, while King Frederick William of Prussia made a secret alliance with Alexander. Talleyrand felt certain: "It is the beginning of the end."

But if Pauline mourned her brother's failure in Russia as well as de Canouville's death in Russia, she did not intend to show it. In January 1813 she received at Hyères—a gift from the emperor—a Sèvres *cabaret*, or tea and coffee service, embellished with the portraits of celebrated women from history. Pauline returned it with the request that the empress go to the manufactory and select instead portraits of her brother to adorn the china. Significantly, however, early that same month, she commissioned the imperial cabinetmakers Jacob to produce a repository that would hold all her jewels—those she had bought, those Napoleon had given her, those Camillo had lavished on her on their marriage, and those that were, in fact, Borghese heirlooms that she treated as her own. It was thus to be of a substantial size, and, with bronze decoration by the imperial goldsmith Thomire, it was to cost fourteen thousand francs.

Pauline was thinking ahead. Although her jewelry collection in this cabinet would not be portable, it could be kept in a safe place, and pieces released for sale should her brother's rule end abruptly. Her mother, who had still a lively remembrance of being a refugee with a family to support twenty years earlier, appears to have supported Pauline's project. She wrote from Paris: "Monsieur Decazes [Madame Mère's secretary] will have informed you of the fine necklace of pearls you have been offered. Four rows of them, and the owner wants 100,000 francs." Mere cupidity was not at stake here, but future survival.

But none of these plans did Pauline confide to her suite, and when she left Hyères for the sea breezes of Nice in February, she continued an imperious mistress. Her *lectrice*, Mademoiselle de Quincy, complained,

"We don't see a living soul, we spend our time watching Her Royal Highness move from bed to bed, and we only dream of attending the Carnival entertainments." Pauline's household has been well dubbed "the Ministry of Caprices," and Dr. Peyre was dismissed after ten years of service, a handsome though inexperienced physician, Dr. Espiaud, taking his place. Captain Duchand, who had traveled with Pauline to Marseille and Hyères, had been declared fit for military duty and had left to join an army that Napoleon was amassing to fight Prussia, which, as had been expected, declared war on the emperor in March. "Never have the French shown more zeal and attachment to their sovereign and their country," wrote Archchancellor Cambacérès to Pauline, informing her of Napoleon's departure for the theater of war.

But there was some point to Pauline's caprices now. More often than not they involved economy. Her financial prudence began when she reduced the salary of her steward, Monsieur Michelot, while informing him in the same letter that he was to dismiss most of the staff of the Hôtel Charost in Paris and sell the horses. Often her caprices involved arrangements for the disposal of assets, as when she offered Montgobert to the Leclerc family, or calculated the value of Neuilly or of the house in Paris. But although she fretted about her health, about her wardrobe—thinking nothing of sending urgently for cashmere shawls to Constantinople—and about her finances, Pauline was curiously cavalier about her personal safety. She resisted all requests from her mother to leave Nice—"I am very worried to think you are so close to the enemy, in the event of an invasion," Madame Mère wrote—and departed for her old haunt, Gréoux-les-Bains, in May only when the heat in Nice became oppressive.

While taking the waters at Gréoux, Pauline had, at least, the consolation of knowing, if she cared, that Duchand had survived the battles of May 1813 at Lützen and at Bautzen, from which Napoleon had emerged victorious. Indeed, in the latter bloody combat, despite having had two horses shot from under him, Duchand had captured a battery. Madame Mère wrote to Pauline in high spirits of the effect on the public mood of the victories: "May a solid and stable peace ensue." But the armistice and peace congress that followed did not result in terms that Napoleon accepted. By August France was back at war with the Allies, whose armies in the field totaled eight hundred thousand. Meanwhile Wellington's June victory over French troops at Vitória, if it had released troops for combat elsewhere, had signaled the end of the Napoleonic Empire in Spain.

Flitting between Gréoux and another former residence, La Mignarde, at Aix-en-Provence, Pauline was back at Gréoux in August when news of fresh losses in Germany reached her. At the Battle of Grossbeeren on August 23, Bernadotte, Désirée Clary's husband, former marshal of France and now, as Crown Prince of Sweden, on the Allied side, defeated Marshal Nicholas Charles Oudinot. The following day the Austrian field marshal Blücher defeated Marshal Macdonald, Pauline's former lover, at Katzbach. Two days later at the Battle of Dresden, a partial victory for Napoleon, the turncoat Moreau was in conference with the czar when his legs were blown off. He died, his last words being "Calm yourselves, gentlemen, it is my destiny."

Pauline, as usual, evinced only confidence in her brother, as the carnage being wreaked in Germany continued. "Thank you for the dress you had embroidered for me," she wrote calmly to Madame Michelot in September from Gréoux. "I leave in a month for Nice, where I will spend the winter." But everything changed when she received news of the disastrous Battle of the Nations, which took place at Leipzig over three days in October, where the French imperial forces suffered losses of at least forty-five thousand. Among them was one of Pauline's most distinguished lovers, General Poniatowski, who had become a marshal of France the day before and was now leading the Polish contingent. Covered with wounds, while retreating over a bridge he fell backward and drowned, or was killed by friendly fire. At Leipzig the Allies had not only inflicted a great defeat on the French emperor, but they thereafter dissolved the Confederation of the Rhine.

"The latest news has affected me badly," wrote Pauline from Nice to her mother's secretary, Decazes. She had enjoined silence, she said, on all her suite in relation to all political affairs. But, besides this censorship, she had a more practical project: "I am sending with this to Paris my valet, Merlin, whom you may trust. Talk openly to him. I need to know the state of my account, for I have offered 300,000 francs to the Emperor." A necklace—a diamond one—that she had recently bought was to be sold, she instructed, to meet this demand on her purse. In addition she required him to have all her remaining jewels placed with Madame Mère. Pauline was preparing herself for all eventualities.

Eight days later, writing from Gotha on October 25, Napoleon conditionally accepted his sister's remarkable offer. "My expenses have been considerable this year," he wrote euphemistically and envisaged that the campaigns of 1814 and 1815 would be similarly expensive. "The will of my people is such that I think I will have the means necessary for campaigns, if the coalition of Europe against France continues. If I don't meet with success [with the Senate], then I'll use your money."

Pauline remained at Nice, her health declining, as the news grew steadily less encouraging. The nature of Pauline's sufferings is unclear, and they may have been nervous in origin, but there was no doubting her weakness. "She has got pitiably thin, and crisis follows crisis," wrote the Comtesse de Cavour in early 1814, adding that the librarian Ferrand guarded Her Imperial Highness's door—"as an Angel bars the door to paradise"—and, with Dr. Espiaud, conspired to keep from the princess all bad news. There was certainly enough of it. The Dutch had ejected the French in November 1813; in December the Austrians occupied Switzerland. "When the Emperor's soldiers report some small victory," the countess continued, "he has the governor fire cannons to please her."

The members of Pauline's suite were anxious for her safety, and for their own. The princess spoke of going to Paris in the spring, and of her eagerness to see her family there. But her household did not think that, in her state of health, she could be moved farther than Lyon, even if an Allied invasion threatened. Meanwhile Pauline appeared impervious to danger, refusing calls from her mother to hurry immediately to Paris. Instead, from her bed she continued to make economies, erasing at a stroke from her different households secretaries, surgeons, valets, lackeys, and sending Mademoiselle de Quincy to gather all liquid cash and other portable valuables in Paris and deposit them with Madame Mère.

Then, in January 1814, the Allies announced that they were fighting against the French emperor alone, as he had rejected terms that, in their stated view, the French people would have accepted. This declaration on the part of the Allies did at last fire up the emperor in Paris to exert himself. "Invaders?" he questioned one doubting Thomas at the Tuileries. "Do you see Cossacks in Paris? They're not here yet, and I haven't lost all my skills." To prove it, as the English advanced northward on France over the Pyrenees from Spain, as other Allied forces moved into the northern and eastern French territories, Napoleon defended his capital in a brilliant "Six Days' Campaign."

Pauline's spirits revived, her health improved, and she rose from her bed to scold Monsieur Michelot and countermand all the orders she had so recently sent him. She was coming to Paris and would be there in six weeks. Her jewels were all to be returned to the Hôtel Charost. "I am sure you acted from good intentions," she wrote graciously, "but you needed to have a little more confidence in the Emperor, and less haste. If the victories continue"—and Pauline appears to have had no doubt that they would—"everything is to be put back just as it was. I don't want any confusion."

But confusion was, regrettably, to be the order of the day. Despite the individual victories of Champaubert, of Montmirail, of Vauchamps, and of Château-Thierry, Napoleon failed to withstand the Allied invasion. In late March the French capital fell to the Allies, and, for the first time since the Hundred Years' War, a foreign army marched down its streets. The Parisians had earlier watched silently as Marie Louise, the three-year-old King of Rome, Hortense, and other members of the Bonaparte clan had departed the city. Napoleon, who had fought his way as far as Fontainebleau, was forced to abdicate on April 11 and accept in lieu the Kingdom of Elba, a small island off the coast of Tuscany. The emperor betrayed no immediate emotion, but five days later he wrote to Josephine, who was at Navarre, to say that he felt a great burden lifted from him. He intended, he said, to write the history of his reign. It would "prove most curious, for till now I have been perceived in profile only. But I shall not tell the whole. I have heaped benefits on thousands of ungrateful wretches, and what have they done? They have betrayed me." Meanwhile, to the throne of France ascended Louis XVIII, an elderly gentleman who had been living elsewhere on the Continent and in England since his brother Louis XVI had been executed in the Revolution twenty years before. "What is a throne?— a bit of wood gilded and covered in velvet. I am the state," Napoleon had said. No longer, and at Fontainebleau on April 20 he said his adieux to the former Imperial Guard, who had served his every wish.

His adieux were not concluded, however. At the Château Bouillidiou, a gloomy country house in the Var near Saint-Raphaël and Fréjus, where Napoleon would in due course embark for Elba, Pauline waited. Others who had been a part of the imperial adventure and who were now fleeing France offered to take her with them. She refused, and the pope's former delegate to Paris, Cardinal Pacca, found her "pale as death but full of spirit." To her sister Elisa's husband, Bacciochi, she was obdurate: "I have not always loved the Emperor as I should, but as my brother he has a claim on my allegiance. The Emperor is passing by here. I must offer him my condolences and, if he wishes it, follow him to Elba."

Was Pauline serious in this? Such were the Allied governments' suspicions of Napoleon's intentions, and of his sister's, following his abdication that they had provided two regiments of Liechtensteiner guards to patrol the park of the château where Pauline waited. Austrian troops, meanwhile, bivouacked close by. One possibility envisaged was that, with his family's help, the former emperor might reignite loyalties in France and return to scotch the restoration of the monarchy. As a result the interview between brother and sister, when it occurred, was closely monitored by the Austrian and British officers who had Napoleon in their keeping.

Nobody was prepared for the cry of outrage that the princess emitted on seeing her brother. On the journey south the former emperor had lost all presence of mind. Sweating and moaning, he had been convulsed by nameless terrors, as well as by palpable fear of the populace who crowded around the carriage. At different times he had changed coats with one of his companions, in an effort to escape the mob's attention, and he appeared before his sister, still flustered, and dressed in the greatcoat of an Austrian general.

"How can I embrace you when you wear the enemy uniform?" Pauline asked, refusing to hold any further dialogue until her brother had changed into his familiar gray redingote. Then she tenderly caressed him. Her actions, the enemy officers observed, had a most marked effect on the former emperor. Losing his fear, he descended into the courtyard of the château and spoke to the local people gathered there. Some of the menfolk had previously been in imperial service, and one of them he recognized.

Upon his return to the princess, brother and sister, who had not met since the spring of 1812, spoke long and intimately of what had passed, and he accepted without demur the offer of her company on Elba. Naturally—Pauline being Pauline—she could not travel there immediately, for she meant first to take the waters on Ischia. That the island of Ischia was part of the Kingdom of Naples and her brother-in-law Murat one of the Allied leaders did not weigh with her. Nor does it appear to have troubled Napoleon. The Allied governments, however, were perplexed to know what sort of plot might be being hatched.

As evidence of her devotion to her brother, that night Pauline—not known for giving up her creature comforts lightly—offered her quarters at the Château Bouillidiou to the emperor and stayed at a less commodious house nearby. While Napoleon set sail next day for Elba, she bent her attention to the interesting question: Which transport should she gratify with her custom? It had been arranged that the English frigate *Undaunted* would return for her after it had taken Napoleon to Elba. But Murat had sent *Laetitia* from Naples, and a Royal Navy officer, Captain John Tower, was offering the use of his frigate, *Curaçao*, which lay at Nice.

In the end Princess Borghese chose to board the Neapolitan frigate at Saint-Raphaël, while the *Curaçao* sailed alongside to await further commands. France and Pauline Bonaparte had looked their last on each other, but in Naples she was her usual *exigeante* self, writing to Madame Michelot, "Please make sure that the bonnets and dresses you send are better packed than the last ones . . . don't forget to send me some new books. . . . Address them to the Neapolitan Minister at Paris. . . . I have arrived, extremely tired and in need of everything."

CHAPTER FOURTEEN

Diamonds on the Battlefield, 1814–1815

ALTHOUGH SHE HAD TRUMPETED her intention of joining the emperor in exile, Princess Borghese delayed at Naples for some months after her arrival there in June 1814. This did not, however, prevent her from lambasting her brother Joseph and sister Elisa, who showed no sign of proceeding to Elba at all. "One should not leave the Emperor all alone," she wrote. (Napoleon had kept his title, under the terms of the Treaty of Fontainebleau, though he had lost the Empire that gave it substance.) "It's now, when he is miserable, that one should show him affection. Or that's how I see it," she wrote to her mother at the end of the month, urging Madame Mère to precede her to the island.

To compound Napoleon's unhappiness, he had suffered a serious loss. His ex-wife, the Empress Josephine, who had been much feted by the Allied sovereigns upon their arrival in Paris in May, had subsequently caught a chill and died. Meanwhile Hortense, who had for some time lived separately from her husband, Louis Bonaparte, and had remained in Paris on her mother's account, did not thereafter leave the capital. This breached Napoleon's directive, the emperor having declared, according to Pauline, that "none of our family could establish themselves in France without it being an act of gross treachery." An exception was apparently made for the empress Marie Louise, who was following a cure at Aix-les-Bains, and whom the emperor affected to believe would soon join him on Elba. But Hortense, upon whom the attractions of Restoration Paris were not lost, chose to believe that her brother-in-law and former stepfather's reign was firmly over. (There were others who had marked his words at Fontainebleau in April: "I shall return when the violets bloom again.") Pauline saw herself, on the other hand, as triumphantly *sans peur et sans reproche* (without fear and without reproach). For not only was she, in due course, going to winter on Elba, but, at the beginning of June, en route from France to Naples, she had stopped overnight to inspect the emperor's new island domain.

VERY DIFFERENT from the Tuileries was I Mulini, the modest house with a garden that surmounted Portoferraio, Elba's harbor, now capital of Napoleon's kingdom. Moreover, there was no glittering throng or splendid officers to adorn receptions in the poorly frescoed rooms. For company—and as, respectively, grand marshal, governor, and military governor—Napoleon had just three generals, Bertrand, Drouot, and Cambronne—all three more loyal than brilliant. The mood could have been somber, after Napoleon's guard had welcomed the princess with salutes and cannon fire. But the Bonapartes proved now as ever adaptable. In the course of twenty-four hours Pauline dined one day with her brother and the next with his generals. She made a tour of inspection of the island, driving out with the emperor, and above all she made energetic arrangements to obtain the disparate elements that, in her opinion, were required to make life palatable upon her return to Elba. Furniture from Paris, a band of musicians, and orange trees for the garden from Naples—there was nothing the princess did not think of or plan for. Up at I Mulini she handed Grand Marshal Bertrand a necklace. It was to be sold, she told him, and a tract of land purchased to provide a country house for her and her brother, away from the humid air of Portoferraio.

Instructions too went to Madame Michelot in Paris, who had so ably and for so many years interpreted Pauline's demands. Madame was not to leave to her husband the important business of selecting the belongings that were to be sent to Elba. "You know better than he what will be useful to me," Pauline wrote. (Twenty packing cases full of mirrors, clocks, and candelabra in due course arrived on the island.) Then she departed the island fiefdom, so hurriedly that it was believed that she and her brother had quarreled. In fact Pauline had interests of her own to address before she could return to Elba and adopt the guise of "comforting angel."

From Naples in June she told her brother Lucien that she had plans to visit Rome: "I count on you to present my homage to His Holiness the Pope and remind him that I hope he will consider me still as one of the most faithful of his flock." Given that the pope had so long been their brother the emperor's prisoner, these remarks warrant some explanation. In May, Allied forces had returned the pope to Rome and restored to the Vatican the territories that had been ruled by the French since 1808. Meanwhile Lucien Bonaparte had been under house arrest in England, though he had played no part in the imperial drama, having quarreled with Napoleon long before. Now the English exile returned to Rome and to his large family. The pope, recognizing Lucien's neutral status, gave him the title of Prince of Canino. As for Pauline, it would seem that, during the pope's imprisonment at Fontainebleau, she had taken pains to preserve her courteous relationship with him from Roman days. At any rate she was now, not unnaturally, keeping her options open on the question of a permanent residence. Not only Lucien but her brother Louis, her mother, and her uncle Fesch had all been accepted by the pope as residents of Rome. If Paris was denied her, Rome, much as she had disliked it when living with Camillo, was now an acceptable alternative.

Relations with Camillo were also on Pauline's mind. "Tell me a little of Borghese," she instructed Lucien in Rome. "He has given no sign of life." In the general and sudden dismemberment of the Napoleonic Empire that had followed after the Allies took Paris in April, Camillo had left Turin and headed south—but not before he had packed up the numerous family treasures he had imported from Rome and dis-

played in the northern Italian city during his period there as French
governor-general. By a curious twist of fate the ship carrying some
of his possessions—among them the famous statue of Pauline, reclining, as Venus Victorious—made landfall at Elba in July. Napoleon,
while awaiting his sister's return, attempted to claim her marble image.
But to no avail. The statue proceeded to Rome, where it was installed
in the Palazzo Borghese.

Camillo, however, was not so fortunate. The pope, though ready to
forgive Bonaparte sins, had been poorly treated as a prisoner in Savona,
part of Governor-General Borghese's fiefdom. Now he refused to allow
the prince to return to Rome, on the ground that he was living an
immoral life. It was true that the prince had, while in Turin, formed an
attachment to a widowed cousin, the Duchessa Lante. Her company
and that of her three daughters had proved congenial after the fireworks of life with Pauline. Now Camillo was forced, with the duchess
and her daughters, to take up residence in his palace in Florence. But
there too he found life agreeable—until Pauline intervened to bedevil
his existence once more.

Camillo had heard that the princess had the Hôtel Charost up for
sale, so he arranged to have the Borghese collection that adorned the
walls of the Paris house returned to Rome. Pauline was immediately up
in arms. "Don't give any picture up, whoever he sends," she instructed
Michelot in mid-July. "Take twenty-five of the best paintings out of
their frames and hide them somewhere safe. If they ask for them, say
you sent them to me." The missing works would, the princess noted
with satisfaction, be useful as bargaining tools in the financial arrangements she expected to make with the prince, now that the Empire was
at an end. As an afterthought, she instructed Michelot to send, with
the twenty cases that were en route to Elba, the Borghese silver that had
graced her dining room in Paris.

Pauline's principal concern, when not arranging for her residence
on Elba, was to rid herself of her properties in France. Although the
Treaty of Fontainebleau had allowed her an income from the French
government—never to be paid—of three hundred thousand francs, she

was not convinced that the Bourbons would long allow her to own the Hôtel Charost, Neuilly, and Montgobert. To avoid sequestration her intention was to sell them one by one, and, by the end of April, she had let it be known that she wished to dispose of her town house. During the Allied sovereigns' May balls to celebrate Louis XVIII's accession to the throne, the Austrian emperor Francis I occupied the house. But it was quite a different power who expressed an interest in the house later in the summer of 1814. And it was no sovereign who wrote, "I have come into her house," on August 29, but Arthur Wellesley, newly created Duke of Wellington, who had earlier trounced Napoleon's forces in Spain.

But for a disagreement between his brother and the British prime minister, Lord Liverpool, the new duke would have been given a position in the London government. As it was, Wellington had been appointed British ambassador to the court of Louis XVIII, and, casting about for a Paris residence, he settled on the Hôtel Charost. (Meanwhile the Prussians bought for their Paris residence Eugène's *hôtel* on the rue de Lille.) After negotiation with Pauline's notary, Edon, the British government agreed to pay "by installments" a sum of 863,000 francs for the house, its sumptuous contents—valued at 300,000 francs and listed in a detailed inventory—and stables.

For some weeks, before his mousy wife, Kitty, arrived to cramp his style, Wellington could revel in Pauline's grand bed, examine his reflection in the princess's mirrors, and entertain in her dining room and grand saloons. Now it was his turn to pay for the candles—in candelabra on tables and on mantelpieces, in chandeliers above, four tiers deep—that illumined the poppy red silk, the bronzes, and bright gold of the *hôtel*'s Empire decor. Honoring the previous enemy occupation, the duke hung Princess Borghese's portrait on one side of a likeness of Pius VII. On the pope's other side, he placed a portrait of La Grassini, the singer who had once granted the "last favors" to Napoleon, and was now energetically lavishing them on the Iron Duke. "Exactly like Our Lord between the two thieves," exclaimed the Comte d'Artois on seeing the trio of portraits. As for the duke's opinion of Pauline, whom he was destined never to meet, he described her to a niece as a "heartless little devil." But on his return to London, when he hung a certain Waterloo chamber, the only portrait of a woman among a mass of field marshals and scenes of battle was that of—Pauline Borghese.

Meanwhile Madame Mère had answered Pauline's call to arms and, leaving Rome for Elba at the beginning of August, settled in unassuming apartments close to I Mulini. Her presence was believed by the Bonaparte family to bring her son comfort. But, as the old lady was increasingly absorbed by the mysticism to which the Abbé Buonavita, a Corsican in her suite, had introduced her, and as Napoleon disliked anything but the most orthodox faith, that comfort was necessarily circumscribed. Nevertheless Sir Neil Campbell, the British commissioner whose responsibilities were now limited to reporting on the emperor's movements, wrote to Castlereagh, the British foreign secretary, in mid-September: "I begin to think he is quite resigned to his retreat." And Madame Ducluzel, once Dermide's governess and now Pauline's attendant, who spent some time quarantined offshore, said, "I would be happy to live at Portoferraio. The town seems to me a little Paris. There are fine grenadiers and handsome Poles on horseback. One would think one hadn't left France."

Following the melancholy into which he had plunged on hearing news of Josephine's death, Napoleon had been cheered by a secret visit from Marie Walewska. She brought with her to a mountain rendezvous in the Elban hinterland their young son, Alexandre, and promised to return. But no such promises were forthcoming from Marie Louise, who had been given the Duchy of Parma by the Allied powers. And the three-year-old King of Rome, now known as the Prince of Parma, remained with his mother. Napoleon was, in consequence, delighted to welcome Pauline when she finally left Naples at the end of October and arrived in Portoferraio on November 1. Though she had delayed, the princess was magnificent when she appeared. At the ball that Napoleon gave to welcome her—and where the orchestra played, as well as the "Marseillaise," the popular air "Où peut-on être mieux qu'au sein de sa famille?" ("Where can one better be than in the midst of one's family?")—her gaiety and beauty greatly enlivened the proceedings. To Pons de l'Hérault, governor of the lucrative island iron mines, whom Napoleon had co-opted to form part of his household, she was Napoleon's "good angel . . . the treasure of the palace." Further, he declared that, such was the princess's obvious attachment to her brother, if the emperor had struck her she would have said, "Let him do it, if it gives him pleasure."

When Pauline appeared in a dress of black velvet that displeased Napoleon, she went to take it off. Her appearance in a white dress caused him to ask if she was dressed *à la victime*. Again she retired to change. And finally, when the emperor directed the princess to put away her fine jewelry, as she outshone the other women, who had none, she complied. In short, while Pauline had not revered her brother as he would have wished when he was emperor of the French, she now paid him full homage—and, leading by example others at the court in exile, she never crossed his path in the dingy drawing room at I Mulini without making a deep curtsey.

An enemy press would later seize upon these examples of Pauline's self-abnegation in Elba to claim that she and Napoleon enjoyed an incestuous relationship at I Mulini. There was certainly the opportunity. Once indeed Pons de l'Hérault saw Napoleon plant a kiss on his sister's mouth. "It is the custom in Corsica," said the emperor. But Pauline was used flagrantly to exercise power over the men whom she was currently bedding, and Pons de l'Hérault and other witnesses noted no such displays. One may conclude that, while the relationship between Pauline and her brother had at different times earlier been sexually charged, on Elba she provided succor rather than sex.

Indeed Princess Borghese found after some weeks that the emperor was growing morose, disenchanted with his island kingdom and with the few entertainments to be had, which, upon his first arrival, he had pursued with energy. Pauline set to and established a small coterie of attractive women—wives of the officers serving on Elba and a Greek interpreter's wife—who could be counted on to coax her brother out of the doldrums. And Napoleon, who had no interest in isolation unless it was to plan military and strategic maneuvers, brightened and acceded to his sister's wishes for parties and picnics—the weather was still clement—and airings and balls.

Although Pauline was pleased with the success of her plans, her health remained an issue, and one that she and her mother took seriously. They were right to be concerned, as her ailments at different times included sacroiliac pain, salpingitis, and even anemia and jaundice, remnants of the bouts of yellow fever she had endured in Saint-Domingue. To this we can probably add gonorrhea, unless the application of leeches in Aix-les-Bains or other medication had cured her. But Napoleon would have no truck with his sister's valetudinarianism. He recommended instead fresh air, as the princess informed Pons de l'Hérault in tragic tones when the governor met her in the lower part of the town. She was being bumped down the steep steps on a litter, and de l'Hérault did wonder if her brother had not just intended her to stand at an open window. But de l'Hérault had grown to understand, as had others who spent time in the princess's company, that she required to be thought of, first and foremost, as an invalid. Indeed, the princess was furious when de l'Hérault said, on New Year's Day 1815, that she looked "as fresh and healthy" as the roses he had seen in the garden that morning.

One of Napoleon's servants, the mameluke Ali, was censorious of Pauline and of her caprices. She dressed like a girl of eighteen, he declared, and yet, under her makeup, she was plainly a woman in her thirties. (Pauline had turned thirty-four in October.) She pleaded illness, then danced vigorously at the balls she gave in her apartments. And she would have gone on till late into the night, he claimed, only her brother intervened to draw the proceedings to a halt. Indeed, for want of any on-island lover Pauline seized upon her brother's generals for partners. But, after an energetic dance, Cambronne declared he would rather risk gunfire again than accompany her once more into the fray, and Drouot was similarly unpromising material who preferred his Bible to the dance floor.

Pauline does not appear to have borne any grudge against the gen-

erals who spurned her. But, perhaps contemplating the revival of a former romance, she wrote to Madame Michelot for news of Duchand,
who had last visited her just before she left for Naples. Meanwhile she
saw to the construction of a theater on the site of a demolished church,
below I Mulini, and arranged a program of plays. She drove out with
the emperor to inspect San Martino, the country house that was being
prepared for their occupancy. And she wrote tranquilly enough: "There
are great winds here, the weather is very changeable. I enjoy being with
my brother, but I am anxious for the future."

Pauline's anxiety was, in part, inspired by her brother's restlessness,
although the failure of Montgobert and Neuilly to find buyers disturbed her too. Napoleon had news that the Allied powers at the Congress of Vienna were quarreling. In Paris, moreover, Louis XVIII had
not proved popular, and a kind of quiet anarchy obtained, in which
hopes that Napoleon would return and overthrow the Bourbons were
openly and covertly expressed. On the Paris boulevards violets, as a
symbol of that hope, were to be seen in hats alongside the Bourbon
white cockade. When Napoleon's supporters met, to the question "Do
you believe in Jesus Christ?" the required response was "Yes, and in his
resurrection." The English were detested, and Pauline's house in Paris
lay empty after the British government thought it politic to remove
Wellington from the capital and send him to Vienna.

Napoleon began to think that a bid for power might yet prove successful, and Pauline, as she told Pons de l'Hérault, found her brother
more inclined to solitude and reverie. Nevertheless, she continued to
plan entertainments in the emperor's honor. She persisted in her guise,
to use Pons de l'Hérault's words, as "the princess, so gay, so sweet, and
whose every word was an expression of grace and pleasure. Whose
lively face and animated regards, whose enchanting smile gave life and
spirit to all who approached her." And among the fetes she planned was
a ball to be held on February 26.

Rarely can the refusal of an invitation to a party have had such an
effect upon the destiny of Europe. For when the British resident, Sir
Neil Campbell, received—on February 16—Pauline's request that he

attend her ball ten days later, he wrote that he was unable to accept. He was bound for Florence, where he intended to consult a doctor, and would not return to Elba until the ball was over. (Campbell suffered from deafness as a result of head wounds incurred in the Spanish campaign. But he was also being economical with the truth, as he had a mistress in Livorno, whom he intended to visit.) Pauline showed this note to her brother, and, so the story goes, once Sir Neil was safely gone, the emperor asked her to bring the ball forward by several days. But he told neither her nor his mother the reason why, until after the ball was over, on the evening of the twenty-fifth. Taking first Madame Mère and then Pauline into the garden of I Mulini, Napoleon explained that the following day he planned to take ship for the southern coast of France. A few hundred men would accompany him, and, from there, gathering support, he would advance on Paris. In his opinion, and according to information he had received, many of the regiments stationed on his route north would declare for his cause. Meanwhile, in Naples, Murat—who had turned his coat once in favor of the Allies—had once more pledged his support, and a substantial number of troops, for the emperor.

Pauline, mournful but practical, offered her brother a diamond necklace worth five hundred thousand francs that could be sold should money be scarce. The stones, upon being accepted, were entrusted to Marchand, Napoleon's valet, but the latter was shocked by the princess's wretched appearance. "Don't abandon him, Marchand. Take care of him," she said. Kissing her hand, the valet thought to encourage her by saying she would be soon reunited with her brother. But Pauline answered that she did not believe she would ever see Napoleon again.

The inhabitants of Elba were hardly less perturbed than Pauline when they learned of the emperor's plans from Napoleon's chamberlain, General Lapi: "Inhabitants of Elba, our august sovereign, recalled by Providence to his glorious career, is about to quit our island. He has left me in charge and, says that, as a proof of his confidence in you, he leaves his mother and sister to your protection." The renown that the small island had enjoyed during Napoleon's stay would now be a thing of the past. But the emperor's arrangements for a swift departure were unstoppable. He shut the gates of the harbor before Lapi made his announcement, so that no shipping could carry the news abroad. And by eight in the evening on February 26, when Napoleon went on board the brig *L'Inconstant* that was to carry him over to France, all his officers, troops, horses, and supplies were embarked and ready to depart on that and other transports.

That afternoon Bertrand, Drouot, Cambronne, and Pons de l'Hérault, who were all to accompany the emperor, had come to say their adieux to the princess. According to de l'Hérault, she was pale, her eyes were bathed in tears, and her lips were without color. He hardly recognized this doleful woman as the gay hostess who had charmed him all winter. "Good-bye, my friends," she said, and kissed each of them in turn. "May success attend you. Take care of my brother. Send me news." And then, after saying a last good-bye to Napoleon, Pauline waited to hear the outcome of his bid for power in France. At the same time she prepared herself for the return of Sir Neil Campbell, and the consequences to herself of her brother's departure from Elba.

It was two days later that the *Partridge* brought a mildly apprehensive Sir Neil back to Portoferraio from Livorno. Campbell had heard, while in Tuscany, that the Polish cavalrymen on Elba were mending their saddles, and that cases of plate belonging to Pauline had been transported to the Tuscan coast. In consequence he wished to assure himself that the emperor was not meditating leaving Elba. But he was not seriously concerned and had recently told Castlereagh that their prisoner appeared to have lost all ambition and had grown fat and idle.

Upon his arrival in Portoferraio, Campbell learned that he had been deceived and that Napoleon "with all his generals, and all his French, Polish and Corsican troops" had evacuated the island. "Your brother has broken his parole," he said to Pauline, "for he promised not to leave the island, but the Mediterranean is full of shipping, and"—predicted Campbell—"he is now a prisoner."

Pauline replied that that was no way to speak to a woman. And in fact news soon came that Napoleon and his six hundred men had landed in the Gulf of Saint-Juan near Antibes on March 1 and were gathering support as they marched north. But, to torment the anguished Campbell, Pauline declared that she was very disturbed by her brother's departure. She "laid hold of my hand and pressed it to her heart," wrote the British resident, "so that I might feel how much she was agitated. However, she did not appear to be so, and there was rather a smile upon her face."

Pauline had apparently shaken off her earlier presentiments that her brother's mission would fail. But in fact, while Campbell left the island in search of Napoleon, and while, in France, increasing numbers of soldiers mustered around Napoleon's standard as he headed for Paris, Pauline organized her own departure from Elba—for Italy. Although the intention had been for her and her mother to join Napoleon in Paris, once he was secure there, she was worried, following threats that Campbell had made in their interview, that she would be interned by the Allied powers. And so she took the decision to strike out on her own and seek sanctuary with Lucien in Rome—whether temporary or permanent remained to be seen. But from that base she intended to negotiate with Camillo.

Leaving Madame Mère at Portoferraio, Pauline and Madame Ducluzel embarked with another attendant, Madame Molo, and her mother, Madame Lebel, in an open felucca on the night of March 4. Lieutenant Monier, one of Napoleon's officers who had been on the dependent island of Pianosa when the emperor left Elba, was their guide, and, after an uncomfortable journey, they landed at Viareggio on the Tuscan coast. Hearing that Signor Raffaello Mansi, who had been such an affable host in Lucca and in Bagni di Lucca, was in residence at his villa in Viareggio, Pauline sent to ask for accommodation. But Mansi had no wish, now that an Austrian grand duke ruled Tuscany, to be associated with Princess Borghese and her Bonaparte clan. He begged off, claiming that his family was in residence at the villa, so there was no room.

Balked, Pauline applied to take up residence in her sister Elisa's former villa at Compignano, which lay between Viareggio and Lucca. In this she was successful. But unfortunately Elisa was disputing with Austria its claim to Lucca and its territories, which included Compignano. (She asserted that the city, anciently a republic, had made an autonomous decision in 1805 to declare her and her husband, Felice Bacciochi, their sovereigns.) Elisa had been interned at Brünn (now Brno, Czech Republic) by the Austrians and could hardly lay claim to her villa at Compignano in person. Nevertheless the Austrian governor at Lucca, Colonel Wercklein, sent a detachment of cavalry to occupy the park, and Princess Borghese was permitted very restricted access to the outside world. One of those allowed through was the priest whom she had asked to come from Lucca. As she took her bath behind a curtain while he said mass on the other side of it, it could be argued that their contact was minimal.

The news that Louis XVIII had fled and that Napoleon had been carried into the Tuileries on March 20, that he was once more emperor of the French, gave Pauline fresh energy. She dictated urgent directives: "She does not wish her household to be named before she arrives, above all she refuses to have back anyone who left her." But it was not only the composition of her household in Paris that occupied her. Although her correspondence was restricted, letters and couriers appeared often enough during April and May for the princess to grasp the salient details of the situation in France.

Once back in Paris, Napoleon was having to present himself as a constitutional monarch to a people who had bad memories of his dictatorship. It was no easy task, but upon it depended his domestic security and that of his family. "I am growing old. The repose of a constitutional king may suit me," he said. "It will more surely suit my son." Moreover, upon hearing the news of Napoleon's advance on Paris, the Allied powers in Vienna had disbanded the congress and each had pledged 150,000 troops to put into the field against the emperor, whom they declared an outlaw. Napoleon could therefore count on fighting an invasion force before he could fully count on the loyalty of his people.

In the circumstances Pauline had no great hope of a long reign in

France for her brother but was eager for him to bring pressure on the Austrian authorities to free her, while he was still in government. Monier, who had remained with her following the flight from Elba, managed to evade the Austrian guards at Compignano in May and bring Pauline's plight to the emperor's attention in Paris. Upon Napoleon's orders the French chargé d'affaires then pleaded in Florence with the Austrian grand duke: "The arrest of a woman is against all received usage. There can be no interest in holding her."

In addition, Napoleon ordered Decrès, now once again minister of marine and colonies, to send a frigate to wait off Viareggio for the princess, should she be freed. But the frigate was never sent, and in the meantime Pauline's health had deteriorated. After doctors from Lucca, from Pisa, and from Viareggio had been summoned to give their opinions of her case, it was judged urgently necessary by all that she take the waters at Bagni di Lucca. Reluctantly Colonel Wercklein let her go, and at the beginning of June, Princess Borghese took up residence in the bathing station where she had last stayed when the news of Dermide's death was broken to her.

Meanwhile, in Paris, growing discontent with Napoleon's "reforms" had culminated in a liberal politician who opposed the emperor being elected president of the Chamber of Deputies at the gaudy Champ de Mai—a ceremonial to ratify the new constitution, in fact deferred till the beginning of June. But the emperor had no time to brood on such setbacks and indeed said that it was not the time to engage in subtle discussions when the enemy ram was at the gates. On June 12 he set off with fewer than two hundred thousand men to do battle for the northeastern frontier of France, where the Allied forces had massed.

Pauline was at Bagni to receive news of the fatal outcome of this battle at Waterloo on June 18, which ended Napoleon's hundred days of power. Napoleon, pale and sluggish in his slate-colored greatcoat, left Marshal Ney to direct operations for much of the encounter. Even when he roused himself to take command, however, he was undone by his belief that the Prussians, under Marshal Blücher, could not come in time to the aid of the British forces commanded by the Duke of

Wellington. The Prussians duly proved him wrong, fighting their way to the battlefield through rain and mud. The Allies triumphed, and Napoleon made for Paris, in hopes that he could organize national resistance. But he soon saw that that was a task beyond even him. "Dare to do it," urged his brother Lucien, who had, those last months, been in Paris, putting aside quarrels with Napoleon to support his brother's bid for power. "I have dared too much already" was the answer. And the emperor abdicated for the second time, paving the way for Louis XVIII to return to Paris in July.

Colonel Wercklein took pleasure in coming in person to inform Princess Borghese of the details of Napoleon's defeat, his abdication, and even his attempted flight to America as they emerged. Although her attendant Madame Molo declared, "Death would be a boon in these circumstances," Pauline remained energetic. Believing, after the emperor had surrendered at Rochefort to an English naval captain, that he would be placed under house arrest somewhere in the United Kingdom, she sent to Metternich, now Austria's foreign minister, imploring him to intervene and arrange that she could live with the emperor. But it became clear that instead the Allied powers intended to embark him for Saint Helena, a rocky outcrop in the Atlantic, where it was decreed he should spend the remainder of his days. Only then did Pauline write to the pope, begging him to give her a refuge in Rome—a request that received a favorable answer.

After remaining a period of months at Bagni di Lucca, in October 1815 Pauline made the journey to Rome, where she at first took up residence in the Palazzo Falconieri in the via Giulia with her uncle and mother. She had yet to come to an accommodation with her husband about the apartments in the Palazzo Borghese, which she declared to be hers as of right, and a struggle lay ahead of her in the Roman law courts. But there was another matter unresolved. One detail of the epic struggle at Waterloo that Wercklein had not known to confide to Pauline was that Napoleon had left his carriage on the field. It contained, besides a sword, its hilt set with diamonds, and a traveling case, all the items in it of gold, the Borghese diamond necklace, which

Marchand had hidden in the lining of the coach before the battle. The valet had then not had time to extract it before he and his master fled for Paris. Accounts of the necklace's fate differ. On the one hand it is said it disappeared from the carriage before the vehicle, captured by the enemy, went on show in London. According to another legend, however, the emperor's trusted companion, Las Cases, took the jewelry and, when he embarked with Napoleon on the *Northumberland,* bound for Saint Helena, had it with him. No reference to the necklace, however, is made by Napoleon or any of his comrades in their accounts of life on Saint Helena.

Schemes and conspiracies now swirled in Europe and in America around the absent but still potent figure of the emperor of the French. Would he yet be persuaded to convert the Borghese necklace—if he had it with him—or other valuables into hard currency and once more, like an eagle, take wing for France? Or would he, as he claimed, be content at Longwood House on Saint Helena to write a memoir of his "distinguished career"? The Allied powers were aware of Princess Borghese's devotion to her brother and were eager to counter any plots and plans in which she might become involved. Though the princess declared herself relieved to have found asylum with her mother and brothers in Rome, they placed her under the most stringent surveillance—a surveillance that Pauline, naturally, delighted in evading.

CHAPTER FIFTEEN

Plots and Plans, 1815–1821

"My FIRST THOUGHT is to thank Your Holiness," Princess Borghese wrote, upon her arrival in Rome in October 1815, to Pius VII. And indeed the pope's clemency, despite his earlier treatment at the hands of Napoleon, in affording a refuge to Pauline and certain other members of the Bonaparte family was worthy of acknowledgment. The Allied powers had decreed Austrian exile for Elisa Bacciochi, Jérôme, and the widowed Caroline Murat, who could potentially muster support for Napoleon in their former principalities and kingdoms. (Murat had been executed, following his support for Napoleon in the Hundred Days, at Pizzo in Italy.) Metternich's police, it was judged, would best keep these Bonaparte siblings under observation. And Pauline had very nearly been added to their number in Graz and Trieste, because she was still viewed as having been a channel of communication between Napoleon and the Murats before the emperor's departure from Elba. But her brother Louis, resident at Rome, had entered upon an adroit correspondence, replete with references to Pauline's status as a Roman princess, with the Austrian and papal authorities. As a result she received the permission of the Allied powers, and that of the pope, to return to Rome.

Henceforward Pauline's conduct would come under scrutiny not only from the Roman police but from Louis XVIII's ambassador to

Rome, the Comte de Blacas, as well as from the Prussian, Russian, and Austrian ministers in that city. Furthermore, should she secure permission to visit Bagni di Lucca or other bathing stations in Tuscany, she would be the subject of Austrian and British police reports. Blacas, for one, was by no means the most impartial of judges. Indeed, upon Napoleon's return to Paris in 1815, the emperor found, among the papers that the count, foreign minister in Louis XVIII's first brief reign, had left behind, a disgruntled letter that one of Pauline's maidservants on Elba had written. Interpolated with accounts of Napoleon's fondness for his sister and of his furnishing apartments for her was, in another hand, the allegation that the brother and sister had slept together. "Good, to print," a royalist minion had written in the margin. But Pauline had never altered her behavior one jot for private or public consumption, not even when Napoleon's creature Fouché had reported on her daily doings in Paris. The knowledge that her activities—as well as those of her other relations in Rome—Madame Mère, Cardinal Fesch, Louis, and Lucien—would now be canvassed by two or more government agencies did not cause her to lose her composure.

Something else, however, greatly distressed Pauline, and she lost no time in informing the pope himself of her anxiety—namely, Camillo's "extraordinary and inexcusable behavior." During the Hundred Days, Prince Borghese had remained at the Palazzo Borghese in Florence, the Duchessa Lante at his side, and there he now appeared to have every intention of remaining. But hostilities had broken out while Pauline was still in Bagni di Lucca and making arrangements for her residence in Rome. Camillo had expressly forbidden her to take up residence in her apartments in the Palazzo Borghese there. "Extraordinary" as Pauline claimed to find her husband's order, when she received word to this effect from Gozzani, the Borghese steward in Rome, she had, in fact, expected nothing less. For, as she knew well, Camillo had long wished to secure a separation, then a divorce, and marry the Duchessa Lante. Denying Pauline a home, following her brother's fall from power, was a first step in this direction.

While she had no wish to live with Camillo, Pauline was determined, following the loss of her imperial titles and estate, to remain married and keep the rank of "true" Roman princess—and the Borghese residences, carriages, and jewels as well. "I am ready to accede to whatever Your Holiness should decide," Pauline wrote winningly to the pope, begging him to intervene. "As proof, I ask you to choose one or more judges to settle in private and without appeal all the differences between the prince and me."

So illustrious in Rome was the Borghese name—though its current holders might not lend it distinction—that several cardinals were directed to break their heads upon the divisions between Pauline and Camillo. Lucien Bonaparte had tried without success to broker a settlement in 1814 while Napoleon was confined at Elba. But Camillo had then insisted upon the return of the Borghese jewels, which he had given into Pauline's eager grasp in 1803 upon their marriage. Lucien, without dwelling upon the presence of the Duchessa Lante in Camillo's house, had replied that, as there was no official separation, there was no reason for his sister to return the stones. Now it was Louis Bonaparte's turn to champion his sister. While Pauline presented herself as a much injured wife, taking up residence in an underheated villa on the via Nomentana, Louis weighed in with some judicious remarks on Camillo's morals, which he addressed to one of the pope's cardinals.

"A wife is not a friend," wrote Louis, whose own wife, Hortense, had for some years elected to live separately from him. "No matter how cool the relations between the spouses, in all Christian countries, legal judgment must precede a formal separation. A husband cannot refuse to receive his wife without doing her great injury." And he wrote again, now specifically attacking Camillo's cohabitation with the Duchessa Lante in Florence: "It is not enough for him to live publicly with another woman in his wife's apartments. . . . He causes even greater scandal in the Capital of Christianity [Rome]." It was outrageous that Pauline, Camillo's wedded wife, should be "obliged to ask for judges to secure her entry to her husband's house."

Such indeed was the cardinals' conclusion, and it was of no avail for Camillo to write a memorandum detailing Pauline's neglect of almost every wifely duty. (Adulterous behavior was not an offense with which he could directly tax her, given his relationship with the duchessa.) Pauline had wished, wrote Camillo, throughout their marriage to live "separate and independently." Indeed, only the previous year, when electing to join the emperor on Elba rather than meet him in Italy, she had written, "Adieu, Camillo, I have known for a long time that our personalities are not compatible, so it is better to live separately and not make each other unhappy." But Pauline was proof against such truths, and now she wrote a beguiling letter to Camillo, hoping that they could put aside the differences that had so cruelly divided them and live together once more. The prospect of this so alarmed the prince— as was the princess's intention—that he gave up his objections to an unofficial separation. Thereby all his hopes for a judicial separation, from which divorce and remarriage could follow, dissolved.

By June 1816 terms had been agreed. Apartments in the Palazzo Borghese were ceded to Pauline, two carriages apportioned to her, and besides the twenty thousand francs a year she already received from Camillo, fourteen thousand scudi were to be hers annually. (Scudi, Roman currency, were worth five francs each.) In addition she was to have the wherewithal to buy a villa removed from the mephitic air of the Tiber, the river that lay beneath the windows of her palace. Then there was the use of the Casino Don Francesco at Frascati to be mentioned—and finally the Borghese jewels. These Camillo did ask to be separated from the other jewels in Pauline's collection and to be kept in a safe-deposit box—as was the custom in Rome—from which she could remove individual pieces upon submitting a request. Pauline tossed her head, refused to surrender any stones to such a repository, and called the Parisian jeweler Devoix to Rome. He was to witness that no one could now tell which were Borghese and which had been acquired from other sources, as she had had them all set and reset so many times. Her victory was complete, although characteristically she told Monsieur Michelot in Paris that she had made "great sacrifices" in coming to an arrangement with the prince.

Pauline had spurned Rome as a residence when she lived there with

Camillo in 1804 and had made little effort to charm its inhabitants. But now Paris, for which she sighed, was the domain of Louis XVIII, Neuilly was French crown property, and a new British ambassador, Sir Charles Stewart, occupied the Hôtel Charost. Accordingly Princess Borghese, having won from her husband all that she had wanted and more, set about, with an energy that would have bewildered those who had known her as a languorous invalid in the south of France, establishing herself as a "little queen" in Roman society. She made her receptions, soirees, and concerts the most sought-after invitations in town, though, as George Ticknor, a young American scholar touring Europe, noted, the Roman nobility was at a loss to know how to treat the Bonapartes: "for they belong, now at least, to no nation, and live at home as among strangers. Their acquaintance, however, is more sought after than that of any persons in Rome, and, as for myself, I found no societies so pleasant." As for Pauline herself, said Ticknor, she was "the most consummate coquette I ever saw . . . she has an uncommonly beautiful form and a face still striking, if not beautiful. When to this is added the preservation of a youthful gaiety, uncommon talent, and a practical address . . . it will be apparent she is . . . a most uncommon woman."

Pauline's apartments in the Palazzo Borghese were described by the Irish novelist Lady Morgan as "beyond beyond" when she attended a concert that the princess gave there. On another day, when Lady Morgan dined with Pauline, the princess invited the company to see her jewels, among them the emerald tiara set with diamonds that she had worn at Napoleon's coronation in Notre-Dame. "We passed through eight rooms en suite to get to her bedroom," the visitor reported. "The bed was white and gold, the quilt point lace and the sheets French cambric, embroidered." We know that Camillo installed a bathroom in Pauline's quarters, and, as she found no fault with it, we may assume it was appropriately luxurious.

Pauline's jewels were, of course, magnificent, but the princess was also happy, upon occasion, to show the Canova statue of herself as Venus, which now resided in Camillo's apartments. During its years in

Turin a mechanism had been installed within a painted base that allowed the statue to revolve before the spectator. Seen at night, illuminated by the light of small torches, the life-size portrait of Pauline on her marble mattress took on a fleshy tone, and, from the grave head to the cocked toes, by way of a titillating display of derriere, became one of the sights of Rome. There was no shortage of tourists, now that the long European wars were over and the borders open. Indeed, not being one to hold a grudge, Pauline told Camillo in the autumn of 1816 that "all the foreigners" agreed with her that the Villa Borghese, his property set in a capacious parkland, incorporating a lake and temples, and extending over the Pincio hill, was "the finest in Rome."

Pauline had herself bought and had fitted out over the summer of 1816 a charming small villa with a garden close to Porta Pia in the shadow of the Aurelian Wall. She liked to drive to it from the Palazzo Borghese through the grounds of the Villa Borghese—not least because those strolling or driving on the Pincio hill could admire her appearance. Apparently she thought of naming her new property, previously the Villa Sciarra, Villa Bonaparte, but her mother complained that the house was not of an order to bear the family name. (Despite Napoleon's fall from grace, Madame Mère's servants wore imperial livery and, in general, the Bonaparte residences in Rome boasted a splendor and sophistication not found elsewhere in the city and included such items as abundant fires and carpets throughout.)

Princess Borghese named her new plaything Villa Paolina instead, and soon appreciative guests came to dine, to attend concerts, or simply to walk in the gardens and take refreshments. Lady Morgan records a spring morning there, enjoying a *déjeuner* with an assortment of Roman and German princes, English milords and ladies, and American businessmen. "We were served pastries, ices, light wines, and coffee. . . . The principal entertainment was to walk in the elegant apartments and wander through the gardens, admiring the ancient walls that surrounded it, and where once the praetorian guard had done sentry duty."

Lady Morgan, noting the cardinals and bishops among the

princess's habitual guests, observed that "not since the time of Pope Joan had a woman been so surrounded by cardinals as la belle Pauline." But it was rather the presence of Englishmen and Englishwomen at Pauline's table, at her *cercles* and receptions, as well as the pretty attentions she paid them, that others noticed. Napoleon, informed in Saint Helena of the situation, merely smiled: "Then I will have a few enemies the less." But Lucien Bonaparte's intimate the painter Charles de Chatillon remonstrated with the princess, having been present while she entertained a Scottish peer, the Marquess of Douglas, who was heir to the Duke of Hamilton: "Do you forget Saint Helena?"

For reply de Chatillon received a flea in his ear. "Forget Saint Helena?" said Pauline. "Didn't you see how the Marquess of Douglas suffers all morning, standing more than an hour, for all his rheumatism, assisting at my toilette, and handing pins to my maid like a clown? . . . As for the evening—I employ him as my footstool. Imagine the joy I feel to have under my feet one of the grandest milords of Great Britain, one of the first peers of the land. So I, the sister of an unhappy prisoner, treat his assassins."

But Pauline was being disingenuous, and Prince Metternich in Vienna understood the situation better, when he noted in December 1816: "Members of the British opposition are frequenting the Bonapartes in Rome." For it was not all the English—or Scots—whom Pauline welcomed, but members of the British Whig Party, many of whom were at Rome in the winter of 1816–17 with their wives and families. According to Lady Frances Shelley, a correspondent of the Duke of Wellington, "The immaculate Pauline Borghese, and the Bonaparte family . . . receive the homage of the Jerseys, the Lansdownes, the Cowpers, the Kings, in short the regular Opposition. They have made Pauline Borghese their bosom friend. This causes surprise to the foreigners generally," added Lady Frances, herself of the Tory persuasion, "who do not understand that, with us, politics play a grand role, in cementing or destroying friendships."

Pauline had found common cause with the Whigs because both she and they wished to protest against the conditions of Napoleon's exis-

tence on Saint Helena. The Tory government in London, led by Lord
Liverpool, resisted any such demands. In this they were supported by
the Prince of Wales, who had been prince regent ever since his father,
George III, was declared unfit to rule in 1812. (George III was never to
recover and was still inhabiting a twilit world of delirium when he died
in 1820. The regent then succeeded as King George IV.) In Rome,
Pauline concentrated on charming the Whig tourists, and in this she
succeeded admirably. Lord Gower, his sister-in-law, Lady Granville, in
Paris heard, was "dying" for her. Pauline, Lady Granville was told, was
"as pretty as a princess in a fairy tale, but fiendish, truly fiendish. She
asks if her hair is as well styled as the day before, or whether it was better some other day. Then says no, that day some braid, some plait was
less successful."

Lord Jersey became quite besotted with Pauline, to the indignation
of his wife, one of the "Queens" of Whig society. In raptures he said
that she was "clever and delightful." Exclaiming over her habitually elegant pose on a sofa, he said, "her foot looks as if it never had a shoe on."
But in England, Lord Holland, the Whig leader in the upper house,
was the great hope of Pauline and her relations. Although there was little hope that Lord Liverpool's Tory government would fall on this or
any other issue, Holland commanded sufficient respect that a remonstrance on the subject of Napoleon's treatment that he submitted to the
House of Lords in March 1817 was the occasion of feverish interest in
the British and foreign press.

When Napoleon had hoped for asylum in England following
Waterloo, he invoked the example of an Athenian leader who had first
warded off a Persian invasion, then, when ostracized, found asylum
with Artaxerxes, the Persian king. "I have terminated my political
career," Napoleon wrote from Rochefort to the new prince regent, "and
come, like Themistocles, to share the hospitality of the British people.
I place myself under the protection of their laws, and I claim that from
Your Royal Highness as the most powerful, the most constant, and the
most generous of my enemies." But the prince and his Tory government, headed by Lord Liverpool, were not inclined to clemency.

Instead "General Bonaparte"—for so the Allied powers now dubbed the emperor—was dispatched to the basalt rock of Saint Helena out in the South Atlantic, to be guarded by patrolling British ships and a host of troops.

When Sir Hudson Lowe, the British commissioner entrusted with Napoleon's custody, arrived on the island in 1816, he bore with him instructions from Lord Bathurst, the British colonial secretary, which the former emperor viewed as sadistic. Among them was the requirement that, to confirm his presence on the island, "General Bonaparte" should show himself twice a day at Longwood House, the dingy bungalow he shared with the officers and their families who had accompanied him from Europe to this remote—but not unpopulated or unvisited—location. (Saint Helena had previously belonged to the East India Company and continued, as British Crown property, to serve the watering needs of ships traveling between Western Europe and India and farther east. Besides, the island's location in the South Atlantic, with Brazil to its west and the Cape of Good Hope to the southeast, made it a convenient stopping place for traffic between the Americas and the East.) Both residents and travelers in transit heard that Lowe's treatment of Napoleon was demeaning.

Even the Austrian and Russian commissioners who visited the island to see the conditions in which the prisoner of state was held were appalled by the manner in which Lowe followed Bathurst's instructions to the letter. Napoleon was denied access to newspapers. Books he had requested from Europe were not forthcoming. His exercise ground was curtailed, and the budget for his household was slashed, while, it was alleged, his family's correspondence was withheld from him. Slowly, these ignominious conditions of Napoleon's exile became known in England. But when Lord Holland addressed these grievances in the House of Lords, Lord Bathurst belittled them. And, in particular, he declared that no letters had been received in government quarters from any members of his family for "General Bonaparte"—except one from his brother Joseph, which had been forwarded to him.

The Bonaparte family was immediately up in arms. Madame Mère requested that letters for her son that she had, through the medium of an English peer, Lord Lucan, sent to England, be located. In the meantime Pauline dispatched to Lord Holland another letter for Napoleon and a list of items that she wished to have sent out to her brother in Saint Helena. Holland's reply came in May 1817. He was pleased to learn that his "feeble efforts" had met with the approval of Napoleon's relations. As for Pauline's letter to Napoleon, Lord Bathurst had assured him that this and any subsequent communications would be sent out. Should she write "Private" on the envelope, none but the colonial secretary would read the enclosure. Regarding the objects she had requested, however, Bathurst had said: "Napoleon cannot need so many things." Holland enclosed a list of what the colonial secretary had sent out to Saint Helena the previous year. "Lady Holland has compared that with the list of items you wish me to send. We will send first those items that are not on Lord Bathurst's list." As for the other items, "if you think them necessary, you have only to let me know." And there, in a very British manner, the Opposition remonstrance ended.

But Pauline did not confine herself to wooing the English—according to police authorities in Rome, at least. In those early years following Napoleon's imprisonment on Saint Helena, there were plots aplenty to free him—not only in Europe, but in North and even South America, where many French "malcontents" had gone to live, following the Bourbon restoration. It was believed that, should Napoleon only be freed and take up residence in the Americas, he could, from there, once more build support in France.

Every project of the Bonapartes' devising was suspect. When Lucien Bonaparte asked permission to go with his son, Charles, to his brother Joseph, who was living in style in Philadelphia—there was a plan afoot to marry the boy to Joseph's daughter Zenaïde—it was refused. The voyage was viewed as a pretext for Lucien to rouse support in America for his brother. In Rome, Pauline and Lucien were carefully watched, every visit to their palazzi noted by the papal, French, and Austrian secret police. It was thought that Lucien, long a resident in Rome, performed introductions of "disaffected elements" to his sister, and that she then supplied these dissidents with money. A visit to the Palazzo Borghese, for instance, from one Casamarte—a Corsican sailor whose mother had been the Bonapartes' wet nurse—occasioned a flood of reports. Meanwhile a Polish officer, Charles Piontkowski, who had served Napoleon in Elba, then in Saint Helena, feared to carry reports of the former emperor to his relations in Rome, believing that he would be arrested there as a spy. Pauline's annual requests to take the waters at Bagni di Lucca, although ultimately approved, resulted each summer in a flurry of speculation and conjecture about her intentions there.

In short, rumor and myth swirled about Pauline and the other Bonapartes in Rome, although on Saint Helena Napoleon himself stoutly denied that he would ever agree to leave the island, except with the concordance of the Allied powers. As a fugitive in America, he said, he would be an easy prey for a hireling's bullet that the French govern-ment would be only too glad to pay for. For her part Pauline neither encouraged nor discouraged the rumors. Her focus was still Napoleon, although her appearance, her toilette, and her health naturally contin-ued to be matters for concern. At Bagni di Lucca, where she summered in 1818, the French foreign minister, the Duc de Richelieu, heard, "She has succeeded with the English without exception." At a ball she gave in the bathing station, wrote the duke's agent, she performed her duties as hostess with "the address of a classic courtesan." And although every winter she succumbed to bouts of ill health, in the spring she reemerged, phoenixlike, to fascinate Roman society once more. An English invalid, Henry Matthews, felt his heart beat more strongly when he saw her promenading on the Pincio hill "with a bevy of admirers; as smart and pretty a little bantam figure as can be imagined. The symmetry of her figure is very striking." Sometimes Pauline's out-fit was pink, sometimes a becoming pearl gray taffeta or satin, set off by a matching bonnet trimmed with blond lace. The politics of Restora-tion France were not to her taste, but the Parisian dressmakers contin-ued to supply her wants.

.   .   .

As TIME PASSED it was Napoleon's health, rather than the restrictions on his liberty, that preoccupied Pauline. Reports came that he was suffering in the damp climate of Saint Helena, where liver complaints, dysentery, and inflammation of the bowel were widespread among the population and often proved fatal to Europeans. When news came that O'Meara, the surgeon on Saint Helena, had found a swelling on Napoleon's right side and diagnosed hepatitis, Madame Mère wrote—as "an afflicted mother"—to the Allied powers who were gathered at the Congress of Aix-la-Chapelle of 1818, begging them to sanction the removal of Napoleon to a healthier environment. Others, including the pope, wrote too, but the British government was adamant. Napoleon must remain where he was, and reports that the former emperor's legs were swollen and his digestion was shot to pieces did not alter that determination.

Anxious and frustrated, Pauline lost that sublime confidence in her looks that had till now distinguished her. "I confess I do not see that exquisite beauty she was so celebrated for," Lady Morgan wrote in 1819. "She is, she says, much altered, and grown thin fretting about her brother." Laure d'Abrantès, visiting Rome the previous year, observed that, beneath a necklace of large pearls, the princess's once lovely neck was grown thin. And when Laure wished to see the Canova of Pauline as Venus, the princess was impatient. Indeed, now that she had lost the perfect curves that had won her such admiration, which she had loved to display in silhouette, Pauline took against the statue that revealed them, and wrote to Camillo asking him not to allow it to be shown anymore. "The nudity of the statue approaches indecency. It was created for your pleasure. Now it no longer serves that purpose and it is right that it remains hidden from the gaze of others," she insisted. She ignored the fact that she herself had happily exhibited it to the curious until recently. The truth may have been, as she expressed it to Laure, that she suspected the motives of those who viewed the statue, then came calling on her "to inspect the ravages that sorrow has inflicted on me. . . . They are not content to poison my poor brother with suffering on Saint Helena. They wish to see me here exhibit the same symptoms."

Pauline did not come off entirely victorious in her battle with her husband. For, although the statue was put under lock and key, Camillo's steward, Gozzani, could still be persuaded to show it. And in 1820 no less a personage than the vicar-general of Rome, Cardinal Litta, addressed the prince at Pauline's behest. She was "very saddened and aggrieved," wrote Litta, that this statue was shown to foreigners, and "she was willing to do anything she could to stop the scandal." So reluctant, indeed, was the princess now to have others see her flesh made marble, Litta added, that she was even willing to reimburse the prince for its purchase price, if the offending item could be locked away. Indeed she offered to sit to Canova for another, more "respectable" statue. Camillo continued to protest that no one had access to the statue, Pauline to counterclaim that Gozzani, his steward, was open to bribery. And meanwhile every year Pauline's own flesh grew a little more lined, a little more yellow, as bilious and "putrid" fevers first contracted in Saint-Domingue, and from which she had since suffered increasingly in Europe, took their toll.

More significantly Pauline had been recently vanquished in another combat—this time with her mother and uncle. In a concession to the Bonaparte family in 1819, the Allied powers had agreed to allow a doctor, selected by Madame Mère and Cardinal Fesch, to proceed to Saint Helena. Grand Marshal Bertrand had written to Madame Mère, painting a pitiful picture of his master's health and asking for medical aid in the wake of surgeon O'Meara's departure from the island. Following numerous deaths on the island, Bertrand also asked for a cook and a steward, as well as priests to act as secretaries. To Napoleon's chagrin, however, when these gentlemen eventually arrived on the island, it transpired that the doctor, Francesco Antommarchi, was a student of anatomy and useless as a physician. Meanwhile, of the priests, Buonavita was an ignorant fellow who also suffered from palsy and whose diction, in consequence, was badly affected. The other, Vigani, was a youth and was barely trained.

In an extraordinary twist of events, under the influence of an Austrian mystic, the elderly duo, Madame Mère and Fesch, had come to believe that Napoleon was no longer on Saint Helena but had been transported to a nameless elsewhere. According to them the choice of doctor and of priest was therefore of no importance, and they blindly ignored the offer made by Foucault de Beauregard, Napoleon's former physician at the Tuileries and on Elba, to travel out to Saint Helena. Indeed Madame Mère and Fesch believed that, before Antommarchi, Buonavita, and Vigani reached Saint Helena, they would be miraculously diverted to that nameless other place where Napoleon now was.

Pauline and Louis attempted to make their mother and uncle see reason. "You cannot believe what scenes and quarrels there were," wrote Pauline, reflecting later upon the schism that developed between the older and younger generations. But it was Madame Mère and Cardinal Fesch whom the Allied powers had authorized to respond to Bertrand. Pauline and Louis had no redress. And although Napoleon, in dismal spirits, asked that companions for his exile be sought, after all, in Paris rather than in Rome, the British government considered that no further correspondence on the subject was necessary.

At least the new arrivals on Saint Helena could bring Napoleon news of his family. When Antommarchi told the former emperor that, the moment he sent word, Princess Borghese was ready to leave Rome and come to him, he replied: "Let her remain where she is. I would not have her see me insulted like this." He asked if she was still young and beautiful, and Antommarchi, to whom Pauline had given audiences at Rome, replied, "Still." "Ah, she has only ever cared for her toilette and for pleasure," said her brother.

In Rome, as if in response to the conversation on Saint Helena, Pauline had recovered her beauty. A young musician, Giovanni Pacini, encountered in the winter season at the Teatro della Valle, had reawakened in her the lust that had lain dormant during these years of exile. To the Palazzo Borghese came other musicians, among them Rossini. Pacini, in his memoirs, described the scene in fanciful prose: "Her palace was a new Olympus, where Venus did the honors." Pauline now was once more confident of her power to charm and fascinate— supremely confident, as Madame Hocheneck, a German lady, discovered when she was bidden with a Roman lady, Princess Ruspoli, to attend the princess's toilette. Upon entering, they found Pauline "in a delicious boudoir . . . casually lying on a chaise longue, with her little feet on show. . . . A page as pretty as a cupid, and dressed in a tabard, came in," records Madame Hocheneck. He "bore a silver basin, linen, perfumes, and cosmetics," and set a velvet stool beside the sofa on which the princess then placed one of her feet. While the page, kneeling, pulled down the princess's stocking—"even her garter too"—she chatted to her visitors. And as the page washed and dried and perfumed each foot, Madame Hocheneck and Princess Ruspoli—not to mention Pauline herself—admired the "truly incomparable" extremity.

But although Napoleon had declared that her toilette and pleasure were Pauline's only concerns, she was increasingly worried about his well-being. At the end of June 1821 she wrote to Lady Holland: "I have heard from Lord Gower that you are in Paris. Have you heard anything about my brother's health?" Pauline had hoped to hear, she said, from the priest who had traveled out to Saint Helena, but no reports had as yet been forthcoming. Less than two weeks later, on July 11, Pauline was paying her mother a visit in the latter's apartments that overlooked the Piazza Venezia, when she became convinced that Madame Mère was suppressing some news or information. Under questioning, her mother revealed that the Abbé Buonavita, in ill health, had returned from Saint Helena and was actually elsewhere in Madame Mère's apartments. Upon his being brought forward, Pauline found that Comte Montholon, one of Napoleon's companions, had entrusted to Buonavita, when the abbot left the island in March, a letter addressed to her. It made sad reading:

Madame, Napoleon charges me to tell you the deplorable state of his health. The liver complaint from which he has been suffering for several years, and which is endemic and fatal on the island, has made frightening progress these past six months. . . . He is extremely weak, he can barely endure a drive of half an hour, he cannot walk without help. And then his intestines are also under threat. . . . His stomach rejects all food . . . he lives on jelly. . . . He is dying without aid on a frightful rock, his agony is terrible.

For Pauline it was a clarion call to action. The same day that she extracted from Buonavita the letter that Montholon had written on March 17, she sent a copy of it to the British prime minister, Lord Liverpool. And she wrote:

> In the name of all the members of his family, I beg the English government that he [Napoleon] be moved to a different climate. If that request is refused, it's a death sentence for him, and I ask permission to go and join him, and be there when he breathes his last.
>
> Please have the goodness, milord, to authorize this, so that I can leave as soon as possible. The state of my health does not allow me to travel by land. Hence it's my intention to embark at Civitavecchia and go from there to England, where I will take the first ship for Saint Helena. However, I will need to come in to London, to procure what I will need for such a long voyage.

Pauline added: "I know Napoleon has not long to live, and I would reproach myself for ever if I had not tried by every means in my power to soften his last hours, and prove to him my devotion."

This letter was most unwelcome to Lord Liverpool and his government, who were busily combating the claims of George IV's estranged wife, Queen Caroline, to attend that monarch's coronation. (It was to take place on July 19.) They wanted nothing less than to have to combat this new potential source of disorder and disaffection. And Pauline begged Liverpool to send a copy of her letter and of the enclosure to Lady Holland, "who had always shown such an interest in Napoleon's fate." Pauline in London, en route to Saint Helena, with the backing of her Whiggish friends, could easily inflame a populace whose radical sensibilities had been whipped to fever pitch the previous year during the trial of Queen Caroline for adultery.

In the event Pauline never did go to London, and Liverpool was saved a reply. For only a few days after Pauline had written to the British prime minister news came that "General Bonaparte" had died in his bed at Saint Helena on May 5, Montholon and Antommarchi at his side, Grand Marshal Bertrand closing his eyes. At the end the former emperor's mind had roamed, and he had spoken of Josephine, of France, and of his beloved son the King of Rome, known since 1815 as the Duc de Reichstadt. Writing to her sister-in-law Hortense from Frascati in August 1821, Pauline echoed her brother, who had named in his will the "English oligarchy," or Tory government headed by Lord Liverpool, as his "assassins." "I have made a vow to receive no more of the English," she declared. "Without exception they are all butchers." Pauline was now waiting to hear with the rest of the family whether their mother's application to Lord Liverpool for Napoleon's remains to be brought back to Europe would be successful. While she was vengeful, she was also in great distress. "Dear Hortense," she wrote. "I cannot accustom myself to the idea that I will never see him again. I am in despair. Adieu. For me life has no more charm, all is finished. I embrace you." It remained to be seen how Pauline, who had for so long regarded the interests of her brother as paramount, would fare in a world without him.

CHAPTER SIXTEEN

"Great Remains of Beauty,"
1821–1825

Pauline's efforts on her brother's behalf during the last few months of his life and before the news of his death in May reached Rome had already taxed her strength. In particular, Montholon's letter of March that the Abbé Buonavita had given her in July, deploring Napoleon's health and begging her intercession with the British government, had seen her screw her courage to the sticking point, determined not to fail the ailing ex-emperor.

The same day that she wrote to Lord Liverpool, she started writing an account of her mother's and uncle's dependence on the Austrian mystic, and of their insistence that Napoleon was no longer on Saint Helena. This was for Planat de la Faye, one of her brother's former officers, who had received permission to go out to Saint Helena and—knowing nothing of Napoleon's death—was in England readying himself for his journey. Pauline stayed up four nights in a row to complete the letter that she meant de la Faye to carry out to Napoleon, and ended with a flourish that she would see her correspondent when she herself reached Saint Helena. "In taking these steps," she wrote to Montholon, "I have consulted only my heart. . . . I trust my strength will sustain me so that I can prove to the Emperor that no one loves him so much as I do."

The shock of learning, days after she finished her missives to Planat de la Faye and to Montholon, that Napoleon was dead, confounded the princess's health and destroyed her boldness. While she had assailed the British government, had contemplated with equanimity the test of nerve that would be the journey to Saint Helena and a residence there, now she shrank from action and shunned company. When Leclerc had died, when her son Dermide had died, Pauline—the young widow and mother—had sheared her hair, prostrated herself before their graves. But after their deaths, though she carried with her that gilded funerary urn, her life had resumed its butterfly quality. She was older now, and her bereavement following Napoleon's death was of a different order. There was no rending of hair or garments. Remaining at Frascati throughout the summer months of 1821, Pauline offered to contribute to the costs of transport, should her mother's campaign to have Napoleon's body returned to Europe succeed. "Milord," wrote Letizia Bonaparte to Lord Castlereagh, "the mother of the Emperor Napoleon begs to claim from his enemies the ashes of her son." The petition went unheeded, for, following instructions received from Lord Bathurst, the colonial secretary, Governor Lowe had buried the imperial captive on Saint Helena. On this issue Pauline corresponded with her mother, but she did not visit Letizia or any others of her family in Rome. Preferring to remain alone in her desolation at Frascati, she wrote to Hortense in August of spending the winter by the sea in Genoa: "The sea air will do me good. My spirits are so oppressed, I am in need of travel."

There was now nothing to stop members of the Bonaparte clan moving freely about Europe. With the death of the great man, their surveillance by the secret police of the European powers was at an end. Now Napoleon's brothers and sisters, who had once been kings and queens, who had been suspected many times over the previous five years of playing a part in plots to rescue the deposed emperor and restore Napoleonic rule in France, were declared "sans importance," or irrelevant. Their children too, some now in their late teens and early twenties, were free to travel. Lacking either firm homeland or roots, they headed for America, where Joseph lived in style as the Comte de Survilliers. In due course marriages there were arranged for his daughters—heiresses both to the gold that Joseph had acquired when king of Spain. Zenaïde was married to Lucien's eldest son, Charles, and Charlotte to Louis's elder son, Napoléon Louis—unions that had long been contemplated by their elders and that were in keeping with the Corsican tradition of intermarriage between cousins.

Princess Borghese, however, showed no interest in joining her brother and younger members of the family in America. And indeed she did not, after all, spend the winter of 1821 in Genoa. Instead she received in Rome the companions of her late brother, who, in accordance with the instructions that Napoleon had issued before his death, came bringing news of his last moments, bearing his will, and carrying items that had been bequeathed to her in that testament and in its codicils. In August, Pauline had begged Hortense to send her any details of Napoleon's last days that she might hear from his companions who now returned to Europe, promising that she would perform the same service for her sister-in-law. That autumn she interrogated Dr. Antommarchi minutely when he reached Rome and gave an account of his imperial patient's last days, of his death, of the autopsy. "Although suffering, she still admitted me," wrote the doctor, "and wanted to know everything, understand everything. She showed the most vivid regret when she heard the outrages and agonies that Napoleon had endured."

Pauline herself later recalled just how agitated she was during this period of bereavement: "When they read his [Napoleon's] will and I heard the passage concerning me, I fell back, on the floor, as if dead." Coursot, Napoleon's valet on Saint Helena, brought her the smaller items mentioned in the will—a lock of hair, Chinese chains and necklaces, some medals made from iron ore mined on Elba. The villa of San Martino on Elba, on the other hand—complete with provincial frescoes of the emperor's Egyptian campaigns—which had been purchased with the princess's money and which Napoleon had now bequeathed her, was not a legacy of which she could expect to make much use. Nevertheless the bequest was to provide Pauline with an idea for a memorial to her life with her brother.

Slowly Pauline returned to health, and her interest in those around her quickened. Her brother on Saint Helena, barred the company of the great and grand, had amused himself with the children on the island, playing blindman's buff with one family and giving General Bertrand's daughter a bonbon box that had once been Pauline's. The princess had always been kind to children, especially, of course, members of her family. Lucien's elder daughters, who had once been playmates of Dermide, were now married, and she welcomed them with their husbands at the Villa Paolina in Rome, which continued to offer, as one visitor put it, "English neatness, French elegance and Italian taste." Lucien's teenage son Paul was something of a favorite, as was Louis and Hortense's second son, Napoléon Louis, who had been born some months after Dermide's death. By virtue of his brother's death in Holland in 1807 he was now his parents' elder son, Charles-Louis-Napoléon, the future Napoleon III, having been born in 1808.

In general, the princess's relations with all her family were good, and, with Bonaparte migration now allowed, her Murat nephews and nieces visited from Trieste, where the widowed Caroline had made her home. So there was all the more reason for the Bonaparte clan to be outraged in the winter of 1821 when Princess Borghese made a pet of a newcomer to Rome, the sixteen-year-old Jerome Bonaparte-Patterson. This young American, who had the Bonaparte "classical profile," was her brother Jérôme's son by his first marriage to the American Elizabeth Patterson—a woman whom Jérôme had divorced long before, at Napoleon's insistence, so that he could marry Princess Catherine of Württemberg. But now mother and son had traveled to Rome, following assurances from the American fur king, John Jacob Astor, who had visited the city a year earlier, that the princess would receive them.

Meanwhile Jérôme and Catherine, who had married in 1808, were still living in Trieste but had plans to move to Rome with their three young children—Jérôme, Napoléon, and Mathilde. In the circumstances Jérôme viewed his sister's reception of his son by his first marriage as an insult—to his wife, Catherine, and to himself. Indeed, as Pauline was fond of Catherine, her championing of young Jerome seems at first sight a contrary act. On the other hand Napoleon's death and his will had made a great impression on Pauline. We have the evidence of Elizabeth Patterson that, while she and her son were in Rome, the princess was engaged in making her own will. And Pauline spoke of arranging a marriage between the young man and one of her brother Lucien's daughters. Pauline, now having no use for the considerable sums of money that she had kept in reserve for Napoleon, was casting about for an heir. Just as Joseph's daughters were promised in marriage to their first cousins, thus ensuring that Lucien's and Louis's stock would share in Joseph's inheritance, so Pauline herself thought of dividing her considerable wealth and property between two branches of the family by leaving it to a Bonaparte husband and wife.

For some time in pursuit of this plan Elizabeth Patterson, a handsome brunette, and her son were to be seen everywhere with the princess—at the Palazzo Borghese, at the Villa Paolina, out in her carriage in the Pincio gardens. And then the relationship soured, and Elizabeth Patterson, returning empty-handed to America, spat venom on the subject of her erstwhile benefactor: "Every day she [Pauline] makes a new will and will end by leaving her property to complete strangers. She has quarreled with all the world, and, even to win her inheritance, no one can put up with her caprices which are so bizarre it's impossible not to think her touched with madness. All I was told about her was not a half of the truth."

Pauline was to remember her nephew Jerome in her will, but not to the tune his mother, Elizabeth, would have liked. Meanwhile, the breach apparently healed, Jérôme and Catherine concluded their move to Rome, swelling the Bonaparte numbers in the city and settling with their children into the Palazzo Núñes, close to the Pincio gardens. But from now on Pauline's relations began to wonder and speculate who would be her heir, as in Paris—before the birth of the King of Rome—they had once speculated who would inherit Napoleon's throne.

As if wishing to sharpen her relations' lust, in the new year of 1822 Pauline acquired two properties in Tuscany that, with the Villa Paolina in Rome, she would be free to leave to whomever she wished. (The apartments in the Palazzo Borghese and her residence in Frascati would, at her death, revert to the Borghese family.) The princess's relationship with Giovanni Pacini, the young singer whom she called "Nino," which had continued by fits and starts during her year of mourning her brother, prompted both purchases. Pacini had taken up a position as chapel master to Maria Luisa, the former Queen of Eturia now restored as Duchess of Lucca, in September 1821. The following summer Pauline bought from the Arnolfini family a villa on the San Quirico hill above Lucca, which she renamed Villa Paolina.

This purchase allowed her to be nearby when Pacini was occupied with his duties at the Lucca court. At the same time she began the process of having built on the shoreline at Viareggio a villa that would be shaded by a plantation of pines on the eastern front but whose loggia to the west would be open to the beach and to the sun and sea breezes. "Every week she changes residence, rents and leaves houses at Bagni di Lucca or at Viareggio," gossiped an elderly Tuscan diplomat, "while she waits for her pavilion there to rise from the ground and offer a comfortable home for next winter. . . . Her health," he added, "gives the prince great hopes that he will soon need to go into mourning."

Pacini himself had a villa at Viareggio, which explains, in part, the choice of location for this residence, which Pauline yet again named Villa Paolina. But it was also here at Viareggio that the princess had landed when she left Elba, where she had last seen Napoleon before the Hundred Days began. From her villa, when completed, she would be able to gaze across the sea at the distant bulk of Elba. Moreover, the decoration of her villa she modeled after that of the villa on Elba that her brother had left her, while adding to the Egyptian and trompe l'oeil elements of the frescoes in that villa Chinese and pastoral scenes.

At Viareggio, Pauline, bathing herself in the rays of the noonday sun she so unfashionably loved, constructed a residence where, should she so wish, she could pass her mind over her days on Elba with Napoleon and further back, to those days in the south of France with Forbin, even as far back as those childhood days in Corsica, which had ended in flight from a burning home in Ajaccio. It was, in a sense, a memorial to a past that had been always illuminated by the existence of her brother Napoleon. Few visitors came to the Villa Paolina at Viareggio to distract Pauline from her memories or from the disturbing truth that, where all had been sumptuous and gorgeous, now there were only shadows.

Pauline could, alternatively, live in the moment with Pacini—but as the months progressed the affair with him grew less satisfactory. The truth was that Pacini was not enamored of the princess, as had been her previous lovers. He was happy to stage his opera *The Slave of Baghdad* in her home, or set verses by Tasso to music for her, compose pieces for her to play on the piano or the harp. But he was the one rather to accept homage from the princess. Pauline, once the most beautiful woman of her generation, was growing older, and years of illness had marked her face. Moreover, her public bathing arrangements, her determination to dress in the latest fashion, as she had for the last twenty years, were beginning to mark her out, elegant though she still was, as odd, eccentric, even a remnant from another age. A description of her during the winter of 1822, when she inhabited apartments in the Palazzo Lanfranchi on the Arno in Pisa, bears this out. She wore, according to a young girl later to become Princess Corsini, "a white dress embroidered with gold. Her hair was curled on her forehead, a little bonnet on her head. Pale and transparent, she was like a fluttering sylphide [forest nymph], excelling in little attentions, compliments, and blandishments."

Jean-Jacques Coulmann, a young Frenchman and Bonaparte enthusiast who brought to Pauline at Pisa, at the author's request, a copy of Las Cases's *Memorial of Saint Helena,* an account of conversations with Napoleon there, was embarrassed to find Pauline still behind a screen, bathing, when he was shown in. Other gentlemen were conversing in the room, and when the princess emerged he was struck by her appearance. He wrote: "Events and emotions seemed to have used and desiccated her. Her features were still noble and regular, her eyes expressed benevolence but determination too. And her figure was still refined and symmetrical. But—her skin had yellowed and the blood seemed to have drained from her veins." Was Pauline aware that her looks had withered? She told her visitor that it was since her brother's death that she had been ill. Coulmann was nevertheless keen to converse with her and show her those passages that concerned her in the book he bore. He regarded the dialogue that followed as "a page of history."

Pauline was delighted with Napoleon's assertion, in the *Memorial,* that all the artists agreed her to be "another Venus de Medici." "Oh, as for that," she said, "I never would have claimed that. Before, I was better, it's true." Still she showed the reference with great joy to the other gentlemen present. She repudiated the story that a whole post wagon had traveled daily from Paris to Nice, when she was in the south of France, to bring her new toilettes and alterations. ("My sister is the queen of trinkets," Napoleon declared, according to Las Cases.) But she spoke with more sincerity when she declared that she had read neither the verses of Pierre-Antoine Lebrun on her brother's death nor any others. "Anything that recalls my brother upsets me," she said. Coulmann was fascinated by her and by her scorn for the Bourbon restoration. When Napoleon entered the Tuileries in March 1815, said Princess Borghese, there were "beds not made, tables not cleared. It was a stable. . . . Now we were so clean, there was order and regularity throughout, even flowers on our travels. . . . The Emperor was right to call cleanliness next to virtue. Well, the French will see the difference. Do they regret us?" she ended suddenly.

For, all the time, while Coulmann was attempting to remember her conversation for posterity, Princess Borghese had been busy on other accounts: "Bring me another bonnet. I don't want that one . . . a cashmere shawl for my shoulders. . . . I'll need a warming pan. . . . Doctor, I have a fever. . . . You're going to the Opéra, what's on this evening?" Then the page of history turned, and she swept off to bed.

Later in 1823, when Pauline was back in Rome, there appeared every chance that Prince Borghése in Florence would have the opportunity to wear mourning. Following severe and repeated bilious attacks, she was barred from going out. Her condition worsened, she took communion at Christmas—and it was not expected that she would survive into the new year. And yet she rallied again, so much so that she felt more than able to conduct a flirtation in the spring with the Duke of Devonshire. This grand bachelor Whig was in Rome with the laudable aim of commissioning pieces for a sculpture gallery he had built at Chatsworth, his Derbyshire home. He wrote in his diary after their first meeting: ". . . she is curious to see, great remains of beauty, very civil and gracious to me." Now at last was Pauline's opportunity to appear in a "respectable" pose, and well covered. After lunch in the garden of the Villa Paolina, watched by the duke and by her brother Jérôme, Thomas Campbell, sculptor, took plaster casts of the princess's hand, foot, and nose.

Eventually a reclining statue would emerge, and again much later the duke would record in his *Handbook to Chatsworth:* "She was no longer young, but retained the beauty and charm that made her brother strike the [Andrieu] medal in honour of the Sister of the Graces." At the time of his visit to Rome in 1824, however, the duke was less measured in his admiration for Pauline. His sister Lady Granville heard that he was infatuated, and remarked, "It's *assez de son genre* [quite his style] to squiddle [waste time] with a princess, and he was sure to be taken with all those little clap-traps of embroidered cushions, satin slippers, dressing-gowns of cachemire, morsels of Petrarch with which this one assails our nobility."

Pauline enjoyed the attention and entertained her noble admirer with stories of the imperial court she had once inhabited. After he escorted her to a masked ball at the house of the Russian count Demidov, she was "full of whims and childishness, but now and then very entertaining about her family, and *bellissima,*" he wrote in his diary. He ended, like all visitors to Rome, by relishing Pauline's soirees above all others on offer: ". . . party at Pss Borghese. I was presented to Jerome and his wife. . . . I waltzed with Mme de St Leu—*la reine* Hortense—a very nice person. Pauline danced opposite her in a quadrille, and I thought myself in Paris in the last reign." Upon his return to England the duke took with him as a gift a mourning bracelet that Pauline had had made when Napoleon died, and which now hid a repair to the arm of a Venus that Devonshire had bought in Rome.

But it was the Calabrian, Pacini, not the English duke, who occupied Pauline's heart. And he was proving false. While she was at the Villa Paolina at Viareggio in the summer of 1824, she heard that the composer had been nearby but had never made his presence known to her. Moreover her brother Jérôme wrote from Trieste, where Pacini had professional commitments, to say that the composer had engaged in "gallantries" there. The lies, omissions, and commissions were multiplying, and Pauline was helpless to stop them, though she had laid out considerable sums on Pacini's behalf and had even appointed his sister, Claudia, and her husband, Giorgio, as members of her household, at his request.

"Caro Nino, I write two lines to tell you I am tired and suffering," she began one of many letters in which she expostulated with her lover. "Today I have not slept . . . then Giacomo Belluomini [her Viareggio agent] told me you wanted him not to say you passed by Pescia. Why do you always lie? I don't want to hear any more lies from you, big or small. They cost you my respect. I am ill and sad to think my Nino doesn't speak the truth." But she relented: "Beloved Nino, you are on your travels, you are far from me, but it is so you can win fame and admiration. I am content with what makes you happy. . . . May God make you see that I merit from you a true proof of your affection. This is the moment to prove to me how dear I am to you. Adieu, dear Nino."

But Nino was not destined to prove his affection for the princess. His lies continued, and Pauline knew better, in the end, than to continue the flawed relationship. "I told him at the beginning that the first lie would end it all," she wrote to Belluomini, who was a friend of Pacini's:

I have pardoned him since, so many times. I am tired of being deceived by a man that I have heaped with benefits. I have taken the firm resolution to break with him and leave him to his lies and falsehoods. . . . My health is in a dangerous state, and I don't want to endure waiting two months perhaps and then risk being disappointed in my plans. In short I feel wounded to my heart, I

did not expect such coldness. It is an insult he'll regret one day.
Then he'll understand what he's lost. . . . I will not reply to his
letters, which will be returned to him unopened. There is the
decision that will let me at last be at peace.

And from now on Princess Borghese, having shed Pacini—and
indeed his sister and brother-in-law—was indeed at peace, although
she was not well. She had spent some time, following Pope Pius VII's
death in 1823, pursuing the idea of a new settlement with Camillo in
the Vatican courts, for she declared she had submitted to papal juris-
diction in 1816 only from a disinclination to trouble that benevolent
churchman. Now that Leo X was pope, it occurred to her that she
might wrest some extra scudi from her husband, on the ground that
the 1816 settlement did not reflect adequately the arrangements for a
jointure in her nuptial contact of 1803. But when Camillo declared
himself ready to do battle with her before the Sacra Rota, the Vatican
law court, Pauline formed a new plan. She told Camillo that she would
halt her action if he increased her annual income from fourteen thousand scudi to twenty thousand.

Far from agreeing to this amiable compromise, Camillo submitted
to the Rota a number of documents, including a sixty-page pro memoria in which he wrote feelingly of having been spurned, humiliated,
and ignored by the princess. The auditors, or judges, of the Sacra Rota
viewed with dread the prospect of intervening in the altercation but
judged that the 1816 settlement should stand. At that point Pauline
took to her bed and wrote a charming letter to her husband in May
1824, expressing her hope that she and he could forget their differences
and once more live together. To Camillo's dismay, this was followed by
a letter from the pope declaring that Princess Borghese was a sick
woman and that it was a sad matter for a good Catholic, and especially
for a Roman prince, to live separately from his wife. Pauline's health
had indeed deteriorated, and it would seem likely that she was now suffering from liver cancer.

Camillo, knowing when he was beaten, made only one condition.

He would take in his wife, but he would have none of her "band of comedians"—by which he meant Pacini and his relations. As she had already parted with those characters, Pauline happily acceded to his condition and prepared for the journey to Florence. A disconsolate Camillo made arrangements for the Duchessa Lante and her daughters, who had moved with him from Turin into apartments in the Palazzo Borghese at Florence, to live elsewhere.

Initially Pauline and Camillo dealt extremely well together, once they had recovered from the surprise of cohabitation after so many years apart. The Palazzo Borghese, a fifteenth-century stronghold close to the Duomo, had recently been redecorated by Camillo, and its costly interiors were thick with gold—which met with Pauline's approval. Camillo's appearance was rather less appealing. If Pauline's beauty was now paper thin, the prince's good looks were almost lost under flesh and jowls so that, in profile, he resembled one of the more decadent Roman emperors on a coin. But he remained kind as ever and took his wife out on airings in his carriage. They walked arm in arm in the Cascine, the fashionable Florentine park. He invited Florentine society to receptions, concerts, and balls, and they flocked to the palace. Indeed, the reunion of the Borghese couple—so unexpected, so miraculous an event—inspired a local poet to write an ode on the subject of their matrimonial felicity.

Pauline's health, however, took a turn for the worse in the spring of 1825, and she began to fret. She grumbled that her apartments let in no noonday sun, the Prussian minister heard. But in fact the princess was at last relinquishing the tenacious hold on life that had seen her survive so many crises. Her sufferings did not abate, and she wrote to Louis in May 1825: "I am in pain and I suffer, I am reduced to a shadow. They are mending the cobbles in the street outside and the noise is frightful. I can't stay here, so the Prince is renting me a villa a mile away, where I'll spend May." In her state of health, she added, she could not think of traveling to her villa at Lucca.

The prince rented the Villa Fabbricotti up on the Montughi hill above Florence, and there Pauline was moved during the month of

May. With her went Sylvie d'Hautmesnil, a bedchamber woman who had been with her for some years. But the princess's ailments were not such as could respond to a change of air, or to quiet. Camillo kept an anxious watch over her. Pauline's brothers were sent for. Jérôme arrived at the beginning of June. Louis had not yet arrived when, in the night of June 8, the doctors reported that the end was at hand and she should be given the last rites. But Pauline, ill though she was, said, "I'll tell you when I am ready. I still have some hours to live." Not until eleven the following morning did she agree to receive the priest who had been hovering outside. And even at the moment of communion, when the priest wished to speak a few words, Pauline, on easy terms with the Church to the last, stopped him and spoke herself. It was a discourse, wrote Sylvie d'Hautmesnil, who was present, most touching in its piety.

Matters spiritual having been so admirably and concisely dispatched, Pauline was free to attend to the material in her last precious hours of life. Out went the priest and in came a Florentine notary and companions, who had been summoned to take down and witness her last earthly wishes. "These were all strangers," Sylvie d'Hautmesnil informs us, "but the princess put them at their ease, spoke to them charmingly and apologized for disturbing them. One would have thought her a person in perfect health."

From her bed, dressed "as ever" with elegance, Pauline dictated the terms of her will. It was a lengthy document, for there were many family members of whom to make mention. To Zenaïde and Charles Bonaparte fell the Villa Paolina at Lucca. Napoléon Louis and Charlotte won the villa at Rome, and sister Caroline was left the seaside residence at Viareggio. (In addition, to Caroline passed the gilt urn containing the embalmed hearts of Leclerc and of Dermide.) The American Jerome gained by Pauline's will, and her nephew Paul, too, although not his father Lucien—"for reasons," she wrote, as a child might. But Princess Borghese was not finished. She left sums of money to the children of her wet nurse in Ajaccio—"should they still be living." Meanwhile Camillo's brother, Don Francesco, received the

Gérard portrait of the princess's husband. To a Luccan neighbor, the Marchesa Torrigiani, went a travel toilet mirror. And her British admirers were not forgotten. She left the Elban medals that Napoleon had bequeathed her to the Duke of Devonshire and to the Duke of Hamilton, whom she had used, when he was Marquess of Douglas, as a footstool, a magnificent traveling case filled with gold implements.

IT WAS THE CHRONICLE of a life that had ranged near and far, a life that was now nearly over. "I die in the middle of cruel and horrible sufferings," she declared, and indeed her bedchamber woman wrote that Pauline had not been free from pain for over eighty days, her liver, lungs, and stomach all causing her torment. At the end, as Napoleon had done before her, Pauline asserted that she was a good Catholic. "I die without any feelings of hatred or animosity against anyone, in the principles of the faith and doctrine of the apostolic Church, and in piety and resignation."

Having signed the will, Pauline handed the pen to Sylvie to place back on her *écritoire*, or writing desk, and the notary exited, leaving the princess to say a punctilious good-bye to the members of the household. To Sylvie, Pauline gave cool instructions about the toilette and the *parure* in which her embalmed corpse was to be attired. Apparently she called for a mirror to inspect her appearance. More certainly Pauline Borghese's last act before she died was to hand her keys—the keys securing the jewels and coffers and apartments over which they had fought so long—to the prince. Her affairs were in order, and she died at one in the afternoon on June 9, 1825. The cause of her death, like that of her father years before in Montpellier, was given as a *scirro*—or tumor—on the stomach.

A lock of hair cut from the princess's head an hour after death and preserved in Florence—in a drawer of that toilet mirror bequeathed to the Marchesa Torrigiani—is still a rich, dark chestnut color. Pauline's body, after embalming, was taken, as she had wished, to Rome and laid in its coffin in the Borghese family vault in the Basilica of Santa Maria

Maggiore. It had been a remarkable journey from the tenement house in Ajaccio, where the Bonapartes' sixth child was born in October 1780, and from the small font in the dark cathedral there, where she was baptized Maria Paoletta, to this opulent resting place. There her coffin lies to this day, in the company of the Borghese pope, Paul V, and of Cardinal Scipione Borghese, who laid out the Villa Borghese. Famous men in their day, today their renown is eclipsed by that of the parvenu princess, the Corsican cuckoo in their midst.

For many Pauline's true memorial lies in the titillating pink perfection of the Canova figure, lying seductively on that marble mattress in the Villa Borghese. Even copies of this statue can arouse admiration, and two Quaker ladies in Philadelphia were once embarrassed to stand by while Pauline's brother Joseph extolled his sister's beauties. He "stood some time perfectly enraptured before it [his copy of the statue], pointing out to us what a beautiful head Pauline had; what hair; what eyes, nose, mouth, chin, what a throat; what a neck; what arms; what a magnificent bust; what a foot—enumerating all her charms one after another, and demanding our opinion of them. Necessity made us philosophers, and we were obliged to show as much sangfroid on the subject as himself; for it was impossible to turn away without our prudery's exciting more attention than would be pleasant." How Pauline would have enjoyed both her brother's praise and the ladies' discomfiture! One can almost hear her laugh echo through the halls of Joseph's lavish mansion.

NOTES

ALL TRANSLATIONS are the author's own, unless otherwise indicated. All original text is in the language of source, whether archive or publication, unless otherwise indicated. Some of Napoleon's many bons mots come from the *New Cambridge Modern History*, vol. 9, edited by C. W. Crawley (1961), others from the great variety of biographies attached to his name.

ABBREVIATIONS

Arch. Borghese   Archivio Borghese
ASV   Archivio Segreto Vaticano, Rome
Segr. Stato   Segretaria di Stato

Chapter One / Dinner at Marseille, 1796

3   Victor Emmanuel Leclerc: Champion, *Général Leclerc*, 8; Arnault, *Souvenirs*, vol. 2, 219.

4   commonplace book, which survives him: Versini, *M. de Buonaparte*, 155.

4   in that town's archives: Saint-Maur, *Pauline Borghèse*, vol. 2, document 1.

4   less knowing than Paoletta: Napoleon, *Correspondance générale*, vol. 1, 112–13.

4   "pull up skirts than undo breeches": Marchand, *Mémoires*, 134.

4   even scribble on the walls: Larrey, *Madame Mère*, vol. 2, 529.

6   in the town garrison: Champion, *Général Leclerc*, 8.

6   that of a "Persian viceroy": Arnaud, *Fils de Fréron*, 332.

7   "he has behaved well there": Napoleon, *Correspondance générale*, vol. 1, 270; 300; 309.

7   "as Petrarch loved Laura": *Revue Rétrospective*, vol. 3, 99–100.

8   taught her—to other lovers: d'Abrantès, *Mémoires*, vol. 14, 311–12.

9   "to smooth all obstacles": *Revue Rétrospective*, vol. 3, 101; 108–9.

10   to have no occupation: Napoleon, *Correspondance générale*, vol. 1, 272.

10   "No money, no match": d'Abrantès, *Mémoires*, vol. 1, 251.

11   "when I present her": *Revue Rétrospective*, vol. 3, 101.

12   garrison commander at Marseille: Napoleon, *Correspondance générale*, vol. 1, 299.

12 commendation from de la Poype: Champion, *Général Leclerc*, 3–8.

13 "Tell my brother": Napoleon, *Correspondance générale*, vol. 1, 423; 465; 397.

14 "masters of all Lombardy": Napoleon, *Correspondance générale*, vol. 1, 397–98; 400.

17 "P.B.'s every day": *Revue Rétrospective*, vol. 3, 102–9.

18 "amo, si amatissimo amante": Ibid., 106–7.

18 Italian headquarters at Milan: Napoleon, *Correspondance générale*, vol. 1, 698.

Chapter Two / Garrison Bride, 1797–1798

19 "the Army of Italy": someone said. Arnault, *Souvenirs*, vol. 2, 334.

20 "lose themselves in pleasure": Napoleon, *Correspondance générale*, vol. 1, 914.

20 The envoy of Pauline's brother: Champion, *Général Leclerc*, 9; Fonds Masson, box 67, 3.

21 had added to her attractions: Arnault, *Souvenirs*, vol. 2, 335.

22 "at Milan in a fortnight": Napoleon, *Correspondance générale*, vol. 1, 698–99; 705.

23 their own execution: Arnault, *Souvenirs*, vol. 3, 12.

24 from Pontoise on February 22: Fonds Masson, box 67, 3.

25 "the right thing only by caprice": Arnault, *Souvenirs*, vol. 3, 30; 34–35.

25 a contemporary, the Duchesse d'Abrantès, put it: d'Abrantès, *Mémoires*, vol. 9, 106.

26 the nuptial benediction was given: Fonds Masson, box 67, 4–5 (Italian).

26 "unlimited confidence in our destinies": Marmont, *Mémoires*, vol. 1, 296.

26 "the blond Bonaparte" as a compliment: Thiébault, *Mémoires*, vol. 3, 201.

26 "get rid of this one too": Arnault, *Souvenirs*, vol. 3, 33–34.

26 the Bonaparte family property: Champion, *Général Leclerc*, 9.

27 "not much bigger than a lentil": Arnault, *Souvenirs*, vol. 3, 338–39.

28 in the Palazzo Graziani: Fonds Masson, box 67, 6–9.

28 "I would have to have you with me": Champion, *Général Leclerc*, 10, n. 40.

29 an Austrian archduke had been born: Frédéric Masson, in Masson, *Napoléon et Sa Famille*, vol. 1, 230.

29 and Guastalla, for 160,000 francs: Fonds Masson, box 67, 205–52.

29 he was transferred to Paris: Fonds de Blocqueville, album C, 429.

29 "around us wherever we went": Reinhard, *Une Femme de diplomate*, 13.

Chapter Three / Madame Leclerc in Paris, 1798–1799

30 who commanded the Army of England: Champion, *Général Leclerc*, 9.

31 calling them "Poulot" and "Poulotte": Cornuau, *Correspondance*, 28.

31 "put off the party till six": Ibid.; 42.

32 the *diligence*, the public coach service: Fonds de Blocqueville, album A, 173 ff.; 139.

32 had been dictated by herself: Cornuau, *Correspondance,* 43–45.

33 "did not know how to read or write": Fleuriot de l'Angle, *La Paolina,* 52.

33 "improving," he wrote in 1801: Fonds de Blocqueville, album A, 115.

37 "You are quite deluded": d'Abrantès, *Mémoires:* vol. 2, 215; 211–20.

37 "an affection tender but chaste": Cornuau, *Correspondance,* 28.

39 not so long before: d'Abrantès, *Mémoires,* vol. 2, 333; 314–15; 261.

40 to continue their relationship: Ibid., 319, 325, n. 1; vol. 19, 282.

42 "c'est l'ordre du général": Furet and Richet, *La Révolution,* 332.

43 within hours as first consul: d'Abrantès, *Mémoires,* vol. 2, 338.

Chapter Four / Sister to the First Consul, 1800–1802

45 she said firmly. "Quite different": d'Abrantès, *Mémoires,* vol. 3, 333–34.

46 four hundred were dead and six hundred taken prisoner: Forges, *Général Leclerc,* 13–14.

46 and indulgent toward others: Fonds de Blocqueville, album C, 1.

46 "but that the first consul would": d'Abrantès, *Mémoires,* vol. 6, 82.

47 Leclerc was to declare: Hardy, *Correspondance,* 205–10

47 to support her pelvis: Fonds de Blocqueville, album A, 225.

48 "with your big stomach?": Cornuau, *Correspondance,* 42.

49 a name for himself in Paris: Fonds de Blocqueville, album A, 189, 193, 197, 179.

49 that he could do no more: Ibid., 177.

50 "as a servant girl," she wrote: Cornuau, *Correspondance,* 43.

50 "now you must wake up": George, *Mémoires,* 17.

50 "once they have finished planting": Fonds Masson, box 67, 20.

50 a swing in the garden: Fleuriot de L'Angle, *La Paolina,* 57.

51 "let you come to Paris": Fonds de Blocqueville, album C, 69.

51 "even in his place": Champion, *Général Leclerc,* 13

52 "five centuries behind France": Fonds de Blocqueville, album A, 105; 115.

52 "I will be obliged to you": Masson, *Napoléon et Sa Famille,* vol. 2, 33–34.

52 "the vines we planted": Fonds de Blocqueville, album A, 213; 179.

53 "who are so dear to me": Ibid., 123.

53 "to the most senior general": Napoleon, *Correspondance générale,* vol. 3, 802–3.

56 "said Leclerc, extending his hand": Norvins, *Souvenirs,* vol. 2, 305–6.

56 military career out there: Fonds de Blocqueville, album A, 97.

56 Hardy wrote optimistically to his wife: Hardy, *Correspondance,* 259.

56 "appointed at the last minute": Hohl, "Papiers du Général Leclerc," 179.

58 "Oh," said Pauline. "So you are": d'Abrantès, *Mémoires,* vol. 6, 64ff.

58 their property on death: Fonds de Blocqueville, album A, 147.

58 had property in Saint-Domingue: Saint-Maur, *Pauline Bonaparte,* vol. 2, document 12.

58 this prime command: Nabonne, *Pauline Bonaparte,* 70.

59 "All France is come to Saint-Domingue": Hardy, *Correspondance,* 266, n. 1.

Chapter Five / Expedition to Haiti, 1802

60   were nearly as lucrative: Smith, *Wealth of Nations,* 450.

62   "aware of the destruction": Norvins, *Souvenirs,* vol. 2, 348–49.

62   the ominous red clouds: Hardy, *Correspondance,* 268ff.

63   would be a crime: Tulard, "Général Leclerc," 147.

63   a June day in France: Hardy, *Correspondance,* 271.

64   "recovered her spirits": Roussier, *Lettres du Général Leclerc,* 116.

64   "my brother's private guard": Bro, *Mémoires,* 10.

64   "to return to France": Roussier, *Lettres du Général Leclerc,* 114; 116–17.

64   "I have seen in my life": Champion, *Général Leclerc,* 30.

65   had perverted its cause: James, *Black Jacobins,* 257–58.

65   "whom they intended to kill": Champion, *Général Leclerc,* 33–34.

65   native to the colony: Descourtilz, *Voyage d'un naturaliste,* 31ff.

66   "to the town's renaissance": Norvins, *Souvenirs,* vol. 2, 387

66   "fine and brilliant": Roussier, *Lettres du Général Leclerc,* 145.

66   was like beef: Ibid., 148.

66   "not those of nature?": Descourtilz, *Voyage d'un naturaliste,* 40.

67   "to regain it," he warned: Champion, *Général Leclerc,* 34.

67   Madame Hardy at home: Hardy, *Correspondance,* 288.

67   "Apollo of the French army": Blond, *Pauline Bonaparte,* 82.

67   "the ardor of her passions": Pasquier, *Histoire de mon temps,* vol. 1, 403.

67   to see which she preferred: Barras, *Mémoires,* vol. 4, 191.

68   "in love and tender friendship": Napoleon, *Correspondance générale,* vol. 3, 934; 1012.

69   Davout on May 8: Champion, *Général Leclerc,* 45.

69   infuriated and alarmed the French: Norvins, *Souvenirs,* vol. 2, 398.

71   "when we had them dance": Ibid., 389–92.

71   "its roots are numerous and deep": James, *Black Jacobins,* 271.

71   "once more in combustion": Roussier, *Lettres du Général Leclerc,* 183.

72   "five of my aides-de-camp": Hohl, "Papiers du Général Leclerc," 183.

72   "death emptied them," wrote Norvins: Norvins, *Souvenirs,* vol. 2, 398.

72   "and still isn't discouraged": Roussier, *Lettres du Général Leclerc,* 181.

72   "warriors of the army of Saint-Domingue": Hohl, "Papiers du Général Leclerc," 180.

73   "heading for Saint-Domingue,": Napoleon told him: Roussier, *Lettres du Général Leclerc,* 305–6.

73   "have to change their tune": Hohl, "Papiers du Général Leclerc," 180.

73   at a picturesque spot: Fonds de Blocqueville, album A, 243; 247; 239.

74   "no longer fatal in that season": Champion, *Général Leclerc,* 38–39.

74   victim to yellow fever: Hohl, "Papiers du Général Leclerc," 183.

74   "indeed agreeable for me": Roussier, *Lettres du Général Leclerc,* 190–91.

Chapter Six / Pestilential Climate, 1802–1803

75   "but licentiousness operates": Roussier, *Lettres du Général Leclerc*, 190; 182.

75   massacre of all the Europeans: Tulard, "Général Leclerc," 151.

76   linked, was already dead: Champion, *Général Leclerc*, 39–40.

76   "you will never get it back": Tulard, "Général Leclerc," 152.

77   over which they bent: Norvins, *Souvenirs*, vol. 3, 7.

78   "'I don't want to go anymore'": Norvins, *Souvenirs*, vol. 3, 22ff.

78   butterflies of the island with a net: Ibid., vol. 3, 10.

78   "from the reality": Champion, *Général Leclerc*, 41–42.

78   "easily heated in winter": Hohl, "Papiers du Général Leclerc," 183.

79   the parrots and monkeys: Norvins, *Souvenirs*, vol. 3, 25.

79   "I will go down to Le Cap": Cornuau, *Correspondance*, 44.

81   determination of a Spartan woman: Norvins, *Souvenirs*, vol. 3, 36ff.

81   "my men whom the yellow fever spares": Hohl, "Papiers du Général Leclerc," 181.

81   "since I have been in this country": Roussier, *Lettres du Général Leclerc*, 239.

82   "well worthy to be your sister": Ibid., 256; 230; 260.

82   "imprinted on history": Napoleon, *Correspondance générale*, vol. 3, 1168–69.

82   their immediate entourage: Fonds de Blocqueville, album A, 259.

83   "the general had suffered": Roussier, *Lettres du Général Leclerc*, 36.

84   "My father is dead!": Norvins, *Souvenirs*, vol. 3, 43.

84   "her son will inherit his virtues": Dupâquier, "Pauline Bonaparte," 172.

84   "gauge of her conjugal love": Fonds de Blocqueville, album C, 371.

84   "Pauline, who is truly unhappy": Masson, *Napoléon et Sa Famille*, vol. 2, 231.

85   may not have pleased Leclerc's mother: Fonds de Blocqueville, album C, 374.

85   David and Jonathan: Champion, *Général Leclerc*, 24, n. 98.

87   "consolation for your unhappiness": Napoleon, *Correspondance générale*, vol. 4, 22.

88   "what I wanted, which was three hundred thousand francs": Norvins, *Souvenirs*, vol. 3, 67; 69–70.

Chapter Seven / Union with a Roman Prince, 1803

91   "I will kill myself": d'Abrantès, *Mémoires*, vol. 7, 207.

91   (. . . of long standing): Masson, *Napoléon et Sa Famille*, vol. 2, 241.

92   her first encounter with the prince: d'Abrantès, *Mémoires*, vol. 7, 208.

93   anyone more demanding in Paris: Masson, *Napoléon et Sa Famille*, vol. 2, 245

95   "the happiest of his life": Angiolini, *Correspondance*, 50–51.

95   "to ask for her hand": Masson, *Napoléon et Sa Famille*, vol. 2, 251–52.

96   remarrying so quickly: Saint-Maur, *Pauline Borghèse*, vol. 1, 21.

96   "the first family in Rome": Angiolini, *Correspondance*, 75, n. 1.

96   "from her head to her toes she is all Roman": Larrey, *Madame Mère*, vol. 1, 335.

97   "suffer a little longer": Angiolini, *Correspondance*, 67; 81; 85.

98   joint guardians to the child: Fonds Masson, box 67, 12–18.

99   "all the jewels of the Borghese house": Saint-Maur, *Pauline Borghèse*, vol. 1, 20ff.

99   "I am a princess, a real princess": d'Abrantès, *Mémoires*, vol. 7, 209–210.

99   the design that had attracted such attention: Saint-Maur, *Pauline Borghèse*, vol. 1, 20ff.

100   "I love you": Napoleon, *Correspondance générale*, vol. 4, 439.

100   But she had to admire his spirit: Saint-Maur, *Pauline Borghèse*, vol. 1, 23–25.

101   until the dress she required had arrived from Paris: Cornuau, *Correspondance*, 44.

101   his brother and his new wife: Saint-Maur, *Pauline Borghèse*, vol. 1, 46–48.

102   as he told Angiolini in March 1804: Angiolini, *Correspondance*, 92.

102   "meet again soon in France": Masson, *Napoléon et Sa Famille*, vol. 2, 406.

102   "neither force nor a show of authority will deter them": Angiolini, *Correspondance*, 93; 95.

103   women in Paris lived differently: Napoleon, *Correspondance générale*, vol. 4: 666; 668.

104   momentous news came from Paris in May: Angiolini, *Correspondance*, 96.

104   "harsh words between him and my brother": Saint-Maur, *Pauline Borghèse*, vol. 1, 80–81.

Chapter Eight / Bitter Summer, 1804

106   "it is more important to be good and esteemed": Napoleon, *Correspondance générale*, vol. 4, 668.

107   "on lions at the Farnesina": Chateaubriand, *Mémoires d'Outre-Tombe*, vol. 1, 856; vol. 2, 1990–91.

107   "advantages of nature": Saint-Maur, *Pauline Borghèse*, vol. 1, 44.

107   "created for your pleasure": *Venere Vincitrice*, 125.

109   "Every veil must fall before Canova": Chastenet, *Pauline Bonaparte*, 109.

109   "He looks more belligerent than pacific": Angeli, *I Bonaparte a Roma*, 90.

111   claimed to have won Letizia's approval: Cornuau, *Correspondance*, 45.

111   "my accusers play false": Saint-Maur, *Pauline Borghèse*, vol. 1, 43–44.

112   she ended as usual: Fonds Masson, box 68, 33–34.

112   "to see the princess undressed": Saint-Maur, *Pauline Borghèse*, vol. 1, 93; 126; 93–94.

113   marshal of the Empire and governor of Paris: Murat, *Lettres*, vol. 3, 142.

113   "the greatest honors possible": Kühn, *Pauline Bonaparte*, 95, n. 1.

114   "give dinners continually, and often balls": Angiolini, *Correspondance*, 105–6.

115   "with all economy possible": Cornuau, *Correspondance*, 46

115 a "more or less sweet tête-à-tête": Saint-Maur, *Pauline Borghèse*, vol. 1, 94.

116 "I cannot live without him": Cornuau, *Correspondance*, 46.

119 her son's last days: Saint-Maur, *Pauline Borghèse*, vol. 1, 96–101.

119 "this terrible blow": Cornuau, *Correspondance*, 46.

120 agreed to everything: Saint-Maur, *Pauline Borghèse*, vol. 1, 102–4.

120 "until after the coronation": Cornuau, *Correspondance*, 46–47.

123 in the first week of December: Saint-Maur, *Pauline Borghèse*, vol. 1, 127; 137–40; 143.

Chapter Nine / The Borgheses at War, 1804–1807

126 licensed to satisfy "every fantasy": Rémusat, *Mémoires*, vol. 1, 203–5.

126 "as it is possible to be": Metternich, *Mémoires*, vol. 1, 312.

127 "the patrimony of our father the king": d'Abrantès, *Mémoires*, vol. 9, 99.

129 might not have wholly concurred: Larrey, *Madame Mère*, vol. 2, 364.

130 "always in the same manner": Angiolini, *Correspondance*, 124.

130 "you must live to a great age": [Stewarton?], *Female Revolutionary Plutarch*, vol. 3, 200–201.

131 (. . . a further layer of jewelry): Rémusat, *Mémoires*, vol. 2, 347–48.

131 the insufficient food and drink: d'Abrantès, *Histoire des Salons*, vol. 6, 281.

133 "I don't recall": Dumas, *Mes Mémoires*, vol. 1, 152–54.

134 "I would have come to Paris": Angiolini, *Correspondance*, 146.

135 "I never doubted his aptitude": Murat, *Lettres*, vol. 4, 2.

135 "devour" it: Angiolini, *Correspondance*, 155.

135 "I have just received letters from him": Kühn, *Pauline Bonaparte*, 109.

135 "shut, even to her mother": Angiolini, *Correspondance*, 159.

135 "monotonous life that doesn't suit me": Murat, *Lettres*, vol. 4, 164.

136 "and forgets us all": Hortense, *Mémoires*, vol. 1, 237.

137 styling her husband "His Serene Idiot": [Goldsmith?], *Court of St. Cloud*, vol. 2, 131.

138 "such liberties are permitted": [Goldsmith?], *Secret History, Cabinet of Bonaparte*, 494.

138 "You always go too far," Napoleon replied: [Goldsmith?], *Court of St. Cloud*, vol. 2, 131–132.

138 one of his wife's ladies in revenge: Masson, "La Princesse Pauline," 799.

139 wrote a lady at court: Ducrest, *Mémoires*, vol. 2, 26.

139 "material for lengthy discussion": Potocka, *Mémoires*, 209.

Chapter Ten / Messalina of the Empire, 1807

141 pervaded by the smell of sour milk for months to come: Stiegler, *Récits de guerre*, 77–78.

141 a "little red sea": Napoleon, *Lettres à Josephine*, 279–80.

142 specifically her fallopian tubes: Parlange, *Étude médico-psychologique*, 67.

142 "she had to be carried everywhere": Barras, *Mémoires*, vol. 4, 191–92.

143 she rushed again from the room: Favre, *Les confidences d'un vieux palais*, 215–17.

143 "At length she acknowledged it": Morris, *Diary and Letters*, vol. 2, 491–92.

145 "increases greatly my chagrin": Masson, "La Princesse Pauline," 803.

146 "the class into which he had risen": Crawley, *New Cambridge History*, vol. 9, 321.

148 "his pretty white horses": Masson, *Napoléon et Sa Famille*, vol. 3, 343.

149 "Violets look terrible in black hair": d'Abrantès, *Histoire des Salons*, vol. 6, 285–88.

151 "be open with me when you reply": Kühn, *Pauline Bonaparte*, 117–18.

152 "in front of her in Paris": Masson, *Napoléon et Sa Famille*, vol. 4, 429–33.

153 "a pretty gauze muslin to your taste": Cornuau, *Correspondance*, 48.

153 his expenditure was for nothing: Laflandre-Linden, *Les Bonaparte en Provence*, 147–48.

154 "a way to water the route": Thibaudeau, *Mémoires*, 223–24.

154 "and agitate me a little": Cornuau, *Correspondance*, 48.

155 "I would never have authorized it": Masson, *Napoléon et Sa Famille*, vol. 4, 430–35.

Chapter Eleven / Southern Belle, 1807–1808

158 a punishment she would remember: Thibaudeau, *Mémoires*, 224–27.

159 (. . . his stomach as a footrest): Barras, *Mémoires*, vol. 4, 192.

161 "other women under her feet": Nadaillac, *Mémoires*, 305; 199–201.

163 "'spent two days with us'": Blangini, *Souvenirs*, 138–50.

164 and four equerries: Fonds Masson, box 68, 61ff.

165 *à la cosaque* for airings: Masson, *Napoléon et Sa Famille*, vol. 4, 443.

166 prove equally biddable in Turin: Constant, *Mémoires sur la vie de Napoléon*, vol. 6, 245–59.

167 for Rome as Camillo's bride: Masson, *Napoléon et Sa Famille*, vol. 4, 444.

167 "vive le prince, vive la princesse!": Constant, *Mémoires sur la vie de Napoléon*, vol. 6, 280–85.

169 "nothing other than the wish for Paris": Masson, *Napoléon et Sa Famille*, vol. 4, 444–46.

Chapter Twelve / Agent for Divorce, 1808–1812

170 "after his return from Germany": Masson, *Napoléon et Sa Famille*, vol. 4, 447.

171 "in the name of France": Caulaincourt, *Mémoires*, vol. 1, 274.

173 "her sole occupation was pleasure": Metternich, *Mémoires*, vol. 1, 312.

173 "the pleasure of being beautiful": de Girardin, *Journal et souvenirs*, vol. 4, 383.

173 Clary slyly adds: Clary, *Trois mois à Paris*, 301; 222

174 "in going there, despite her beauty": Kühn, *Pauline Bonaparte*, 159–61, quoting Friedrich, *40 Jahren aus dem Leben eines Toten*, 3 vols. (Tübingen, 1848–49).

176 "a distraction from the divorce": Hortense, *Mémoires*, vol. 2, 42–43.

176 attended all the *cercles:* Murat, *Lettres*, vol. 6, 514.

177 "arranges the rendezvous for His Majesty": de Girardin, *Journal et Souvenirs*, vol. 4, 339.

177 "Tell Madame de M. to await me": Cornuau, *Correspondance*, 30–41.

177 her beloved Malmaison: Hortense, *Mémoires*, vol. 2, 43–55.

178 "sweetness and contentment, not headaches": Cornuau, *Correspondance*, 38.

179 "had to pick it up again": Clary, *Trois Mois à Paris*, 78–80.

179 "economize on the details": Kühn, *Pauline Bonaparte*, 159.

180 "'. . . for the rabble,'" wrote de Girardin: de Girardin, *Journal et Souvenirs*, vol. 4, 390–91.

182 "sent to Russia": Ducrest, *Mémoires*, vol. 2, 23–26.

182 sighs to make the candles gutter: Thiébault, *Mémoires*, vol. 4, 443.

183 "He can still dance": Kühn, *Pauline Bonaparte*, 169–70.

183 a letter meant for Napoleon's eyes: Ibid., 180.

185 the reflected face of "France": d'Abrantès, *Mémoires*, vol. 14, 186.

185 "to do anything of the kind": Hortense, *Mémoires*, vol. 2, 139–40.

Chapter Thirteen / Survival, 1812–1814

187 "and Angélique [from *Le Malade imaginaire*]: d'Abrantès, *Mémoires*, xiv, 262.

188 "uncertainty that destroys me": Cornuau, *Correspondance*, 17; 13.

190 "a good drubbing": Cornuau, *Correspondance*, 12; 19.

191 "From your oldest friend at Aix": d'Abrantès, *Mémoires*, vol. 14, 293–301.

191 "to beg you for more": Fleuriot de l'Angle, *La Paolina*, 204, quoting original letter then in possession of Comte de Meribel.

192 (. . . featured as a matter of course): Parlange, *Étude médico-psychologique*, 70.

193 in very histrionic fashion: d'Abrantès, *Mémoires*, vol. 14, 310–11.

194 "find no more on earth . . .": Petrarca, *Rime, Trionfi e Poesie Latine*, 359; 388.

194 "So I have restrained myself": *Lettres d'Amour de Talma*, 69–70.

195 brilliants, that depicted the princess: Ducrest, *Mémoires*, vol. 2, 26–27.

196 "and her health is altered": Masson, *Napoléon et Sa Famille*, vol. 7, 381–82.

196 "the stones I bought from Picot": Fonds Masson, box 69, 493.

197 "what you've read in the *Moniteur*": Cornuau, *Correspondance*, 5.

197 "announced later to the nation": Caulaincourt, *Mémoires*, vol. 2, 193.

198 "to commemorate the emperor's coronation": Cornuau, *Correspondance*, 21.

198 "but I shall yet recoup": Caulaincourt, *Mémoires*, vol. 2, 373.

198 "trace of fatigue on his face": Cornuau, *Correspondance*, 26.

198 "those who had died in Russia": Fezensac, *Souvenirs Militaires*, 356.

199 "It is the beginning of the end": Harris, *Talleyrand: Betrayer and Saviour,* 387, n. 10.

199 "the owner wants 100,200 francs": Cornuau, *Correspondance,* 9.

200 "attending the Carnival entertainments": Masson, *Napoléon et Sa Famille,* vol. 8, 335.

200 departure for the theater of war: Cornuau, *Correspondance,* 25.

200 of the house in Paris: Masson, *Napoléon et Sa Famille,* vol. 8, 330–31.

200 "solid and stable peace ensue": Cornuau, *Correspondance,* 9.

201 "I will spend the winter": Ibid., 49.

202 "offered 300,000 francs to the Emperor": Kühn, *Pauline Bonaparte,* 205.

202 "fire cannons to please her": Masson, *Napoléon et Sa Famille,* vol. 8, 350; 354; 359.

203 "I don't want any confusion": Ibid., vol. 10, 72.

204 "They have betrayed me": Napoleon, *Lettres à Josephine,* 400–401.

204 "follow him to Elba": Masson, *Napoléon et Sa Famille,* vol. 10, 76; 78.

205 she tenderly caressed him: d'Abrantès, *Mémoires,* vol. 18, 246.

206 "in need of everything": Cornuau, *Correspondance,* 49.

Chapter Fourteen / Diamonds on the Battlefield, 1814–1815

207 to precede her to the island: Masson, *Napoléon et Sa Famille,* vol. 10, 328.

207 "an act of gross treachery": Kühn, *Pauline Bonaparte,* 215.

209 "useful to me," Pauline wrote: Cornuau, *Correspondance,* 50.

209 adopt the guise of "comforting angel": Pons de l'Hérault, *Souvenirs,* 238.

209 "given no sign of life": Masson, *Napoléon et Sa Famille,* vol. 10, 316–17.

210 installed in the Palazzo Borghese: Corsini, *I Bonaparte a Firenze,* 214.

210 graced her dining room in Paris: Masson, *Napoléon et Sa Famille,* vol. 10, 318–19.

211 trounced Napoleon's forces in Spain: Longford, *Wellington: Years of the Sword,* 369.

211 a detailed inventory—and stables: Ronfort and Augarde, *À l'ombre de Pauline,* 21.

212 "heartless little devil": Longford, *Wellington: Years of the Sword,* 383.

212 "resigned to his retreat": Campbell, *Diary,* 130.

212 "one hadn't left France": Cornuau, *Correspondance,* 51.

213 "if it gives him pleasure": Pons de l'Hérault, *Souvenirs,* 238.

214 in the garden that morning: Ibid., 241–42.

214 a woman in her thirties: Mameluck Ali, *Souvenirs,* 64–65.

215 "anxious for the future": Kühn, *Pauline Bonaparte,* 226.

215 "and in his resurrection": Longford, *Wellington: Years of the Sword,* 378.

215 "all who approached her": Pons de l'Hérault, *Souvenirs,* 238.

216 ever see Napoleon again: Marchand, *Mémoires,* 155–56.

216 "and sister to your protection": Campbell, *Diary,* 183, n. 89.

217 "Send me news": Pons de l'Hérault, *Mémoire,* 118–19.

218 "a smile upon her face": Campbell, *Diary,* 184–85.

219 their contact was minimal: Sforza, "Pauline Bonaparte a Compignano," 150.

219 "she refuses to have back anyone who left her": Masson, *Napoléon et Sa Famille,* vol. 12, 78.

221 Pauline remained energetic: Ibid., 81.

222 life on Saint Helena: Constant, *Mémoires intimes,* vol. 1, 206–08; Marchand, *Mémoires,* 225.

Chapter Fifteen / Plots and Plans, 1815–1821

223 in October 1815, to Pius VII: ASV, Segr. Stato, Interni, packet 565, bundle 9, letter of Oct. 18, 1815, "Beatissimo Padre."

224 a royalist minion had written in the margin: O'Meara, *Napoleon in Exile,* vol. 1, 225.

225 "differences between the prince and me": ASV, Segr. Stato, Interni, packet 565, bundle 9, letter of Oct. 18, 1815, "Beatissimo Padre."

225 "doing her great injury": Borghetti, "Davanti alla Sacra Rota," 103.

225 "entry to her husband's house": ASV, Segr. Stato, Interni, packet 565, bundle 9, letter of Jan. 10, 1816, "Monsignor, la position pénible."

226 "not make each other unhappy": ASV, Segr. Stato, Interni, packet 565, bundle 9, "Pro Memoria per il Principe Borghese."

226 and live together once more: Kühn, *Pauline Bonaparte,* 243.

226 an arrangement with the prince: Fonds Masson, box 70, 227.

227 "a most uncommon woman": Ticknor, *Life, Letters, Journals,* vol. 1, 181–82.

227 "the sheets French cambric, embroidered": Morgan, *Memoirs,* vol. 2, 122–23, 129–30.

228 "the finest in Rome": Guerrini, *Paolina,* 526–27.

229 "by cardinals as la belle Pauline": Morgan, *Italy,* vol. 2, 418, n.; vol. 3, 51.

229 "a few enemies the less": Masson, *Napoléon et Sa Famille,* vol. 13, 266.

229 "treat his assassins": Kühn, *Pauline Bonaparte,* 247.

229 "frequenting the Bonapartes in Rome": Masson, *Napoléon et Sa Famille,* vol. 12, 286.

229 "cementing or destroying friendships": Shelley, *Diary,* vol. 1, 359.

230 "it never had a shoe on": Granville, *Letters,* vol. 1, 111–13.

230 "most generous of my enemies": Napoleon, *Correspondance publié par ordre de Napoléon III,* vol. 28, 348.

232 "you have only to let me know": ASV, Segr. Stato, Interni, packet 565, bundle 9, letter of May 19, 1817, "Je suis extrémement flatté."

233 her intentions there: Ibid., bundle 1; police report, Apr. 30, 1817; bundle 9, passim.

233 "a classic courtesan": Fleuriot de l'Angle, *La Paolina,* 271.

233 "her figure is very striking": Matthews, *Diary of an Invalid,* 127–28.

234 a healthier environment: Larrey, *Madame Mère,* vol. 2, 183.

234 "fretting about her brother": Morgan, *Memoirs,* vol. 2, 252.

234 "from the gaze of others," she insisted: *Venere Vincitrice,* 125, n. 13.

234 "exhibit the same symptoms": Kühn, *Pauline Bonaparte,* 249.

235 another, more "respectable" statue: ASV, Arch. Borghese, packet 346, "1820. Posizione concernente la statua fatta da Canova,"; letter of Jan. 17, 1820, "Eccellenza, da qualche tempo."

236 the older and younger generations: Planat de la Faye, *Rome et Sainte-Hélène,* 21.

236 "for pleasure," said her brother: Antommarchi, *Derniers Moments,* vol. 1, 70.

236 "where Venus did the honors": Pacini, *Memorie,* 23.

237 the "truly incomparable" extremity: Montet, *Souvenirs,* 400–401.

237 "anything about my brother's health?": Holland, *Foreign Reminiscences,* 340–41 (French).

238 "his agony is terrible": Antommarchi, *Derniers Moments,* vol. 2, 205–6.

238 "prove to him my devotion": Ibid., vol. 2, 207–8.

239 "all is finished. I embrace you": Guerrini, *Paolina,* 542–43 (French).

Chapter Sixteen / "Great Remains of Beauty," 1821–1825

240 "no one loves him so much as I do": Montholon, Comtesse de, *Souvenirs,* 222–23.

241 "the ashes of her son": Larrey, *Madame Mère,* vol. 2, 266.

241 "I am in need of travel": Guerrini, *Paolina,* 542 (French).

242 "agonies that Napoleon had endured": Antommarchi, *Derniers Moments,* vol. 2, 148.

242 "on the floor, as if dead": Coulmann, *Réminiscences,* vol. 2, 200.

243 "French elegance and Italian taste": Morgan, *Italy,* vol. 2, 418.

245 "to go into mourning": Kühn, *Pauline Bonaparte,* 261–64.

246 "compliments, and blandishments": Silvagni, *La corte e la società romana,* vol. 3, 65–66.

247 she swept off to bed: Coulmann, *Réminiscences,* vol. 2, 198ff.

248 "very civil and gracious to me": Devonshire Collection, Sixth Duke's Papers, Diary transcript, Feb. 15, 1824.

248 "the Sister of the Graces": Devonshire, *Handbook to Chatsworth,* 92–93.

248 "this one assails our nobility": Granville, *Letters,* vol. 1, 267.

248 "in Paris in the last reign": Devonshire Collection, Sixth Duke's Papers, Diary transcript, Feb. 26, 1824; Feb. 19, 1824.

249 "Adieu, dear Nino": Lazzareschi, *Paolina,* 241–43.

250 "at last be at peace": Campetti, "Lettere di Paolina Bonaparte," 74–75 (French).

250 ignored by the princess: Lumbroso, *Miscellanea Napoleonica,* vol. 5, lxxiv–lxxxiv.

251 Pacini and his relations: Chastenet, *Pauline Bonaparte,* vol. 5, 234.

251 their matrimonial felicity: Gorgone, "Paolina Bonaparte, principessa inquieta," 22.

251 the Prussian minister heard: Kühn, *Pauline Bonaparte,* 277.

251 traveling to her villa at Lucca: Guerrini, *Paolina,* 544 (French).

252 dictated the terms of her will: Fonds Masson, box 70, 285–87.

252 (. . . of Leclerc and of Dermide): Fonds de Blocqueville, Campan Correspondence, letters of 1834.

253 "in piety and resignation": Guerrini, *Paolina,* 548–64.

253 so long—to the prince: Fonds Masson, Box 70, 285–88.

253 a *scirro*—or tumor—on the stomach: Gorgone, "Paolina Bonaparte, principessa inquieta," 24.

253 rich, dark chestnut color: Author visit to Palazzo Torrigiani, Florence, 2006.

254 "than would be pleasant": "A Sketch of Joseph Bonaparte," *Godey's Lady's Book* (Apr. 1845), 187.

SOURCES

I AM GREATLY INDEBTED throughout my narrative to the thirteen volumes of Frédéric Masson's *Napoléon et Sa Famille,* for which he drew on his massive collection of Bonaparte papers. Many of those are now conserved in the Fonds Masson, Bibliothèque Thiers, in Paris. Joachim Kühn's *Pauline Bonaparte* has much to recommend it, but, as readers wishing to locate quotations in the text and turning to the Notes will see, many other biographies have individual merits.

MANUSCRIPT SOURCES

Archivio Borghese, Archivio Segreto Vaticano, Rome
Cavour Papers, Fondazione Cavour, Santena, Turin
Devonshire Collection, Chatsworth, Derbyshire
Fondo Borghese, Archivio Segreto Vaticano, Rome
Fonds de Blocqueville, Archives Départementales de l'Yonne, Auxerre
Fonds Masson, Bibliothèque Thiers, Paris
Fonds Napoléon, Archives Nationales, Paris
Hamilton Papers, Lennoxlove, Scotland
Leveson-Gower Papers, Staffordshire County Record Office
Royal Archives, Windsor
Segretaria di Stato, Interni, Archivio Segreto Vaticano, Rome

PUBLISHED SOURCES

Angeli, Diego. *I Bonaparte a Roma.* Rome, 1938.
Angiolini, Luigi, Chevalier. *Correspondance: Angiolini et le Prince Camille Borghèse; Le Mariage de Pauline Bonaparte.* Edited by B. Sancholle-Henraux. Paris, 1913.
Antommarchi, Francesco. *Les Derniers Moments de Napoléon, 1819–1821.* 2 vols. Edited by Désiré Lacroix. Paris, 1898.
Arnaud, Raoul. *"Fils de Fréron, 1754–1802": Journaliste, Sans-Culotte et Thermidorien.* Paris, 1909.
Arnault, Antoine Vincent. *Souvenirs d'un Sexagénaire.* 4 vols. Paris, 1833.
Barras, Paul-François-Jean-Nicolas, Vicomte de. *Mémoires.* edited by George Duruy. 4 vols. Paris, 1895–96.

Beal, Mary, and John Cornforth. *British Embassy, Paris: The House and Its Works of Art.* London, 1992.

Blangini, Felice. *Souvenirs . . . 1797–1834.* Edited by Charles-Maxime-Catherinet de Villemarest. Paris, 1834.

Blond, Georges. *Pauline Bonaparte: La nymphomane au coeur fidèle.* Paris, 1986.

Bonaparte, Napoleon.. *Correspondance générale, 1784–1804.* vols. 1–4. Edited by Thierry Lentz, Henry Laurens, Gabriel Madec, Jean Tulard, and François Houdecek. Paris, 2004–7.

———. *Correspondance de Napoleon Ier publié par ordre de l'Empereur Napoléon III.* 32 vols. Paris, 1858–70.

———. *Lettres d'Amour à Joséphine.* Edited by Chantal de Tourtier-Bonazzi and Jean Tulard. Paris, 1981.

Borghetti, Giuseppe. "Paolina Borghese davanti alla Sacra Rota." *Nuova Antologia: rivista di lettere, scienze ed arti* (1932, Sept. 1): 102–13.

Bro, Général. *Mémoires, 1796–1844.* Edited by Baron Henri Bro de Comères. Paris, 1914.

Bruce, Evangeline. *Napoleon and Josephine: An Improbable Marriage.* London, 1995.

Campbell, Sir Neil. *Napoleon on Elba: Diary of an Eyewitness to Exile.* London, 2004.

Campetti, P. "Lettere di Paolina Borghese." *Bollettino Storico Lucchese* 10 (Oct. 1932), 72–75.

Canova e la Venere Vincitrice. Edited by Anna Coliva and Fernando Mazzocca. Exhibition catalog. Rome, 2007.

Carrington, Dorothy. *Portrait de Charles Bonaparte, d'après ses écrits de jeunesse et ses mémoires.* Ajaccio, 2002.

Caulaincourt, Général de, Duc de Vicence. *Mémoires.* 3 vols. Edited by Jean Hanoteau. Paris, 1933.

Champion, Jean-Marcel. *Le Général de Division Victoire-Emmanuel Leclerc (1772–1802): Éléments pour une biographie.* Pontoise, 1979.

Chastenet, Geneviève. *Pauline Bonaparte: La fidèle infidèle.* Paris, 1986.

Chateaubriand, François-René de. *Mémoires d'Outre-Tombe.* Edited by Jean-Paul Clément. 2 vols. Paris, 1997.

Chevallier, Bernard. *La douce et incomparable Joséphine.* Paris, 1999.

Clary et Aldringen, Prince Charles de. *Trois mois à Paris lors du marriage de l'Empereur Napoléon Ier et de l'Archiduchesse Marie-Louise.* Edited by Baron de Mitis and Comte de Pimodan. Paris, 1914.

Constant [Wairy], Louis. *Mémoires intimes de Napoléon Ier.* Edited by Maurice Dernelle. 2 vols. Paris, 1967.

———. *Mémoires sur la vie de Napoléon.* 6 vols. Paris, 1830.

Cornuau, Pierre. *Correspondance Inédite de Napoléon Ier, de la Famille Impériale et de divers Personnages avec Pauline Borghèse, provenant de la succession de M. Lacipière, Hôtel Drouot, Vente du 20 juin 1939.* Paris, 1939.

Corsini, Andrea. *I Bonaparte a Firenze.* Florence, 1961.

Coulmann, Jean-Jacques. *Réminiscences*. 3 vols. Paris, 1862–69.

Crawley, C. W., ed. *The New Cambridge Modern History*. Vol. 9, *War and Peace in an Age of Upheaval, 1793–1830*. Cambridge, 1965.

d'Abrantès, Duchesse. *Histoire des Salons*. 6 vols. Paris, 1837–38.

———. *Mémoires*. 25 vols. The Hague/Brussels, 1831–37.

de Girardin, Louis-Stanislas-Cécile-Xavier, Comte. *Discours et opinions, journal et souvenirs*. 4 vols. Paris, 1828.

Descourtilz, Michel Étienne. *Voyage d'un naturaliste en Haiti, 1799–1803*. Edited by Jacques Boulenger. Paris, 1935.

Devonshire, William, Sixth Duke of. *Handbook to Chatsworth and Hardwick*. Privately printed, 1844.

Ducrest, Georgette. *Mémoires sur l'Impératrice Joséphine, ses contemporains, la cour de Navarre et de la Malmaison*. 3 vols. Paris, 1828.

Dumas, Alexandre. *Mes Mémoires, 1802–1833*. Edited by Pierre Josserand. 2 vols. Paris, 1989.

Dupâquier, Jacques. "Pauline Bonaparte, Femme Leclerc," *Mémoires de la Société historique et archéologique de Pontoise, du Val d'Oise et du Vexin* 86 (2005): 165–181.

Favre, Louis. *Le Luxembourg 1300–1882: Récits et confidences sur un vieux palais*. Paris, 1882.

Fezensac, Duc de. *Souvenirs Militaires de 1804 à 1814*. Paris, 1863.

Fleuriot de l'Angle, Paul. *La Paolina, Soeur de Napoléon*. Paris, 1946.

Forges, M. A.-P. de. *Le Général Leclerc . . . notice historique et biographique d'après les documents officiels*. Paris, 1869.

Furet, François, and Denis Richet. *La Révolution du 9-Thermidor au 18-Brumaire*. Paris, 1966.

George, Mademoiselle. *Mémoires inédits*. Edited by Paul Arthur Cheramy. Paris, 1908.

Godey's Lady's Book and Ladies' American Magazine, 127 vols. Philadelphia, 1830–93.

[Goldsmith, Lewis?]. *The Secret History of the Cabinet of Bonaparte, Including His Private Life, Character, Domestic Administration, and His Conduct to Foreign Powers*. London, 1810.

———. *The Secret History of the Court and Cabinet of St. Cloud*. 2 vols. London, 1845.

Gorgone, Giulia. "Paolina Bonaparte, principessa inquieta." In *Il rifugio di Venere: La villa di Paolina Bonaparte a Viareggio*. Edited by Glauco Borella and Roberta Martinelli. Exhibition catalog pages 13–25. Lucca, 2005.

Granville, Harriet, Countess. *Letters, 1810–1845*. Edited by Hon. Edward Frederick Leveson-Gower. 2 vols. London, 1894.

Guerrini, Teresa Luzzatto. *Paolina*. Florence, 1932.

Hardy, Jean, Général. *Correspondance intime de 1797 à 1802*. Edited by Général Hardy de Perini. Paris, 1901.

Harris, Robin. *Talleyrand: Betrayer and Saviour of France*. London, 2008.

Hohl, Claude. "Les Papiers du Général Leclerc au Musée d'Eckmühl." *Bulletin de la Societé des Sciences historiques et naturelles de l'Yonne* 107 (1975): 173–88.

Holland, Henry Richard, Lord. *Foreign Reminiscences.* Edited by Henry Edward, Lord Holland. London, 1851.

Hortense, Reine. *Mémoires de la Reine Hortense.* Edited by Prince Napoléon and Jean Hanoteau. 3 vols. Paris, 1928.

James, C. L. R. *The Black Jacobins: Toussaint L'Ouverture and the San Domingo Revolution.* London, 1980.

Kühn, Joachim. *Pauline Bonaparte (1780–1825).* Translated from the German by G. Daubié. Paris, 1937.

Laflandre-Linden, Louise. *Les Bonaparte en Provence.* Nice, 1987.

Larrey, Baron Hippolyte. *Madame Mère (Napoleonis Mater).* 2 vols. Paris, 1892.

Lazzareschi, Eugenio. *Le sorelle di Napoleone: Paolina.* Florence, 1932.

Lettres d'amour inédits de Talma à la Princesse Pauline Bonaparte. Edited by Hector Fleischmann. Paris, 1911.

Longford, Elizabeth. *Wellington: The Years of the Sword.* London, 1969.

Lumbroso, Alberto. *Miscellanea Napoleonica.* 6 vols. Rome, 1895–98.

Mameluck Ali [Louis-Étienne Saint-Denis]. *Souvenirs sur l'Empereur Napoléon.* Edited by Gustave Michaut. Paris, 1926.

Marchand, Louis-Joseph. *Mémoires de Marchand, premier valet de chambre et exécuteur testamentaire de l'Empereur.* Edited by Jean Bourguignon. Paris, 1985.

Marmont, Maréchal, duc de Raguse. *Mémoires de 1792 à 1841.* Edited by Auguste Frédéric Viesse de Marmont, duc de Raguse. 9 vols. Paris, 1857.

Masson, Frédéric. *Napoléon et sa Famille, 1769–1821.* 13 vols. Paris, 1897–1919.

———. "La Princesse Pauline, 1805–1809." *La Revue de Paris* 7, no. 2 (Feb. 15, 1900): 791–823.

Matthews, Henry. *The Diary of an Invalid . . . in the Years 1817, 1818 and 1819.* London, 1820.

Metternich, Clément, Prince. *Mémoires, documents et écrits . . .* Edited by Prince Richard de Metternich and Alphons von Klinkowstroem. 8 vols. Paris, 1880–84.

Montet, Marie-Henriette-Radegoude-Alexandrine Fisson, Baronne du. *Souvenirs, 1785–1866.* Paris, 1904.

Montholon, Comtesse de. *Souvenirs de Sainte-Hélène, 1815–16.* Edited by Comte de Fleury. Paris, 1901.

Morgan, Sydney, Lady. *Italy.* 3 vols. 1820–21.

———. *Memoirs: Autobiography, Diaries and Correspondence.* Edited by William Hepworth Dixon. 2 vols. London, 1862.

Morris, Gouverneur. *Diary and Letters.* Edited by Anne Cary Morris. 2 vols. London, 1889.

Murat, Joachim. *Lettres et documents, 1767–1815.* Edited by Prince Joachim-Napoléon Murat and Paul Le Brethon. 8 vols. Paris, 1908–14.

Nabonne, Bernard. *Pauline Bonaparte: La Vénus Impériale: 1780–1825.* Paris, 1948.

Nadaillac, Marquise de, Duchesse d'Escars. *Mémoires.* Edited by Marquis de Nadaillac. Paris, 1912.

Norvins, Jacques de. *Souvenirs d'un historien de Napoléon: Mémorial.* Edited by L. de Lanzac de Laborie. 3 vols. Paris, 1896–97.

O'Meara, Barry Edward. *Napoleon in Exile: Or, a Voice from St. Helena.* 2 vols. London, 1822.

Pacini, Giovanni. *Le mie memorie artistiche.* Edited by Luciano Nicolosi and Salvatore Pinnavia. Lucca, 1981.

Parlange, Henri. *Étude médico-psychologique sur Pauline Bonaparte.* Lyon, 1938.

Pasquier, Étienne Denis, Chancelier. *Histoire de mon temps: Mémoires.* Edited by Edme Armand Gaston, duc d'Audiffret-Pasquier. 6 vols. Paris, 1893–95.

Petrarca, Francesco. *Rime, Trionfi e Poesie Latine.* Edited by F. Neri, G. Martelloti, E. Bianchi, and N. Sapegno. Milan, 1951.

Planat de la Faye, Nicolas-Louis. *Rome et Sainte-Hélène de 1815 à 1821.* Paris, 1862.

Pons de l'Hérault, André. *Mémoire aux Puissances Alliées.* Edited by Léon-G. Pelissier. Paris, 1899.

———. *Souvenirs et Anecdotes de l'Île d'Elba.* Edited by Léon-G. Pelissier. Paris, 1897.

Potocka, Comtesse de. *Mémoires (1794–1820).* Edited by Casimir Stryienski. Paris, 2005.

Reinhard, Madame. *Une Femme de diplomate: Lettres à sa mère, 1798–1815.* Edited by Baronne de Wimpffen. Paris, 1900.

Rémusat, Claire Elisabeth Jeanne Gvavia de Vergennes, Comtesse de. *Mémoires, 1802–08.* Edited by Paul de Rémusat. 3 vols. Paris, 1880–81.

Revue Rétrospective, ou bibliothèque historique, contenant des mémoires et des documents authentiques, etc. 5 vols. Paris, 1833–34.

Ronfort, Jean Nerée, and Jean-Dominique Augarde. *À l'ombre de Pauline: La Résidence de l'ambassadeur de Grande-Bretagne à Paris.* Paris, 2001.

Roussier, Paul. *Lettres du Général Leclerc, commandant en chef de l'armée de Saint-Domingue en 1802.* Paris, 1937.

Saint-Maur, Madame de. *Pauline Bonaparte jugée par une femme: Mémoires.* Edited by René Hinzelin. 2 vols. Paris, 1948.

Sforza, Giovanni. "Paolina Bonaparte a Compignano e ai Bagni di Lucca nel 1815." *Revue Napoléonienne* 2, no. 1 (Oct.–Nov. 1902): 144–83.

Shelley, Lady Frances. *Diary, 1787–1873.* Edited by Richard Edgcumbe. 2 vols. London, 1912–13.

Silvagni, David. *La corte e la società romana nei secoli XVIII e XIX.* 3 vols. Naples, 1967.

Smith, Adam. *An Inquiry into the Nature and Causes of the Wealth of Nations.* London, 1870. First published 1776.

[Stewarton?]. *The Female Revolutionary Plutarch: Containing Biographical, Historical and Revolutionary Sketches.* 3 vols. London, 1806.

Stiegler, Gaston, *Récits de guerre et de foyer: Le Maréchal Oudinot, duc de Reggio, d'après les souvenirs inédits de la maréchale.* Paris, 1894.

Thibaudeau, Antoine Claire, Comte. *Mémoires, 1799–1815.* Paris, 1913.

Thiébault, Général Baron. *Mémoires.* Edited by Fernand Calmettes. 5 vols. Paris, 1893–95.

Ticknor, George. *Life, Letters and Journals.* Edited by G. S. Hillard. 2 vols. London, 1876.

Tulard, Jean. "Général Leclerc." *Mémoires de la Société historique et archéologique de Pontoise, du Val d'Oise et du Vexin* 86 (2005): 137–62.

———. *Nouvelle bibliographie critique de mémoires sur l'époque napoléonienne.* Geneva, 1991.

Venere Vincitrice: La sala di Paolina Bonaparte alla Galleria Borghese. Edited by Claudio Strinati. Exhibition catalog. Rome, 1997.

Versini, Xavier. *M. de Buonaparte, ou le livre inachevé.* Paris, 1977.

INDEX